WHAT YOUR FOURTH GRADER NEEDS TO KNOW

THE
CORE KNOWLEDGE
SERIES

RESOURCE BOOKS FOR
GRADES ONE THROUGH SIX
BOOK IV

DOUBLEDAY

New York   London   Toronto   Sydney   Auckland

THE·CORE·KNOWLEDGE
SERIES

WHAT YOUR FOURTH GRADER NEEDS TO KNOW

FUNDAMENTALS OF A GOOD FOURTH-GRADE EDUCATION

Edited by

E. D. HIRSCH, JR.

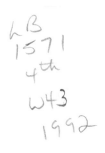

This Book is Dedicated to
Nancy Brown Wellin,
Tireless Supporter and
Generous Benefactor of Core Knowledge,
Activist and Idealist

PUBLISHED BY DOUBLEDAY

a division of Bantam Doubleday Dell Publishing Group, Inc.
1540 Broadway, New York, New York 10036

DOUBLEDAY and the portrayal of an anchor with a dolphin are trademarks of Doubleday, a division of Bantam Doubleday Dell Publishing Group, Inc.

Previously published material is acknowledged on p. 384.

Library of Congress Cataloging in Publication Data
What your fourth grader needs to know: fundamentals of a good fourth-
    grade education /edited by E. D. Hirsch, Jr.— 1st ed.
        p.   cm. — (The Core Knowledge series; bk. 4)
      1. Fourth grade (Education)—United States   2. Curriculum.
    planning—United States.   I. Hirsch, E. D. (Eric Donald), 1928–
    II. Title: What your fourth grader needs to know.   III. Series.
    LB1571 4th.W48   1992
    372.19—dc20   91-38578
                                                           CIP

ISBN 0-385-41118-9

Acknowledgments

This series has depended upon the help, advice, and encouragement of some two thousand people. Some of those singled out here know already the depth of my gratitude; others may be surprised to find themselves thanked publicly for help they gave quietly and freely for the sake of the enterprise alone. To helpers named and unnamed I am deeply grateful.

Project Manager: Tricia Emlet

Editors: Tricia Emlet (Text), Rae Grant (Art)

Artists and Writers: Nancy Bryson (Physical Science), Jacques Chazaud (Illustration), Leslie Evans (Illustration), Jonathan Fuqua (Illustration), Julie C. Grant (Illustration), Marie Hawthorne (Science Biographies), John Hirsch (Mathematics), John Holdren (History & Mythology), Pamela C. Johnson (History & Geography), Blair Logwood Jones (Literature), Phillip Jones (Illustration), Bethanne H. Kelly (Literature and Activities), Gail McIntosh (Illustration), Elaine Moran (Visual Arts), Susan Nees (Illustration), A. Brooke Russell (Geography, Life Science, Physical Science), Peter Ryan (Music & Mythology), Lindley Shutz (Language & Literature), Joel Smith (Illustration), Helen Storey (Sayings), Guiseppe Trogu (Illustration)

Art and Photo Research: Rae Grant

Research and Editing Assistants: Raphael Alvarado (Art), Jennifer Howard (Text), Bethanne H. Kelly (Text), Elaine Moran (Text), Kimberly A. C. Wilson (Text), Carl A. Young, Jr. (Art and Photo)

Permissions: Martha Clay Sullivan

Advisers on Multiculturalism: Minerva Allen, Frank de Varona, Mick Fedullo, Dorothy Fields, Elizabeth Fox-Genovese, Marcia Galli, Dan Garner, Henry Louis Gates, Cheryl Kulas, Joseph C. Miller, Gerry Raining Bird, Dorothy Small, Sharon Stewart-Peregoy, Sterling Stuckey, Marlene Walking Bear, Lucille Watahomigie, Ramona Wilson

Advisers on Elementary Education: Joseph Adelson, Isobel Beck, Paul Bell, Carl Bereiter, David Bjorklund, Constance Jones, Elizabeth LaFuze, J. P. Lutz, Jean Osborne, Sandra Scarr, Nancy Stein, Phyllis Wilkin

Advisers on Technical Subject Matters: Richard Anderson, Holly DeSantis, Andrew Gleason, Eric Karell, Joseph Kett, Michael Lynch, Joseph E. Miller, Margaret Redd, Mark Rush, Ralph Smith, Nancy Summers, James Trefil, Nancy Wayne

Conferees, March 1990: Nola Bacci, Joan Baratz-Snowden, Thomasyne Beverley, Thomas Blackton, Angela Burkhalter, Monty Caldwell, Thomas M. Carroll, Laura Chapman, Carol Anne Collins, Lou Corsaro, Henry Cotton, Anne Coughlin, Arletta Dimberg, Debra P. Douglas, Patricia Edwards, Janet Elenbogen, Mick Fedullo, Michele Fomalont, Nancy Gercke, Mamon Gibson, Jean Haines, Barbara Hayes, Stephen Herzog, Helen Kelley, Brenda King, John King, Elizabeth LaFuze, Diana Lam, Nancy Lambert, Doris Langaster, Richard LaPointe, Lloyd Leverton, Madeleine Long, Allen Luster, Joseph McGeehan, Janet McLin, Gloria McPhee, Marcia Mallard, Judith Matz, William J. Moloney, John Morabito, Robert Morrill, Roberta Morse, Karen Nathan, Dawn Nichols, Valeta Paige, Mary Perrin, Joseph Piazza, Jeanne Price, Marilyn Rauth, Judith Raybern, Mary Reese, Richard Rice, Wallace Saval, John Saxon, Jan Schwab, Ted Sharp, Diana Smith, Richard Smith, Trevanian Smith, Carol Stevens, Nancy Summers, Michael Terry, Robert Todd, Elois Veltman, Sharon Walker, Mary Ann Ward, Penny Williams, Charles Wootten, Clarke Worthington, Jane York

The Three Oaks Elementary School: Constance Jones, Principal; Cecelia Cook, Assistant Principal

Teachers: Joanne Anderson, Linda Anderson, Nancy Annichiarico, Deborah Backes, Katherine Ann Bedingfield, Barbara Bittner, Michael Blue, Coral Boudin, Nancy Bulgerin, Jodene Cebak, Cheryl Chastain, Paula Clark, Betty Cook, Laura DeProfio, Holly DeSantis, Cindy Donmoyer, Lisa Eastridge, Amy Germer, Elizabeth Graves, Jennifer Gunder, Eileen Hafer, Helen Hallman, Donna Hernandez, Kathleen Holzborn, Robert Horner, Jenni Jones, Zoe Ann Klusacek, Annette Lopez, Barbara Lyon, Cindy Miller, Lelar Miller, Laura Morse, Karen Naylor, Joanne O'Neill, Jill Pearson, Linda Peck, Rebecca Poppe, Janet Posch, Judy Quest, Angie Richards, Angie Ryan, April Santarelli, Patricia Scott, Patricia Stapleton, Pamela Stewart, Jeanne Storm, Phillip Storm, Katherine Twomey, Karen Ward

Benefactors: the Brown Foundation, the Dade County School District, the Exxon Education Foundation, the Lee County School District, the National Endowment for the Humanities, the Shutz Foundation

Morale Boosters: Polly Hirsch, Robert Payton, Rafe Sagalyn, Nancy Brown Wellin

Our grateful acknowledgment to these persons does not imply that we have taken their (sometimes conflicting) advice in every case, or that each of them endorses all aspects of this project. Responsibility for final decisions must rest with the editor alone. Suggestions for improvements are very welcome, and I wish to thank in advance those who send advice for revising and improving this series.

Contents

II. GEOGRAPHY, WORLD CIVILIZATION, AND AMERICAN CIVILIZATION

III. FINE ARTS

How to Use This Book*

FOR PARENTS AND TEACHERS

The book you are holding in your hands is an unusual one. It is a collection made for children, but it is not limited to the usual treasury of best-loved stories and poems. It offers in addition engaging accounts of language, literature, history, geography, science, fine arts, and math—the core academic subjects that our children need in this new age of global information. It also contains knowledge that may help them become fulfilled and productive people. But it is not a textbook or a workbook filled with exercises. It offers the academic core—the sort of core knowledge that the best educational systems provide to children all over the world—written in a lively and absorbing manner that includes tips for making those knowledge domains come alive. But such a book must also leave much to you and to your child in the way of additional conversation and practice.

Each book in *The Core Knowledge Series* builds upon knowledge presented in previous books. We know from learning theory that we learn best by building upon what we already know. Hence, this fourth-grade book refers back to previous books. Moreover, the sections of the fourth-grade book also refer you to other sections of the same book. Because subjects and interests cut across disciplines, we encourage you to help your child see connections between art and math, history and literature, physical sciences and language just as we have tried to do. And you should also feel free, using the tables of contents or the indexes, to make your own connections among the books of the series.

We have tried to make this book attractive and interesting by using an interactive, storybook format. We address the child directly as reader, asking questions and suggesting projects that he or she might do. Advice to parents and teachers about teaching specific subject matter is provided in the introduction to each section. You can help your child read more actively both by conversing while you are reading and by bringing the subjects up at a later time when connections occur to you. You and your child

*For a general introduction to the research behind this series and the careful process by which consensus was achieved regarding its content the reader may consult the "General Introduction" in earlier books of this series.

can read the sections of this book in any order. You need not begin at the beginning and work your way through to the end. In fact, we suggest that you skip from section to section, and that you reread as much as your child likes.

To help your child use this book, you might think of it as a guidebook that tries to be as informative and suggestive as possible in a concise format. We encourage you to help your child find ways to explore further what she or he reads here. If possible, take your child to plays, museums, and concerts; help your child find related books (some are suggested here). In short, this guidebook recommends places to visit, and describes what is important in those places, but only you and your child can make the actual visit, travel the streets, and climb the steps.

Bon voyage!

I.

LANGUAGE ARTS

Introduction to Stories and Speeches

FOR PARENTS AND TEACHERS

In Book Four, we include stories from Native American and Asian traditions. We hope these fine tales will become widely familiar. As in Book Three, we also include great speeches from history in the belief that these belong to our literary tradition as fully as stories do.

Because we recognize that fourth grade is a watershed year in reading comprehension, we include more excerpts of novels than previously. Some children will still prefer tales, but others will want to take in longer, more complex forms of prose. When a child is ready and interested, he or she can read the *full* novels that we have excerpted here. A parent or teacher can gauge the child's ability and desire to read full novels, and steer him in that direction when the time comes.

Children recognize the power of story-telling every time they tell a story of their own. Encouraging them to narrate their own stories has many benefits, including, of course, the practice of language skills. You can help draw children into a story they are reading or that you are reading to them if you sometimes ask questions about the story. For example, you might ask, "What do you think is going to happen next?" "Why did one of the characters act as he or she did?" "What might have happened if . . . ?"

After reading aloud one of the stories in this book, you might also ask your child to retell it. Don't be bothered when children change events or characters, thus making the story their own. That is in the best tradition of story-telling, and explains why we have so many different versions of traditional stories.

You can combine story-reading with writing and drawing by encouraging children to write and illustrate their own stories. Some children may be interested in keeping a journal, either as an autobiography or as a way to collect their own stories. This is a fine way for children to enjoy the fun of story-telling and to develop their own writing skills. Adults can also make a game out of collecting new and unfamiliar words and hunting for their meanings in the dictionary.

Stories and Speeches

A Voyage to Lilliput
(adapted from *Gulliver's Travels*, Part I, by Jonathan Swift)

Here Mr. Lemuel Gulliver recounts the events of November 5, 1699, just after his ship was split apart upon a rock somewhere near Tasmania. The rest of the crew perished, and he alone managed to swim to the nearest shore, where he fell asleep from exhaustion.

When I awoke, it was just daylight. I attempted to rise, but was not able to stir; for as I happened to lie on my back, I found my arms and legs were strongly fastened on each side to the ground; and my hair, which was long and thick, tied down in the same manner. I likewise felt several slender ligatures across my body, from my armpits to my thighs. I could only look upward; the sun began to grow hot, and the light offended my eyes. In a little time I felt something alive moving on my left leg, advancing over my breast, and coming almost to my chin. Bending my eyes downward as much as I could, I perceived it to be a human creature not six inches high, with a bow and arrow in his hands. In the meantime, I felt at least forty more of the same kind following the first. I roared so loud that they all ran back in fright, but they soon returned, crying out in shrill voices, *"Hekinah Degul!"* Struggling to

get free, I managed to break the strings and wrench out the pegs that held my left arm and hair to the ground, but the creatures ran off again before I could seize them. I heard one of them cry, *"Togol phonac!"* and instantly felt above a hundred arrows discharged upon my left hand, which pricked me like so many needles. I now thought it prudent to lie still, and when the people observed I was quiet, they discharged no more arrows.

So famished was I that I could not forbear putting my finger frequently on my mouth to signify that I wanted food. Soon, over one hundred inhabitants appeared, laden with baskets full of meat, sent by order of the Emperor. They watched in astonishment at my appetite as I swallowed two or three miniature legs of mutton or several tiny loaves of bread in a single gulp. I was then brought two hogsheads of delicious wine, each of which I finished at a draft. They then began to dance with delight upon my chest, and though I was tempted to seize them and dash them to the ground, I refrained from harming them because of the hospitality they had shown me. In my thoughts I wondered at the intrepidity of these diminutive mortals, who ventured to walk upon me without trembling.

They daubed an ointment upon my hands and face, which, along with a sleeping potion they had placed in my wine, soothed me into a deep slumber. When I awoke, I found myself on a large cart, being carried toward Lilliput, the capital city of my captors, who were called Lilliputians. The Emperor of Lilliput and his court rode forth to greet me, and I was taken to a huge empty temple outside the city where I was to lodge, my legs bound with many chains and padlocks.

The Emperor held frequent councils to debate what course should be taken with me. They feared my breaking loose, or causing a famine due to my huge diet. Some suggested starving me, or shooting me with poison arrows, but they were unsure how to dispose of me safely once I was dead. When the Emperor saw how gently I treated his people, however, he decided to provide me with sufficient food and to grant me certain liberties on the grounds that I swear a peace treaty with him and his kingdom. When I agreed, he sent two of his officers to search my person. They climbed into my pockets and removed the contents, and shortly afterward I was granted my freedom.

I now saw an opportunity to make myself useful to the Emperor of Lilliput by helping him to defeat the Emperor of Blefuscu. These two Emperors were at war because they could not reach an agreement on whether to break their eggs at the larger or the smaller end. Having learned that the Blefuscudians were preparing an invasion by sea, I proposed to seize their entire fleet, which I had seen through my telescope to be lying at anchor in the harbor. By royal warrant, I procured a strong cable, about the size of a packthread, which I then trebled to increase the strength. Then, putting off my coat, shoes, and stockings, I walked into the sea and soon arrived at the harbor. The enemy sailors were so frightened when they saw me that they leaped out of their ships and swam to shore. As I fastened the ships together with the cable, the Blefuscudian sailors fired thousands of arrows, which stuck in my hands and face and would have blinded me had I not thought to put on my spectacles for protection. I cut the anchors of the ships with my knife, took up my cable, and with great ease drew fifty of the enemy's largest men-of-war after me.

I returned to the Lilliputian capital crying, "Long live the most powerful Emperor of Lilliput!" and was received with such appreciation that the Emperor created me a Nardac upon the spot, which is the highest title among them. But because I would not agree to help him make slaves of the defeated enemy, proposing instead to make peace with them, the Emperor would never forgive me. In private council, urged on by my enemy the admiral Skyresh Bogolam (who from the very first had taken a dislike to me for no particular reason), His Imperial Majesty decided that I should be punished as a traitor.

One night I was secretly visited by my friend Reldresal, who held a high position at court. He told me that the Emperor planned to spare my life, but intended to have me blinded. Furthermore, Reldresal said, the council had secretly agreed that I should slowly be starved to death. I was to be arrested in three days' time.

I determined to escape arrest by fleeing to the Emperor of Blefuscu, who had cordially invited me to visit in gratitude for my efforts to make peace with them. About three days after my arrival in Blefuscu, by a lucky accident I happened to spy an overturned boat of my own size not far out to sea. With the help of the Blefuscudians, I was able to retrieve and outfit it, and within about a month I departed for home, well supplied with provisions and money. On the way, I was taken in by a merchant ship returning to England, and so kindly did the captain treat me that I rewarded him with a gift of two hundred sprugs, which is what the Blefuscudians call their money, along with a tiny cow and a sheep big with young.

Gulliver's next voyage takes him to the land of Brobdingnag, where he is surrounded by giants. Later he visits the land of the Houyhnhnms, a race of horselike creatures who are extremely wise. You can read more about these journeys in the book called Gulliver's Travels.

The Tongue-cut Sparrow
(retold from the Japanese)

There once lived an old couple who had no children, no money, and a lot of hard work to do. The old man's only happiness was a sparrow, who lightened his worries with sweet singing. One morning while the old man was cutting wood, his wife was washing the clothes. She had scrubbed the shirts and hung them to dry, when the little sparrow swooped down and ate the rice starch she had planned to use for her ironing.

"Nasty sparrow," the woman bawled. "How could you eat my starch?"

"I'm sorry," the sparrow said sweetly. "I thought this was food you made for me."

The old woman was angry, for she and the old man barely had enough to eat for themselves. In a fit of anger, she fell upon the sparrow with scissors and snipped her tongue out. The little bird flew off.

That night when the old man returned, his wife told him what had happened. The old man waited for the light of the next morning, and then went into the woods to look for the sparrow. Everywhere he went he cried: "Sparrow, oh, tongue-cut sparrow, where is the home of the sparrow?"

The woods grew thicker and darker, and the old man became tired. "Oh, sparrow," he cried, "I hope that you are still alive!"

Suddenly, he heard the whirring of the sparrow's wings and the little bird was there beside him. To his delight, she began to sing brightly.

"Old man, you are very kind," she sang. "I'd like to show you to my home." She led him farther into the woods, to a bamboo house that shone like the stars. Inside, where hundreds of candles flickered, the old man was greeted by other sparrows, and they served him a sumptuous meal. The old man ate until he no longer felt the hunger that had lingered in him for years. Then the sparrows danced for him with intricate moves they had never before shown a human being. Finally, the old man said, "Thank you for your kindness. This is the richest night I have ever known, but I must go home before my wife worries."

"Before you go," his friend said, "you must select a present." In front of the man sat two wicker baskets. "One," said the sparrow, "is very heavy, and one is very light. But whichever you choose, you must not open the basket until you reach home."

"I am an old man, and cannot carry something heavy," he said, and slung the lighter basket upon his back.

When the old man arrived at his home, he told his wife the whole story. "And I chose the lighter basket," he said. Then they opened the basket together. It spilled over with jewels that shone brighter than animals' eyes.

"Fool," his wife cried. "Why didn't you take the heavier basket?" Without another word, she dove into the woods to find the sparrow. Finally she stumbled into the sparrow's glistening bamboo home. She pounded on the door.

"Sparrow, sparrow, let me in!" she cried. When the sparrow opened the door, gone were the flickering candles and the sweet-scented food her husband had described. The sparrow led the old woman into a dirty kitchen and gave her a bowl of thin gruel.

"After all the times I fed you, this is what you give me?" the old woman scoffed. "I don't want your gruel. Give me the heavier basket. I am younger and stronger than my husband. I can carry it back."

"Fine," said the tongue-cut sparrow. "But don't open it until you reach home."

The old woman grabbed the basket and scurried for home. But the basket was heavy, and each step became harder, and heavier, and slower to take. Finally, she thought her back would break. She fell down beside a crooked old tree. "One look," she thought, "just one glance would lift my spirits enough to carry me home." Pulling the basket into the moonlight, she opened it. Something gleamed. Something glimmered. "Gold and silver chains," the woman whispered. "And a jewel that gleams like the green of my cat's eye." The old woman reached in the basket and then shrieked.

Out of the basket, toads and snakes slithered! They crawled up her arm and wrapped themselves around her body. The old woman swatted at them, but they clung and hissed at her. When she was finally able to free herself, she ran home, shuddering and weeping. Her husband greeted her at the door, and she fell into his arms. Now, at last, she was happy with what she had.

Now when you pass their house, you can hear the old woman singing sweetly, while the old man enjoys her songs.

This tale is also available in an illustrated version retold by Katherine Paterson (Dutton, 1987), and in a collection of stories retold by Virginia Haviland, Favorite Fairy Tales Told in Japan *(Little Brown, 1967).*

Robinson Crusoe
(retold from the novel by Daniel Defoe)

NOTE TO PARENTS AND TEACHERS: *Robinson Crusoe is well-known as a tale of survival, perseverance, and ingenuity, even by those who have never read the original novel. It is less recognized, however, as a spiritual autobiography that tells the story of Crusoe's inner, religious life: some of this aspect is preserved in our retelling here.*

As well-known as Crusoe is the figure of Friday, whom modern readers may see in a different light than did the book's first audience. Crusoe was a man of his times and, like his creator, Defoe, he shared the cultural assumptions of his time. You may want to discuss with children certain assumptions behind Crusoe's actions, such as his quick perception of Friday as a potential servant.

I, Robinson Crusoe, was born in the year 1632, in the city of York, of a good family. In the year 1659, I took to sea against the wishes of my father. In times to come I would often recall his warning that I would have leisure to repent my decision, for on the thirtieth of September, I was shipwrecked during a dreadful storm and washed upon the shore of a dismal island, all the rest of the ship's company being drowned, and myself almost dead.

My initial joy at finding myself alive soon gave way to despair as I looked about me and realized that I was alone with no means of sustaining myself. I soon discovered, however, that the bulk of the ship remained intact some distance from shore, and by fashioning a raft from pieces of the wreckage I was able to carry away a quantity of provisions and tools. Among these were a tin of biscuits, some dried meat, a bit of rum and tobacco, several axes and other implements, and several rifles with a quantity of powder and shot which had not been dampened by the sea. With these last I managed to shoot enough birds and wild goats to provide myself with food when my supplies began to give out. And when all my clothes fell to pieces, I made myself a short jacket and breeches of goatskin, as well as a tall shapeless cap to protect my head from sun and rain. With my hairy attire, my sunburned skin, and my growing beard, I would have caused fright or else raised a great deal of laughter had any Englishman been there to see me.

I protected myself from wild beasts and any savages who might roam the island by fashioning a kind of fortress, dug out of a large rocky bank. Using debris from the wreck, I drove a number of high stakes into the ground in the shape of a semicircle about the opening of my cave. I then wove pieces of strong cable between these until I had made an almost impenetrable wall that could be breached only by means of a ladder. Once inside, I could pull the ladder in behind me, thus leaving no means of access for intruders. This was of great comfort to me, for I feared being discovered by the fierce cannibals known to inhabit that part of the world.

With continual labor, I was able to make almost everything I needed to make my dwelling comfortable, including a table and shelves for storing my possessions. I managed to trap and tame a she-goat and her kid, and soon I had acquired an entire flock. For companionship I had a dog and two cats, the only other survivors of the wreck. To these I added two parrots, which I tamed and taught to speak a few words. With my subjects about me, I thought myself quite the master of my little kingdom.

One day I discovered corn and rice sprouting near the entrance to my cave. I carefully watered the shoots until they ripened, then I saved all the grain for planting season. After the next harvest, I again saved the grain for planting, continuing in this manner until I had an ample crop and not allowing myself the least corn to eat until the fourth year.

At first I thought that this corn and rice, which were not native to the island, had sprung up by a miracle, sent by divine providence to relieve my distress. When I remembered spilling a bit of chicken feed saved from the ship, however, I just as quickly lost hope and fell to lamenting my lonely condition. Then I reflected that it was no less a miracle that the grain had fallen in just such a place and in the rainy season when it might best thrive; yet this impression too soon wore off, and my self-pity returned. Indeed, though I had from time to time reflected upon the miraculous nature of my survival—that I alone of all the ship had been saved, along with tools and provisions to sustain me—I had never given thanks to God for my deliverance.

Then, in the dampness of the rainy season, I fell ill with a fever, which left me too weak even to seek water to relieve my fierce thirst. I was racked with chills, and when I finally fell asleep, I had a terrible dream. I saw a man descend from a cloud. Clothed all in flames and carrying a sharp spear, he said in a dreadful voice, "Seeing that all these things have not brought thee to repentance, now thou shalt die."

I can scarcely describe my emotions upon waking. Through all the miseries that had befallen me, I never had so much as one thought that my misfortune might be the will of God, or else just punishment for my selfish life and my rebellious behavior against my father. But now, in my sickness, my conscience began to awake and I began to reproach myself for my past misdeeds. From that day forth, I determined to reconcile myself to the life which God in his wisdom had provided for me.

I had a great mind to see the whole island, and I began my exploration by following the path of a brook through grassy savannas until I reached the point at which the land began to slope downward toward the sea on the island's other side. Here I found wild grapes in abundance, which I gathered and dried as raisins. I also found orange, lemon, and lime trees. The place was so lovely and protected from storms that I built a bower there, which I called my country house, where I might reside during the dry season. From my bower I set out to explore the nearby coast. When I came within view of the sea, I spied a large body of land about twenty leagues away, though whether it was an island or continent, inhabited by friend or foe, I knew not.

During my first three years on the island, I considered often how I might cross to this mainland. My first two attempts failed, for in each case, after I had painstakingly built a boat to carry me, I found it too large and heavy to move to the water's edge. At last I built a small canoe out of a tree trunk. Though too small for crossing the ocean, the canoe would at least enable me to sail around my island. I loaded it with provisions, hoisted my little sail, and set out, staying close to the shoreline. At length, however, I came upon a rocky point around which the current swept in such a way as to send my small vessel out to sea. It was only through great struggle and providence that I was able to steer back to land. When at last I fell exhausted upon the floor of my country bower, I was startled to hear a voice echoing my thoughts, saying, "Poor Robin Crusoe, where are you? Where have you been?" I started up in fear, until I realized that it was my parrot, Poll, repeating the phrases I had taught him.

For fifteen years, I busied myself with caring for my crops and flocks, maintaining my houses, and exploring my island. Then one day as I went to my canoe, I was surprised to see the print of a man's naked foot, very plain in the sand. Thunderstruck, I looked and listened, but neither saw nor heard anyone. Nor were there any other footprints. Terrified, I fled to my fortification, wondering whether I should fear savage cannibals from the mainland or the devil himself.

For the next five years, I kept fearful watch, but saw no other signs of a visitor to the island. Then one day as I came down the hill to the southwest point of the island, I was confounded with horror to see the shore littered with skulls, hands, feet, and human bones. I realized that savages had come over from the mainland, bringing their captured enemies, to kill and eat them here on the shore. Now I had my safety upon my mind. I cared not to drive a nail, much less fire a gun, for fear the noise would be heard. I made charcoal by burning wood under turf, so that I might cook without making smoke. I carefully preserved my remaining powder and shot, and kept all my guns loaded and positioned to defend my fortress.

Then, early one December morning in my twenty-third year of residence, I spied a campfire on the shore, and realized that the savages were on my side of the island. I hid myself in a place where I could observe them through my spyglass and saw that there were at least twenty of them. As I watched, they dragged two miserable wretches from their boats, one of whom they immediately struck down with a club. Suddenly the other captive broke and ran, heading straight toward me. Two of his enemies pursued him, but he easily outstripped them, and as I saw him approach, it occurred to me that he might become the companion and servant I had long wished for. So when the three of them had left the sight of the other savages, I came to the rescue with my pistols, striking down one pursuer with the butt of my gun and shooting the other as he raised his bow and arrow to shoot me. The rescued man threw himself down before me and placed my foot upon his head in a gesture of thanks and servitude. Later, after we buried his fallen enemies and the other savages had left the island, I named my new companion Friday, for it was on that day that I rescued him.

Friday was strong, handsome, and quick to learn. He soon became able to assist me in my work and to speak English. At first he regarded with great reverence the gun with which he had seen me kill his pursuer, for one day I found him speaking softly to it, imploring it not to kill him. With my guidance, however, he soon learned to use it skillfully.

Friday's lessons in shooting proved valuable, for one day, after we had lived together pleasantly for several years, our island was once again visited by savages bringing bound captives upon whom they planned to feast. I saw with horror that one of their prisoners was a bearded man wearing European clothes—perhaps one of my own countrymen. "Friday," I said, "we must resolve to fight them; can you fight?" "Yes," said he, "but there are many of them."

We rushed from the woods and fired upon the cannibals, killing or wounding most of them. The survivors fled to their canoes and escaped, leaving the European alive. We untied him, and gave him food and drink, for which he thanked us in Spanish. Then, hearing a groaning noise, we looked to find an old man lying bound in the bottom of one of the abandoned canoes. When Friday heard him speak and looked in his face, Friday kissed him, embraced him, hugged him, cried, laughed, jumped about, danced, sung, and then cried again. When at last he came to himself, he told me that the old man was his father.

I learned from the Spaniard that he was but one of seventeen of his countrymen who had been cast away on the mainland, and that they were in sore need of provisions. Reflecting that I might help them, I proposed a plan to bring them to the island where there was plenty of food to sustain them while together we might build a bark to take us home. So taking Friday's father with him, the Spaniard left to fetch his companions. I was not to need their assistance in leaving the island, however, for a few days later Friday and I were surprised by the arrival of an English ship. The insolent crew members had taken over the vessel, which they had landed upon our shores for the purpose of disposing of the good captain, his mate, and a passenger. They had not reckoned upon finding the island inhabited, and soon we had rescued the prisoners and subdued the mutineers, who begged for mercy. Seeing that I was governor of the island, the grateful captain gave me leave to dispose of the crew as I saw fit, so when we departed in the English ship I allowed them to escape hanging by remaining on the island where they might find acceptance with the arriving Spaniards.

And thus I left the island, the nineteenth of December as I found by the ship's account, in the year 1686, after I had been stranded seven and twenty years, two months, and nineteen days. I returned with Friday to England to find that the investments I had made many years before had fared well in the hands of honest friends, and that I was a prosperous man. At last my years of hardship were rewarded.

On Thin Ice

(adapted and retold from the novel *Little Women* by Louisa May Alcott)

Louisa May Alcott's novels Little Women *and* Little Men *introduce us to the March family—the sisters Meg, Jo, Beth, and Amy, their beloved mother, "Marmee," and their kindly, often-absent father. At the beginning of* Little Women, *the Reverend Mr. March is away, a chaplain with the Union army during the Civil War. The family is poor because Mr. March has lost a great deal of money trying to help a friend. Despite these hardships, Marmee and her four "little women" manage to celebrate Christmas with warmth and to welcome the New Year gladly. They find the cold New England winter difficult, but they also have amusements. At one party, Meg and Jo meet their young neighbor, a boy named Laurie, with whom they become fast friends. As you will see, the March sisters are very close— but they have their differences, like all brothers and sisters.*

"Where are you going?" Amy asked Jo and Meg, when she found them getting ready to go out. There was an air of secrecy about them that excited her curiosity.

"Never mind; little girls shouldn't ask questions," returned Jo sharply.

Amy bridled at this insult and turned coaxingly to Meg. "Do tell me! Oh, wherever you're going you might let me go, too, for Beth is fussing over her piano, and I haven't got anything to do. And I am *so* lonely."

But Meg and Jo told her that she wasn't invited, and besides, they said, she must remember that she was still recovering from a cold. When Amy guessed that they were going to the theater with Laurie, Meg gave in and said they might take her, if she bundled up in warm clothes. But this made Jo even more irritable.

"Laurie invited the two of us. And it will be rude to drag Amy along. I should think she'd hate to poke herself in where she isn't wanted," said Jo crossly, for she disliked the trouble of overseeing a fidgety child when she wanted to enjoy herself. "You may just stay where you are," she scolded.

Her tone and manner angered Amy, who sat on the floor with one boot on and one off, and began to cry. The two older girls hurried downstairs and left their sister wailing in their bedroom like a spoiled child. Just as the party was setting out, Amy called down over the banister in a threatening tone, "You'll be sorry for this, Jo March; see if you aren't!"

"Fiddlesticks!" returned Jo, slamming the door.

Meg and Jo and Laurie had a charming time at the theater. *The Seven Castles of Diamond Lake* was a play as brilliant and wonderful as any heart could wish. But in spite of the comic imps and gorgeous princesses, Jo's pleasure was not complete. The fairy queen's yellow curls reminded her of Amy. And between the acts she found herself wondering what her sister would do to make her "sorry for this." Both Amy and Jo had quick tempers, and when Amy teased Jo and Jo irritated Amy, explosions occurred, of which both were much ashamed afterward. Jo, the oldest, had a hard time curbing her fiery spirit, but her anger never lasted long and her repentance was always sincere. Poor Jo tried desperately to be good, but her temper was always ready to flame up and defeat her.

When the theatergoers returned, Amy was reading quietly. Jo went straight to her bureau, for in their last quarrel, Amy had turned Jo's top drawer upside down on the floor. Tonight everything was in its place, however.

But it was a mistake to think that Amy had forgiven and forgotten, for the next day Jo burst into the living room. "Has anyone taken my notebook?" she demanded. Amy said nothing. "You've got it!" Jo cried.

"No, I haven't."

"That's a fib!" Jo looked very fierce. "You'd better tell me about it at once."

"Scold as much as you like, you'll never see your silly old book again. I burned it up!" said Amy, getting excited in her turn.

"What! Have you really burned it?" Jo turned pale.

"Yes, I did! I told you I'd make you pay for being so cross yesterday, and I have, so—"

She got no farther, for Jo's hot temper mastered her, and she shook Amy, crying, "You wicked, wicked girl! I can never write it again, and I'll never forgive you as long as I live." Meg rescued Amy, and Jo rushed up to the old sofa in the garret, where she finished her fight alone.

The loss of Jo's notebook was a dreadful calamity to her. She had labored over the half-dozen fairy tales inside, secretly hoping to make something good enough to publish. Her stories were the pride of her heart, and she was regarded by the family as a writer of great promise.

Now Amy was sorry for her crime. Considering its seriousness, Amy felt that no one would love her till she had begged Jo's pardon. At tea, Jo looked so grim and unapproachable that it took all of Amy's courage to say, "Please forgive me, Jo, I'm very, very sorry."

"I shall never forgive you," was Jo's stern answer, and from that moment, she ignored Amy entirely. Mrs. March counseled Jo not to let the sun go down on her anger but Jo said, "It was an abominable thing, and she doesn't deserve to be forgiven." With that she marched off to bed, and there was no merry or confidential chatter among the sisters that night.

In the morning, it was bitter cold. Jo looked like a thundercloud. Amy was much offended that her overtures of peace had been repulsed, and began to feel more injured than ever. Nothing went well; Jo dropped her lunch turn-over, Meg was quiet, Beth looked wistful, and Amy kept making remarks about people who talked about being good and yet wouldn't try, even when others set the example.

"Everybody is so hateful," said Jo to herself. "I'll ask Laurie to go skating. He is always kind and jolly, and will put me to rights, I know." And off she went.

Amy heard the clash of skates and exclaimed to Meg, "There! She promised I should go skating too the next time, and this is the last ice we'll have this year. But it's no use asking such a crosspatch to take me."

"You *were* naughty, and it *is* hard for her to forgive the loss of her precious book, but I guess she will forgive you if you ask her at the right minute," said Meg. "Go after them!"

"I'll try!" Amy ran after Jo and Laurie. They were already skating when Amy reached them, but Jo saw her coming, and turned her back on purpose. Laurie did not see Amy at all, for he was carefully skating along the shore, testing the ice. A warm spell had preceded the cold snap, and he wanted to make sure the ice would bear their weight. "I'll check to the first bend before we begin to race," he said.

Jo heard Amy behind her panting, stamping her feet, and trying to put her skates on, but never turned around, for her anger had grown strong, and taken possession of her, like a demon. Laurie shouted, "Keep near the shore; it isn't safe in the middle!" Jo heard, but Amy, still struggling to her feet, did not catch a word Laurie said. Jo's little demon said in her ear, "No matter whether she heard or not, let her take care of herself."

Laurie vanished round the bend; Jo was just at the turn, and Amy, far behind, struck out toward the smoother ice in the middle of the river. For a minute Jo stopped skating, with a strange feeling in her heart. She resolved to go on, but something turned her round just in time to see Amy throw up her hands and go down. The sudden crash of rotten ice, the splash of water, and Amy's cry made Jo's heart stand still. She tried to call Laurie, but her voice was gone. She tried to rush forward toward Amy, but her feet seemed to have no strength in them. For a second, she could only stand motionless, staring, with a terror-stricken face, at the little blue hood floating above the black water. Something rushed swiftly by her, and Laurie's voice cried out.

"Bring a rail. Quick, quick!"

How she did it, she never knew; but for the next few minutes Jo obeyed Laurie blindly. Laurie was quite self-possessed. Lying flat on the ice, he held Amy up till Jo dragged a rail from the fence and together they got the child out of the freezing water, more frightened than hurt.

"Now then, we must walk her home as fast as we can. Pile our things on her, while I get off these confounded skates," cried Laurie, wrapping his coat round Amy, and tugging away at his straps.

Shivering, dripping, and crying, they got Amy home. After an exciting time of it, she fell asleep, rolled in blankets in front of a hot fire. During the bustle, Jo had scarcely spoken, but flew about looking pale and wild. Her dress was torn and her hands were cut by the ice and rails and skate buckles. When Amy was finally asleep, Mrs. March began to bandage Jo's hurt hands.

"Are you sure she is safe?" whispered Jo. "Mother, if she *should* die, it would be my fault." Jo dropped down beside the bed, sobbing. "It's my dreadful temper. When I try to cure it, it breaks out worse than ever! What shall I do, Mother?"

"Amy is quite safe, dear, for you were sensible in covering her and getting her home quickly," said her mother. "As for your temper, you must never get tired of trying, and never think it is impossible to conquer your fault." She kissed her daughter's cheek tenderly.

"Oh, Mother, you don't know how bad it is. It seems as if I could do anything when I'm in a passion!"

"Jo dear, we all have our temptations, and it often takes us all our lives to conquer them. You think your temper is the worst in the world, but mine used to be just like it."

"Yours, Mother? Why, you are never angry!" For the moment, Jo forgot her remorse in her surprise.

"I've been trying to cure it for forty years. And I have only learned not to show it. I still hope to learn not to feel it, though it may take me another forty years to do so."

The patience and humility of her mother's face was a better lesson to Jo than the sharpest reproof. She felt comforted, too, knowing that her mother had a fault like her own, and had tried to mend it. It made her own fault easier to bear and strengthened her resolution to cure it.

"Mother, are you angry when you fold your lips tight together, and go out of the room sometimes?" asked Jo.

"Yes, I've learned to check the hasty words that rise to my lips," answered Mrs. March as she smoothed Jo's disheveled hair.

As they held each other close, Amy stirred, and sighed in her sleep. Jo, as if eager to begin at once to mend her fault, looked up with an expression on her face that it had never worn before.

"I let the sun go down on my anger, and today, if it hadn't been for Laurie, I might have been too late! How could I be so wicked?" said Jo softly as she leaned over her sister.

As if she heard, Amy opened her eyes, and held out her arms, with a smile that went straight to Jo's heart. Neither said a word, but they hugged one another close, in spite of the blankets, and everything was forgiven and forgotten with one hearty kiss.

Rip Van Winkle
(condensed from the story by Washington Irving)

In a village high in the Catskill Mountains, there lived a simple, good-natured fellow by the name of Rip Van Winkle. He was a kind neighbor, and children would shout with joy whenever he approached. The great error in Rip's nature, though, was his aversion to profitable labor. He could fish all day without a murmur even though he never got a nibble, or trudge through hills and swamps for hours at a time to shoot a few squirrels. In fact, Rip was ready

to attend to anybody's business but his own, assisting a neighbor even in the roughest toil. But as to keeping his own farm in order, he found it impossible, and his children were as ragged as if they belonged to nobody. If left to himself, Rip would have whiled his life away in perfect contentment, but his wife kept continually dinning in his ears about his idleness, his carelessness, and the ruin he was bringing on his family. Rip would shrug his shoulders, shake his head, cast up his eyes, but say nothing. Then he would seek refuge outside of the house.

Rip used to console himself, when driven from home, with the company of a group of sages and fellow idlers who convened on a bench in front of an inn. Sitting beneath a sign bearing the likeness of His Majesty George the Third, for New York was in those days still a province of England, they talked over village gossip and told stories. If by chance an old newspaper should fall into their hands from some passing traveler, they would listen as Van Bummel, the schoolmaster, read them its contents, and it would have been worth any statesman's money to hear the discussions that followed. Nicholas Vedder, a patriarch of the village, made his opinions known by the manner in which he smoked his pipe. Short puffs indicated anger; but when he was pleased, he would inhale the smoke slowly and emit it in delicate clouds. But even so august a personage could not escape the scolding of Dame Van Winkle when she appeared in search of her husband.

One day, seeking to escape the labor of the farm and the clamor of his wife, Rip shouldered his gun and walked high into the Catskills in search of squirrels. All day the mountains echoed with the reports of his gun. Finally he threw himself on a green knoll where on one side he could overlook the country below. On the other side he looked down into a deep glen, wild and lonely. Rip lay musing on the scene as evening gradually advanced, and he sighed as he thought of going home.

As he was about to descend to his farm, he heard a voice hallooing, "Rip Van Winkle! Rip Van Winkle!" He perceived a strange figure toiling up the rocks, bent under the weight of something on his back. He was surprised to see any human being in this lonely place, but supposing it to be one of his neighbors in need of assistance, he hastened down to help. The stranger was a short old fellow with a grizzled beard. His dress was of the antique Dutch fashion—a cloth jerkin strapped around the waist and ample breeches with rows of buttons down the sides—and he bore a stout keg that Rip supposed was full of liquor. He made signs for Rip to assist him with his burden, and together they clambered up a narrow gully. Every now and then, long rolling peals like thunder seemed to issue out of a deep ravine. Passing through this ravine, they came to a hollow that looked like a small amphitheater.

In the center was a company of odd-looking persons bowling at ninepins. The thunderous noise Rip had heard from afar was the sound of the ball rolling toward the pins. Like Rip's guide, they were dressed in an outlandish fashion, with long knives in their belts and enormous breeches. One character had a large beard and small, piggish eyes. Another wore a white sugarloaf hat set off with a little red cock's tail. A stout old weather-beaten gentleman seemed to be the commander. They stared at Rip with such lackluster countenances that his heart turned within him and his knees smote together. His

companion now emptied the keg into large flagons. The company quaffed the liquor in profound silence and then returned to their game. As Rip's apprehension subsided, he ventured to taste the beverage. One taste provoked another, and at length his senses were overpowered and he fell into a deep sleep.

Upon waking, he found himself on the green knoll where he had first seen the old man. It was a bright sunny morning. "Surely," thought Rip, "I have not slept here all night." He recalled the strange men—"Oh! That wicked flagon!" thought Rip. "What excuse shall I make to Dame Van Winkle?" He looked around for his gun, but found only an old firelock encrusted with rust. Suspecting he had been robbed, he determined to revisit the scene of the previous evening to demand the return of his gun. As he rose to walk, he found himself stiff in the joints. With difficulty, he located the gully he and his companion had ascended, but to his astonishment a mountain stream was now foaming down it. No traces of the ravine which had led to the amphitheater remained. Rocks presented a high wall over which the torrent came tumbling. He shouldered the rusty firelock, and, with a heart full of trouble, turned his steps homeward.

As he approached the village he met several people, but none whom he knew. They all stared at him with surprise, and stroked their chins. When Rip did the same, he found to his astonishment that his beard had grown a foot long! A troop of children ran at his heels, hooting after him and pointing at his gray beard. There were houses in the village that he had never seen before, with unfamiliar names inscribed over the doors. He began to wonder whether both he and the world around him were bewitched. "That flagon last night," thought he, "has addled my poor head sadly!"

With some difficulty he found his own house. The roof was fallen in and the door was off its hinges. He entered and called for his wife and children, but all was silent. He hastened to the village inn. Before it hung a flag on which was an assemblage of stars and stripes. He recognized on the sign the face of King George, but now the red coat was blue, the head wore a cocked hat, and underneath the figure was printed GENERAL WASHINGTON. There was a crowd of folk around the door, but no one that Rip knew. He inquired, "Where's Nicholas Vedder?"

There was silence, then an old man replied, "Nicholas Vedder! Why he is dead and gone these eighteen years!"

"Where's Van Bummel, the schoolmaster?"

"He went off to war, and is now in Congress."

Rip's heart died away at hearing of these astonishing changes. He said in despair, "I'm not myself. I was myself last night, but I fell asleep on the mountain. Everything's changed, and I can't tell who I am!"

The bystanders looked at each other and tapped their fingers against their foreheads. Then a comely woman pressed through the throng. She had a child in her arms who, frightened by the gray-bearded man's looks, began to cry. "Hush, Rip," cried she, "the old man won't hurt you." The name of the child and the air of the mother awakened a train of recollections in the mind of Rip Van Winkle. He caught the mother and child in his arms and said to the woman, "I am your father—young Rip Van Winkle once—old Rip Van Winkle now! Does nobody know poor Rip Van Winkle?"

All stood amazed, until an old woman, peering into his face for a moment, exclaimed, "Sure enough! It is Rip Van Winkle! Welcome home again, old neighbor. Why, where have you been these twenty years?"

Rip's story was soon told, for the whole twenty years had been to him but as one night. Many were skeptical, but an old man who was well versed in the local traditions corroborated his story in the most satisfactory manner. He assured the company that the Catskill Mountains had always been haunted by strange beings; that the great discoverer Hendrick Hudson kept a vigil there with his ghostly crew of the *Half Moon,* and his own father had once seen them in their old Dutch clothes playing at ninepins in the hollow of the mountain.

Rip's daughter took him home to live with her, her mother having died some years before when she broke a blood vessel in a fit of passion at a peddler. Having arrived at that happy age when a man can be idle with impunity, Rip took his place once more on the bench at the inn door and was revered as one of the patriarchs of the village. He told his story to every stranger who arrived. Some doubted the truth of it, but the old Dutch villagers almost universally gave Rip full credit. Even to this day, whenever a thunderstorm comes up on a summer afternoon, they say that Hendrick Hudson and his crew are at their game of ninepins; and it is a common wish of all henpecked husbands in the neighborhood, when life hangs heavy on their hands, that they might have a quieting draft out of Rip Van Winkle's flagon.

The Legend of Sleepy Hollow
(condensed from the story by Washington Irving)

Not far from the eastern shore of the Hudson River is a little valley known as Sleepy Hollow. A drowsy, dreamy atmosphere seems to hang over the land as if it were under the sway of some witching power. The whole neighborhood abounds with local tales, haunted spots, and twilight superstitions, but the dominant spirit that haunts this region is the apparition of a headless figure on horseback. It is said to be the ghost of a Hessian trooper whose head was carried away by a cannon ball during the Revolutionary War. The ghost rides forth nightly to the scene of battle in search of his head, and he travels with great speed in order to get back to the churchyard before daybreak.

In this out-of-the-way place there lived a worthy fellow by the name of Ichabod Crane, who instructed the children of the vicinity. He was tall but exceedingly lank, with long arms and legs, hands that dangled a mile out of his sleeves, feet that might have served for shovels, and a frame that seemed only loosely joined together. He had huge ears, large green eyes, and a long snipe nose. To see him striding along a hill on a windy day, one might mistake him for some scarecrow escaped from a cornfield. From his schoolhouse could usually be heard the voices of his pupils, reciting their lessons, interrupted now and then by the voice of the master or by the sound of his birch switch as he urged some unfortunate along the path of knowledge.

According to custom, Ichabod Crane was boarded and lodged at the houses of the farmers whose children he instructed. With each one he lived a week at a time, thus making the rounds of the neighborhood. That he might not burden his rustic patrons, he assisted occasionally in the lighter labors of the farms. Laying aside the absolute authority with which he ruled his little empire, the school, he became wonderfully gentle with the children and thus found favor in the eyes of their mothers.

His appearance at a home was apt to occasion some little stir, for the ladies thought his taste and accomplishments vastly superior to those of the rough country swains. He had read several books quite through, and was a perfect master of Cotton Mather's *History of New England Witchcraft*, in which he most firmly believed. It was often his delight, after school was dismissed, to study old Mather's direful tales until dusk. Then, as he wended his way home, every sound of nature would stir his overexcited imagination: the moan of the whippoorwill, the cry of the tree toad, or the dreary hooting of the screech owl.

He loved to pass long winter evenings with the old Dutch wives as they sat spinning by the fire, and listened with interest to their tales of ghosts and goblins—in particular, the legend of the headless horseman. But the pleasure in all this was dearly purchased by the terrors of his subsequent walk homeward. What fearful shapes and shadows beset his path! How often did he dread to look over his shoulder, lest he should behold some unnatural being close behind him!

In addition to his teaching vocation, Ichabod Crane was the singing master of the neighborhood. Among his musical disciples was one Katrina Van Tassel, the only child of a substantial Dutch farmer. She was a blooming lass of fresh eighteen, ripe and rosy-cheeked as one of her father's peaches. She soon found favor in Ichabod's eyes, especially after he had visited her in her paternal mansion. Old Baltus Van Tassel was a thriving, liberal-hearted farmer and a doting father. Every window and crevice of his vast barn was full to bursting with the treasures of the farm. Sleek porkers grunted in their pens, and regiments of turkeys went gobbling through the farmyard. The pedagogue's mouth watered as he pictured every roasting pig running about with an apple in its mouth, and every turkey daintily trussed up with a necklace of savory sausages. As he rolled his eyes over the fat meadowlands and the orchards burdened with ruddy fruit, his heart yearned after the damsel who was to inherit them. His only study was how to gain her affections.

He was to encounter, however, a host of fearful adversaries: Katrina's numerous rustic admirers. The most formidable of these was burly Brom Van Brunt, a local hero of some renown. His Herculean frame had earned him the nickname of Brom Bones. Riding about on his steed Daredevil, a creature full of mettle and mischief, Brom was always ready for a fight or a frolic. Yet with all his roughness, he possessed a strong dash of good humor at bottom.

On one fine autumn morning, a farmhand came to the school door to extend Ichabod an invitation to attend a merrymaking at Mynheer Van Tassel's. The young scholars were turned loose an hour before the usual time, yelping in joy. The gallant Ichabod then brushed up his only suit of rusty black and primped and fussed over his appearance in front of a broken looking glass. That he might make his appearance in true gentlemanly style, he borrowed a horse. Thus gallantly mounted, he issued forth like a knight in quest of adventure. The horse was gaunt and sway-backed; his rusty mane and tail were knotted with burrs; one eye had lost its pupil and was glaring and spectral, but the other had the gleam of a devil in it. He must have had fire and mettle in his day, for he bore the name of Gunpowder. Ichabod was a suitable figure for such a steed; his elbows stuck out like grasshoppers' and as he rode, the motion of his arms was not unlike the flapping of a pair of wings.

The castle of Mynheer Van Tassel was thronged with all the splendid flower of the adjacent country. It was not the charms of the buxom lasses that caught our hero's gaze as he entered the parlor, however, but the sight of a Dutch country tea table piled high with a rich repast of autumn food. Such heaped-up platters of cakes! There was the doughty doughnut, the tender *oly koek*, the crisp cruller, and a whole family of cakes. And then there were apple and peach and pumpkin pies besides ham and smoked beef; dishes of preserved plums, peaches, pears, and quinces; not to mention roasted chickens and bowls of milk and cream. The motherly teapot sent up its vapor from the midst of it all. As Ichabod sampled every dainty, he chuckled to think that he might one day be lord of all this splendor.

Ichabod danced proudly with the lady of his heart, his loosely hung frame clattering about the room, while Brom Bones sat brooding by himself in the corner. When the revel gradually began to break up, Ichabod lingered behind to have a little talk with the heiress Katrina, fully convinced that he was now on the high road to success. Something must have gone wrong at the interview, though, for he soon sallied forth from the mansion with an air quite desolate. He went straight to the stable, and with several hearty kicks roused his steed.

It was the witching time of night when Ichabod traveled homeward. All the ghost stories he had heard came crowding upon his recollection. The night grew darker; the stars seemed to sink deeper in the sky. He had never felt so lonely. A splash by the side of a bridge caught his ear. In the dark shadow, he beheld something huge, misshapen, black and towering. The hair rose upon his head. He stammered, "Who are you?" but received no reply. The shadowy object put itself in motion, and bounded into the middle of the road. It appeared to be a horseman of large dimensions, mounted on a black horse of powerful frame. Ichabod quickened his steed in hopes of leaving the mysterious horse-

man behind. The stranger, however, quickened to an equal pace. The odd silence of Ichabod's companion was soon terribly accounted for: upon seeing his fellow-traveler in relief against the sky, gigantic in height, and muffled in a cloak, Ichabod was horror-struck to perceive that the figure was headless and carried his head before him on his saddle. In desperation Ichabod rained kicks upon Gunpowder. The specter stayed right with him. Away they dashed, stones flying.

An opening in the trees now cheered him with the hope that the church bridge was at hand, the place where, legend said, the horseman should stop. Ichabod cast a look behind to see if his pursuer would vanish. Instead, he saw the goblin in the very act of hurling his head at him. Ichabod endeavored to dodge, but too late. With a crash, he was tumbled into the dust, while Gunpowder, together with the goblin rider, passed by like a whirlwind.

The next morning the old horse was found cropping grass at his master's gate. The students were assembled at the schoolhouse as usual, but no schoolmaster arrived. The tracks of horses' hooves deeply dented in the road were traced to the bridge. On the bank was found the hat of the unfortunate Ichabod, and close beside it a shattered pumpkin. All shook their heads and came to the conclusion that Ichabod had been carried off by the galloping Hessian.

Several years after, a traveler claimed that Ichabod Crane was still alive somewhere and had turned politician. And Brom Bones, who shortly after his rival's disappearance conducted Katrina in triumph to the altar, looked exceedingly knowing whenever the story of Ichabod was related, and always burst into hearty laughter at the mention of the pumpkin. The old country wives, however, maintain to this day that Ichabod was spirited away. It is said that one may still hear his voice, chanting a melancholy psalm in the solitude of Sleepy Hollow.

The Sun Dance

For many of the Plains Indian tribes, the Sun Dance is the way to ask for or repay a favor granted to them by one of the great powers or gods, such as the Great Mystery (Wakan Tanka) of the Sioux or Tirawa of the Pawnee. Because the dance involves great effort, and sometimes even pain, the dancers undertake it only for the most important reasons. Some dance so that a sick friend might be healed. In the past, some celebrated war victories with the Sun Dance.

Many of the tribes tell stories that explain the origin of the dance. The story of Feather Woman, Morning Star, and Scar Face is a tale told by the Blackfoot Indians.

One summer night, a young girl named Feather Woman left her airless tepee to sleep in the sweet-smelling breeze of the plains. When she woke, she found the Morning Star winking back at her. She lay under his spell, and laughing, said, "Morning Star, I would like to wake to your bright welcome every morning." Then she rose to help her sister gather berries and herbs for the dyeing of buffalo skins.

The sisters wandered far into the woods. They had drifted a great way from each other, when Feather Woman discovered a tall young man standing in the midst of a juniper bush before her. His head was crowned with eagle feathers, and his hands and face glistened as though he had passed through a spider's web.

"Feather Woman," he said, "I am Morning Star. Would you come away with me?"

Feather Woman laughed so hard that she spilled all of her berries on the ground. "Oh, you foolish boy," she said. "Why would I leave my family for a stranger?"

As Morning Star took her hand, Feather Woman felt the warmth of the sun on her skin. "Feather Woman," he said. "I have tried to read your thoughts during the many early mornings that you have lain dreaming on the plain. I would like to marry you and take you to Star Country."

Taking his other hand, Feather Woman stepped onto the silk gloss of a spiderweb. And together they flew into the sky as magically as the spider casts his silken threads.

Feather Woman discovered a country much like her own. The prairie grasses sang in the wind, the star people stitched soft, white deerskins, and women dug for roots to dye them. Morning Star took her to the tepee of his parents, Sun and Moon. Moon welcomed her with smiles; when Sun returned in the evening, weary from his passage across the sky, he bid her to learn the ways of his people if she wanted to stay in the Country of the Stars. He said that Moon would teach her.

Morning Star and Feather Woman were married, and soon had a child, Star Boy. Whenever she went with Moon and the other star women to do their daily work, she would bundle her child in soft clothes and carry him with her.

Moon showed her which roots were edible, and which cast the perfect colors for a painting. She also pointed to a large turnip root, which grew nearly as high as the trees, and told her never to dig there. The turnip root was a mystery known only to Sun.

One afternoon, Moon returned Feather Woman's smiles only weakly, and asked her to go to gather the roots alone while she rested. Feather Woman wandered into the woods, taking her child for company. She sang the songs of her own people, and wondered if her sister had married. Deeply homesick, she discovered that she had wandered near the turnip root. Curious, she forgot Moon's warning and began to dig.

She had made little progress, when two white cranes alighted beside her. They cooed, "Can we help you? Our bills are sharp. We can unearth the root for you."

Not knowing that there was a terrible history between the cranes and the star people, Feather Woman consented. The cranes tore at the turnip's roots, and finally the plant fell to its side, pulling up a great chunk of ground. Gathering her baby close, Feather Woman jumped away from the opening. Urging Feather Woman to "Look, look," the cranes lifted their wings and disappeared.

Feather Woman lay on the ground and peered into the yawning doorway to the earth. Far, far below, she saw her sisters running on the prairie. Her father was returning from a hunt, and echoes of her mother's welcome reached her ears. Her heart yearned for home.

That night when she returned to the tepee, Sun gazed on her face and saw her sadness. Harshly he asked, "You have seen below the turnip root to the earth and your people?" When Morning Star heard her say yes, his hands turned cold.

Sun sighed and said, "There can be no sorrow in the Country of the Stars. You must return to earth."

Morning Star and Moon begged him to allow her to stay, but Sun refused. "She must go," he said. "You can talk to her as you used to, when you traverse the sky."

That night, as Feather Woman's family lay in the prairie grass, they saw a star falling toward them. When they awoke, Feather Woman lay beside them. Her child, scarred on the face by their rapid journey, was crying.

*   *   *   *   *

Feather Woman missed Morning Star more and more as the years went by. To protect her son from hurt, she did not tell him who his father was. They spent much of their time alone. Then one day, when Star Boy tried to wake her, he found that her spirit had left for the sandhills.

Because of the mark on his face, the boy now called Scar Face was treated unkindly by many people in the tribe. His birth was mysterious, and they did not want to be near him. In time, so many called him "Scar Face" that everyone forgot his real name.

When Scar Face was a young man, he fell in love with the daughter of the chief. She talked to him kindly when they met, and she never looked away from his face, but smiled and looked in his eyes. Scar Face wanted to marry her.

But when he asked she said, "I have seen the Sun in my dreams and he told me to wait for him."

Scar Face knew that many men wanted to marry her. They held dancing contests in which each tried to dance better than the others to gain her attention. Scar Face knew that she could marry anyone she chose. Ashamed of asking, he turned away.

Several days later she met him near the river where she was gathering water. "Scar Face," she said. "If you find Sun and ask him, I will marry you. But you must bring me some proof that he has agreed."

"But Sun lives far in the West," he cried. "No one knows how to reach him."

The young woman gave him moccasins she had made and a new shirt. "You will find him," she said.

Scar Face traveled far into the mountains. He climbed until he reached the highest peak farthest to the west. Hoping that he might receive a message from the great forces, he began to fast and pray. One night, the Milky Way seemed to reach down to the peak where he was sitting. Scar Face stepped into the air, and journeyed into Star Country.

Scar Face waited in the path of Sun until he saw that Sun had risen, made his day's journey, and was home to rest. Then he entered the tepee of Sun. "My name is Scar Face," he said. "And I love a young woman who was told by you that she must follow your word all of her life. I have come to ask your permission to marry her."

Sun knew who Scar Face was, for it was Sun who had marked the boy's face as he fell to earth. He wanted to know him as he traveled overhead.

Looking at her husband, Moon knew that Sun felt kindly toward the boy. She smiled and said, "Stay with us while Sun decides. You can keep our son, Morning Star, company."

In Star Country, people do not age as they do on earth, so Morning Star was only slightly older than his son Scar Face, whom he did not recognize. The two became good friends, and both received the words of wisdom that were given to them by Sun.

One day, Sun explained why the cranes were so feared by the stars. "They wait until a star begins to cross the sky, and then they attack, using their bills to tear the fragile ladder that Spider has spun for the stars to climb."

Morning Star explained that the cranes had attacked his brothers when they were very young. Falling, his brothers burst into fire and then disappeared in the black sky.

One afternoon, when Morning Star and Scar Face were hunting, the cranes appeared and began swooping down on them. Morning Star frantically ran for cover. Scar Face waved his spear at them, daring them to come closer. As the birds closed in, Scar Face turned to meet them. He did not care if they threatened to hurt his face; it had always hurt him. He felled them one by one.

When Morning Star saw that his friend had saved him, he gathered the heads of the cranes and scalped them. He was afraid that no one would believe his friend's bravery.

When Sun heard the story, he danced a celebratory dance and Moon sang praises for the young man's courage. Sun took Scar Face to a hole in the sky, and together, they looked down upon the earth. Sun traced its shape with his hand, and when they returned, Moon had gathered willows and used them to build a lodge in the earth's shape. She dug a hole in the center of the lodge and filled it with heated stones. When the people had raised a sun pole outside, the family entered the lodge. Moon poured water over the hot rocks, and the steam rose up to cleanse them.

When they emerged from the lodge, the scar was gone from the boy's face. Instantly, Morning Star knew him as Star Boy, his son. The father and son walked to the edge of the Milky Way and bid each other good-bye. "In the morning," Morning Star said, "look up. I will be watching you and your good wife."

Star Boy found the chief's daughter near the river. When she saw him, she knew that Sun had consented to their marriage, and she was happy. Together, they returned to tell the others. And from Star Boy the people learned the Sun Dance.

Treasure Island

(retold with excerpts from the novel by Robert Louis Stevenson)

This story is told by a boy named Jim Hawkins. "Pieces of eight" are gold coins.

Since I, Jim Hawkins, have been asked to tell this story, I go back to the night when we found the map, on the night of the old captain's death. He had lodged at our inn for many weeks without paying, frightening everyone with his dreadful stories about walking the plank and wild deeds at sea. I remember well the sound of his drunken voice, piping up his eternal song:

> Fifteen men on the dead man's chest—
> Yo-ho-ho, and a bottle of rum!

I supposed "the dead man's chest" to be a big box of his that stood upstairs. I knew it contained something of value, for he confided to me that some of his old shipmates were "after it."

That evening a blind man named Pew grabbed me roughly and demanded to talk with the captain, to whom he delivered a piece of paper marked with a black spot. When Pew left, the captain cried in terror, "We have six hours! We'll do them yet!" Then he reeled, clutched his throat, and fell to the floor, dead.

My mother sent for Dr. Livesay, the local magistrate, to help us. But she was also determined to get from the seaman what he owed us. "We'll have that chest open, if we die for it," she said. Shaking, I took the key from his neck and turned it in the lock. Inside were gold coins of all countries. As we counted it out, we heard the tapping of Pew's cane outside.

"I'll take what I have," said my mother, jumping to her feet, and I picked up an oil-skinned packet to square the count. We ran out and hid nearby, barely eluding a group approaching with a lantern. Pew shouted orders to break down the door. They entered, and another voice shouted, "Bill's dead!"

"Search him, you shirking lubbers, and get the chest!"

"Someone's been here before us. But the money's there."

The blind man cursed the money and cried, "I want Flint's map. That boy's taken it. I wish I had put his eyes out!"

Suddenly the King's officers came galloping, and the buccaneers turned and ran. Pew lurched into the path of a rider and was struck down dead. Other riders pursued Pew's mates to the water's edge, but they sailed clean off in their lugger.

My mother and I came out of our hiding place, and the officers took me to Dr. Livesay and Squire Trelawney. They listened to my story with interest, remarking that the "Flint" Pew named was a notorious pirate. Then the doctor cut open the oil-skinned packet. Out fell the map of an island, with its location noted and one spot marked, "bulk of treasure here." The squire was delighted. "Tomorrow I go to Bristol to get the best ship in England," he said. "Hawkins shall come as cabin boy. You, Livesay, are ship's doctor; I am admiral. We'll find this spot, and we'll have money to roll in!"

Several weeks later our ship, the *Hispaniola*, was ready. The squire employed as the ship's cook a one-legged pub owner named Long John Silver, who carried on his shoulder a parrot he had named Captain Flint, after the pirate. Silver explained that he had lost his leg while serving in the Royal Navy, which so impressed the squire that he entrusted Silver with hiring the crew. Long John seemed to me the best possible shipmate, for as we walked among the quays together, he explained what the sailors were about, told me stories of ships and seamen, and repeated nautical terms until I had learned them perfectly, telling me I was "smart as paint."

We had just begun our journey when our captain, Mr. Smollett, complained to the squire that the crew seemed to know all about the treasure we were seeking, even though none of us had breathed a word to them. He agreed to stay only on the condition that the whereabouts of the map be kept secret. The squire agreed. The crew drove the bars before them, singing: "Fifteen men on the dead man's chest, Yo-ho-ho, and a bottle of rum!" and the anchors were raised.

The voyage went well, until one night I overheard Long John Silver telling a crew member named Dick that if he would "join up," he could "end this cruise with hundreds of pounds in his pockets." "Well, there's my hand on it," said Dick.

"You're a brave lad, and smart as paint," said Silver. The rogue was addressing Dick with the same words he had used to me! I now understood that Silver was nothing more than a common pirate. Now another man approached, to whom Silver said, "Dick's square."

I heard the voice of Israel Hands, the coxswain. "He's no fool, is Dick. But what I want to know is, when do we lay 'em athwart? I've had enough o' Cap'n Smollett, by thunder!"

Long John Silver warned him to be patient until the treasure was safely stowed and the able Smollett had set the course for home. "But when the time comes," he said, "let her rip! I'll wring Trelawney's head off his body with these hands." Suddenly they were interrupted by a shout of "Land Ho!" and as they busied themselves for landing, I sought Dr. Livesay, the squire, and Captain Smollett in their quarters. They were shocked to learn about Silver, and vowed to be on guard and to strike first.

The next morning the captain gave the crew permission to spend the day ashore rather than give them the chance to defy orders. A wild notion entered my head to see the island, so I sneaked aboard one of the small boats. Silver spotted me just as we landed, and called out to me, but by then I was several hundred yards ahead of the rest, and soon I had hidden deep in the undergrowth. After a while I heard voices nearby. It was Long John Silver, trying to convince one of the last honest men to join his side. The man defied him, then boldly turned his back and walked away. Grabbing a tree to steady himself, Long John hurled his crutch, knocking the man dead to the ground. Fearing that I would be next, I ran away as fast as I could.

I ran as I had never run before, scarcely minding the direction of my flight so long as it took me away from the murderers. As I ran, fear grew and grew in me, until it turned into a frenzy. Then suddenly I saw a figure, maybe a bear or monkey, maybe a man, which gave me new reason to flee.

But I was soon brought to a stop. There in a clearing stood a sunburned man, with long hair and beard, clad only in a tattered sail. He ran to me eagerly, crying out that he hadn't seen another human being in years. His name was Benjamin Gunn, he said, and he had been marooned there by some angry shipmates after leading them on an unsuccessful quest for Flint's treasure. He was rich, he confided (which made me doubt his sanity), but he had lived off wild goat's flesh and coconuts all this time. I decided to tell him our story, and he promised to help if he might only escape the island with us, being allowed to keep what was rightfully his. He told me where I might find his little homemade boat, hidden in a cove.

Suddenly I heard the sound of cannon, and looked up to see the Union Jack flying above the trees. I ran toward it, and found the stockade I had seen marked on the map, which was being stoutly defended by my friends. They had fled there with arms and some provisions, and now the pirates led by Long John Silver were approaching. I scaled the wall to welcoming cries, and went to work keeping the guns loaded while my friends fired continually, killing a number of the rogues who scaled the wall or rushed upon the fortress. At last the pirates retreated, leaving many of their own dead, and several of ours. We held a somber meeting and decided that our only chance of success lay in setting the ship adrift while the rogues were encamped on shore, thereby cutting off their supplies and means of escape. No sooner had I heard this than I thought of Ben Gunn's boat, and without a word, I stuck a pistol in my belt and was off.

Soon I had found the little craft, rowed it to the *Hispaniola,* and cut the anchor's rope. I followed the ship as it drifted away, and climbed aboard. Only Israel Hands and one other man were aboard, and they were engaged in a drunken argument, unaware of me. When it was over, the other man lay dead, and Hands nursed a knife wound in the leg. At this point I made my appearance, announcing that I was taking command of the ship. Hands seemed to give in, apparently too injured to resist. First I lowered the hateful Jolly Roger, hurled it overboard, and raised the flag of England. Then I did my best to steer the ship to a cove which I knew from the map to lie at the island's other end. But no sooner had the *Hispaniola* run safely aground there, than Hands was on his feet after me. He chased me as I climbed the mast. I turned and drew my pistol, just as he hurled his knife, pinning my shirt to the mast. I fired, and he plummeted into the cove.

I made my way back to the stockade in the darkness, only to be greeted by Silver's parrot screaming, "Pieces of eight! Pieces of eight!" Immediately I was captured by the pirates, who told me that my friends had exchanged the stockade and the map for their freedom, and had now retreated to another part of the island. Long John decided to keep me, just in case he should need a hostage. "Kill me if you want," I said, "but know that I set the ship adrift and killed Israel Hands!" Silver had barely kept the men from killing me when they heard this, when we saw Dr. Livesay approaching. Silver agreed to let me speak with him only after I gave my word not to run. Relieved to see me alive, the doctor suddenly drew his gun upon Silver and urged me to make a break for it. But having given my word as a gentleman, I told him I must stay. "Well, we'll not leave the island without you," he said. Then he said ominously to Silver, "And when you find the treasure, prepare for squalls!"

Even with the map, it was with some difficulty that the pirates found the spot marked "X." As we approached the tall tree near which it was supposed to lie, we came upon the chilling sight of a human skeleton, its bony hands joined over its head on the ground as if to point the way. Suddenly an eerie voice called out, "Fetch aft the rum, Darby M'Graw!" The men looked up in alarm. "Those were Flint's last words," they said. "It's Flint's ghost!" But Silver listened carefully, then said, "By the powers, that's Ben Gunn's voice, and nobody minds him, alive or dead."

In another moment we had come to the spot. There on the ground was a deep ditch, and the remains of a huge chest, split asunder and emptied of its contents. The crew turned upon Silver angrily and drew their pistols, vowing to kill us both. Just then shots rang out from the other direction, where I turned to see my friends coming, led by Ben Gunn. Some of the buccaneers fell, and the rest quickly surrendered.

Dr. Livesay and the others led me and the captives to Ben's cave, where Flint's entire treasure lay safely stowed as it had been ever since Gunn had found it years before. We loaded it aboard the *Hispaniola* and headed for home, leaving all the pirates save Long John Silver to survive as Ben had done, with the help of some arms and provisions. It was our intent to see Silver brought to justice and hanged, but one evening he jumped ship and eluded us forever.

All of us had an ample share of the treasure and used it wisely or foolishly, according to our natures. I vowed that oxen and ropes would not bring me back again to that accursed island; and the worst dreams that ever I have are when I start upright in bed, with the sharp voice of Captain Flint the parrot still ringing in my ears: "Pieces of eight! Pieces of eight!"

Narrative of the Life of Frederick Douglass
(retold with excerpts from the original by Frederick Douglass)

Frederick Douglass was born a slave in Maryland in 1817. In the South before the Civil War, it was against the law for a slave to learn to read and write. But a few, like Douglass, managed to learn.

When Frederick Douglass was twenty-one, he escaped from slavery and made his way to Massachusetts. Eventually he joined the antislavery movement and began making powerful speeches.

In 1845 he wrote a vivid book about his years in slavery, Narrative of the Life of Frederick Douglass. *The book made him famous. The laws at the time said that an escaped slave living in a free state could be caught and returned to his owner. To avoid being recognized and captured, Douglass left America to give speeches in England. When he returned to America, he bought his freedom, and started an antislavery newspaper. During the Civil War, he recruited African-Americans for the Union Army. Shortly before he died, he became the United States ambassador to Haiti.*

From the time that I was very young, I knew that I would not remain a slave for the whole of my life. I was born in Tuckahoe, Maryland. Like most of those who were born into slavery, I have no knowledge of the year I was born as masters did not like to provide slaves with any such information. Some people have told me that my father was my white slave owner. This was a common practice, as it increased the owner's slave holdings, but it boded ill for the child. My mother was traded to another plantation early on, and I only saw her a few times in my life, and then only at night, so I held a special affection for her.

I have been owned and leased by several masters in my life and worked as a house servant, a field hand (the most cruel of labors), and a ship carpenter. When young, I lived at the Great Farm House. It was considered a great sign of trust for an overseer to permit a slave to collect the pay and supplies there. As he made his way, a slave's singing could be heard throughout the quiet woods. Every tone was a prayer to God for deliverance from his chains. I have been utterly astonished to hear that people in the North often mistake that singing for happiness. A slave's songs represent the sorrows in his heart, and he finds relief through them as if they were tears.

When I was twelve or so, I was leased to my master's relative. For a time, my

Frederick Douglass.

mistress taught me my ABC's, and would have gone further had her husband not forbidden it. He thought that education made a slave unruly and discontent. He was right: the more I learned, the more determined I was to be free. I carried books with me whenever I was sent on an errand, and traded bread for reading lessons from the little white boys playing in the street. When my master's son left school, I secretly copied the handwriting in his practice book, and then challenged the street boys to handwriting competitions. I learned to read and write in the only way possible for a slave: I stole the knowledge.

At sixteen, I was leased again to a Mr. Covey, an overseer with a reputation for breaking untamed slaves. I lived with Mr. Covey for one year. During the first six months, hardly a week passed without his whipping me. I was seldom free from a sore back. Mr. Covey gave us enough to eat, but scarce time to eat it. The longest days were too short for him, and the shortest nights too long for him. I was somewhat unmanageable when I first went there, but a few months of his discipline tamed me.

But then came the turning point in my life as a slave. One morning, Mr. Covey met me with a rope, intent on punishment. For the first time in my life, I resisted. I tossed him to the ground, and fought. When he saw that I meant to persist, he walked off and my long-crushed spirit rose. From then on, I let it be known that the white man who succeeded in whipping me must also succeed in killing me. I had several more fights, but I was never beaten again, though I remained a slave for four more years.

After one failed attempt, I finally succeeded in escaping in 1838. I cannot tell you how or who was kind enough to help me, as this information might be used against those who may attempt freedom later. But I settled in New Bedford with my wife (who was already free), where I have lived with a pleasure never known before. Here, people are far wealthier than any plantation owner—they are rich with freedom. Until I die, I will strive for the abolition of slavery and the freedom of all my brethren.

The Glittering Cloud

(retold with excerpts from *On the Banks of Plum Creek* by Laura Ingalls Wilder)

When Laura Ingalls Wilder was growing up, her family lived in one cabin after another on the western frontier, first in "The Big Woods," and later on the prairie. As the frontier moved west, so did the Wilder family. Many years later, Mrs. Wilder wrote nine books about her childhood. You might enjoy these books, beginning with Little House in the Big Woods. *Here is an episode from* On the Banks of Plum Creek.

One day a dark cloud covered the sun, a cloud unlike anything Ma or Pa or Mary or Laura or Baby Carrie had ever seen. It was a cloud of something like snowflakes, but it was made of bits of stuff larger than snowflakes, and thin and glittering. Light shone through each flickering particle, and the light was queer. Standing in the yard, Laura was frightened.

Plunk! Something hit Laura's head and fell to the ground. She looked down and saw the largest grasshopper she had ever seen. Suddenly, the cloud was raining grasshoppers. Their bodies hid the sun. The rasping whirring of their wings filled the air and they hit the ground and the house with the noise of a hailstorm.

Laura tried to beat them off. They clung to her arms and her hair and crawled under her petticoats. Then Laura heard another sound, one big sound made of millions of tiny nips and snips and gnawing. The grasshoppers were eating the precious wheat crop. Pa hitched the horses to the hay wagon and drove through the wheat field, throwing out piles of hay. Ma followed behind him, lighting a fire in each pile. To save the crop, they would try to smoke the grasshoppers out.

The money from this crop was meant to pay off the debt on the house and feed and clothe the family for the year. But there was nothing anyone could do. The grasshoppers ate through the spring. They ate the wheat, and the grassy knolls, and the tops of the willow trees. In the summer, they laid their eggs, and they ate. Throughout the fall, the whole prairie was bare and brown, and the cows began to starve. During the winter, the insects waited. And in the spring, the snow melted, and the creek began to run, the air grew hot, and like corn popping up through the ground, the grasshopper eggs began to hatch. The days got hotter and hotter, and uglier and uglier, and filled with the sound of grasshoppers eating until it seemed more than could be borne.

* * *

"Oh, Charles," Ma said one morning, "seems to me I just can't bear one more day of this."

Ma was sick. Her face was white and thin, and she sat down tired as she spoke. Pa did not answer. For days, he had been going out and coming in with a still, tight face. He did not sing or whistle anymore. It was worst of all when he did not answer Ma. He walked to the door and stood looking out.

"Caroline," he said. "Here's a strange thing. Come look!"

All across the yard, the grasshoppers were walking shoulder to shoulder and end to end, so crowded that the ground seemed to be moving. As fast as they could, they were all walking west.

Mary asked, "Oh, Pa, what does it mean?" and Pa said, "I don't know. It's the same as far as the eye can see. The whole ground is crawling west."

Pa walked around the corner of the house. When he came back in, he said, "Better shut the upstairs window, they are as thick walking up the east side of the house and they are not going around the attic window." The grasshoppers came pouring in the east windows, side by side and end to end!

That whole day long the grasshoppers walked west, and the second day and the third day. No grasshopper turned out of its way for anything. They walked into Plum Creek and drowned, and those behind them kept walking in and drowning until the live ones could walk right over the stacked bodies. And then on the fourth morning, they spread their wings and lifted from the ground. Like a dark, gleaming, glittering, shimmering bright cloud, they rose and went far to the west until they could be seen no more. The sudden stillness was like the stillness after a storm.

Praying her thanks, Ma went into the house and threw herself down in the rocking chair. Laura and Mary sat on the doorstep, which was clear at last. Pa leaned in the doorway next to them.

"I would like someone to tell me how they all knew at once that it was time to go, and how they knew which way was west—the way towards their ancestral home," he said.

But no one could tell him.

Several of the stories you have read are told by someone who is in a difficult situation and needs to find a way to get out of trouble or improve things. Have you ever been in a situation like this? Write a story about it from your point of view.

Sojourner Truth's "Ain't I a Woman"

Sojourner Truth was born into slavery in New York in 1795, and gained her freedom in 1827, when the state emancipated its slaves. After working as a domestic for several years, she began to speak publicly on behalf of abolition and the rights of women.

In 1851, she attended a women's convention in Akron, Ohio. The convention participants did not support her attendance; they were afraid that their cause, the rights of women, would be damaged if it were associated with the rights of blacks. Just a short way into the meeting, the women were opposed by clergymen in the audience who argued against women's rights. They claimed that Jesus Christ was a man. And they recalled from the Bible the story of Adam and Eve, which tells how Eve tempted Adam to disobey God's orders. The atmosphere of the convention thickened with disagreement.

Sojourner Truth rose from her seat and approached the platform. When Frances Gage, the presider, introduced her, Sojourner Truth was met with hisses. Gage writes that when Sojourner Truth fixed her eyes on the crowd and spoke, her vivid, moving words had a "magical" effect. She had "taken us up in her strong arms and carried us safely over the slough of difficulty turning the whole tide in our favor." Here are her words:

Well, children, there is so much racket there must be something out of kilter. I think that 'twixt the Negroes of the South and the women of the North, all talking about rights, the white men will be in a fix pretty soon. But what's all this talking about?

That man over there says that women need to be helped into carriages, and lifted over ditches, and to have the best place everywhere. Nobody helps me into carriages, or over mud-puddles, or gives me any best place! And ain't I a woman? Look at me! Look at my arm! I have ploughed

Sojourner Truth.

and planted, and gathered into barns, and no man could head me! And ain't I a woman? I could work as much and eat as much as a man—when I could get it—and bear the lash as well! And ain't I a woman? I have borne thirteen children, and seen them most all sold off to slavery, and when I cried out with my mother's grief, none but Jesus heard me! And ain't I a woman?

Then they talk about this thing in my head; what's this they call it? [Intellect, someone whispers.] That's it, honey. What's that got to do with women's rights or Negro's rights? If my cup won't hold but a pint, and yours holds a quart, wouldn't you be mean not to let me have my half-measure full?

Then that little man in black there, he says women can't have as much rights as men, 'cause Christ wasn't a woman! Where did your Christ come from? From God and woman! Man had nothing to do with Him!

If the first woman God ever made was strong enough to turn the world upside down all alone, these women together ought to be able to turn it back, and get it right side up again! And now they is asking to do it, the men better let them.

Obliged to you for hearing me, and now old Sojourner Truth ain't got nothing more to say.

Introduction to Poetry

FOR PARENTS AND TEACHERS

The best way to bring children into the spirit of poetry is to read it aloud to them and encourage them to speak it aloud so they can experience the music in the words.

In choosing poems for this section, we wanted all selections to meet two goals: immediacy of pleasure and quality. Most of the poems in this section use short lines, rhymes, and strong rhythms. The rhythm and vividness of the language should appeal to children.

Until children take pleasure in the sound and sentiment of poetry, there is little reason to study it technically. Robert Frost once said that unless students *like* poetry long before they fully understand it, the teacher of literature should write over the classroom door, "Abandon Hope All Ye Who Enter Here."

A child's knowledge of poetry, then, should come first from pleasure and only later from analysis. But a couple of simple terms—like "line" and "stanza"—can help parents and children, or students and teachers, talk about the particular parts of a poem they like best. Without getting technical, you can ask a child, "What's your favorite line?" or say, "Let's read that last stanza again!"

NOTE TO PARENTS AND TEACHERS: *The poet Kenneth Koch has written two fine books on helping children write poetry and teaching poetry to children. They are:*

Wishes, Lies, and Dreams: Teaching Children to Write Poetry (*Vintage Books*).

Rose, Where Did You Get That Red? Teaching Great Poetry to Children (*Vintage Books*).

A Few Poems for Fourth Grade

Poems About Days

Monday's Child is Fair of Face
Anonymous

Monday's child is fair of face,
Tuesday's child is full of grace,
Wednesday's child is full of woe,
Thursday's child has far to go,
Friday's child is loving and giving,
Saturday's child works hard for a living,
And a child that's born on the Sabbath day
Is fair and wise and good and gay.

Solomon Grundy
Anonymous

Solomon Grundy
Born of a Monday,
Christened on Tuesday,
Married on Wednesday,
Took ill on Thursday,
Worse on Friday,
Died on Saturday,
Buried on Sunday;
This is the end
Of Solomon Grundy.

Poems About Animals

The Rhinoceros
by Ogden Nash

The Rhino is a homely beast,
For human eyes he's not a feast,
But you and I will never know
Why Nature chose to make him so.
Farewell, farewell, you old rhinoceros,
I'll stare at something less prepoceros.

The Frog
by Hilaire Belloc

Be kind and tender to the frog,
    And do not call him names,
As "Slimy skin," or "Polly-wog,"
    Or likewise "Ugly James,"
Or "Gap-a-grin," or "Toad-gone-wrong,"
    Or "Bill Bandy-knees":
The frog is justly sensitive
    To epithets like these.
No animal will more repay
    A treatment kind and fair;
At least so lonely people say
    Who keep a frog (and, by the way,
They are extremely rare).

The Crocodile
by Lewis Carroll

How doth the little crocodile
  Improve his shining tail,
And pour the waters of the Nile
  On every golden scale!

How cheerfully he seems to grin!
  How neatly spreads his claws,
And welcomes little fishes in
  With gently smiling jaws!

Lewis Carroll borrowed the rhythm and rhyme for "The Crocodile" from a poem written earlier by Isaac Watts. Watts' poem, called "Against Idleness and Mischief," begins like this:

How doth the little busy bee
  Improve each shining hour,
And gather honey all the day
  From every opening flower!

How skillfully she builds her cell!
  How neat she spreads the wax!
And labors hard to store it well
  With the sweet food she makes.

When you compare the two poems, you can see that Carroll was up to some mischief himself!

People

Humanity
by Elma Stuckey

If I am blind and need someone
To keep me safe from harm,
It matters not the race to me
Of the one who takes my arm.

If I am saved from drowning
As I grasp and grope,
I will not stop to see the face
Of the one who throws the rope.

Or if out on some battlefield
I'm falling faint and weak,
The one who gently lifts me up
May any language speak.

We sip the water clear and cool,
No matter the hand that gives it.
A life that's lived worthwhile and fine,
What matters the one who lives it?

Dreams
by Langston Hughes

Hold fast to dreams
For if dreams die
Life is a broken-winged bird
That cannot fly.

Hold fast to dreams
For when dreams go
Life is a barren field
Frozen with snow.

Humorous Poems

A Tragic Story
by William Makepeace Thackeray

There lived a sage in days of yore,
And he a handsome pigtail wore;
But wondered much, and sorrowed more,
    Because it hung behind him.

He mused upon this curious case,
And swore he'd change the pigtail's place,
And have it hanging at his face,
    Not dangling there behind him.

Says he, "The mystery I've found—
I'll turn me round,"—he turned him round;
    But still it hung behind him.

Then round and round, and out and in,
All day the puzzled sage did spin;
In vain—it mattered not a pin—
    The pigtail hung behind him.

And right, and left, and round about,
And up, and down, and in, and out
He turned; but still the pigtail stout
    Hung steadily behind him.

And though his efforts never slack,
And though he twist, and twirl, and tack,
Alas! still faithful to his back,
    The pigtail hangs behind him.

The Purple Cow
by Gelett Burgess

I never saw a Purple Cow,
    I never hope to see one,
But I can tell you, anyhow,
    I'd rather see than be one!

Clarence
by Shel Silverstein

Clarence Lee from Tennessee
Loved the commercials he saw on TV.
He watched with wide believing eyes
And bought everything they advertised—
Cream to make his skin feel better,
Spray to make his hair look wetter,
Bleach to make his white things whiter,
Stylish jeans that fit much tighter.
Toothpaste for his cavities,
Powder for his doggie's fleas,
Purple mouthwash for his breath,
Deodorant to stop his sweat.
He bought each cereal they presented,
Bought each game that they invented.
Then one day he looked and saw
"A brand-new Maw, a better Paw!
New, improved in every way—
Hurry, order yours today!"
So, of course, our little Clarence
Sent off for two brand-new parents.
The new ones came in the morning mail,
The old ones he sold at a garage sale.
And now they all are doing fine:
His new folks treat him sweet and kind,
His old ones work in an old coal mine.
So if your Maw and Paw are mean
And make you eat your lima beans
And make you wash and make you wait
And never let you stay up late
And scream and scold and preach and pout,
That simply means they're wearing out.
So send off for two brand-new parents
And you'll be as happy as little Clarence.

The Pobble Who Has No Toes
by Edward Lear

The Pobble who has no toes,
    Had once as many as we;
When they said, "Some day you may lose them all;"
    He replied "Fish fiddle de-dee!"
And his Aunt Jobiska made him drink
Lavender water tinged with pink;
For she said, "The World in general knows
There's nothing so good for a Pobble's toes!"

The Pobble who has no toes,
    Swam across the Bristol Channel;
But before he set out he wrapped his nose
    In a piece of scarlet flannel.
For his Aunt Jobiska said, "No harm
Can come to his toes if his nose is warm;
And it's perfectly known that a Pobble's toes
Are safe—provided he minds his nose."

The Pobble swam fast and well.
    And when boats or ships came near him,
He tinkledy-binkledy-winkled a bell
    So that all the world could hear him.
And all the Sailors and Admirals cried,
When they saw him nearing the further side—
"He has gone to fish, for his Aunt Jobiska's
Runcible Cat with crimson whiskers!"

But before he touched the shore,—
    The shore of the Bristol Channel,
A sea-green Porpoise carried away
    His wrapper of scarlet flannel.
And when he came to observe his feet,
Formerly garnished with toes so neat,
His face at once became forlorn
On perceiving that all his toes were gone!

And nobody ever knew,
From that dark day to the present,
Whoso had taken the Pobble's toes,
In a manner so far from pleasant.
Whether the shrimps or crawfish grey,
Or crafty Mermaids stole them away,
Nobody knew; and nobody knows
How the Pobble was robbed of his twice five toes!

The Pobble who has no toes
Was placed in a friendly Bark,
And they rowed him back, and carried him up
To his Aunt Jobiska's Park.
And she made him a feast, at his earnest wish,
Of eggs and buttercups fried with fish;
And she said, "It's a fact the whole world knows,
That Pobbles are happier without their toes."

Poems About Myself

Life Doesn't Frighten Me
by Maya Angelou

Shadows on the wall
Noises down the hall
Life doesn't frighten me at all
Bad dogs barking loud
Big ghosts in a cloud
Life doesn't frighten me at all.

Mean old Mother Goose
Lions on the loose
They don't frighten me at all
Dragons breathing flame
On my counterpane
That doesn't frighten me at all,

I go boo
Make them shoo
I make fun
Way they run
I won't cry
So they fly
I just smile
They go wild
Life doesn't frighten me at all.

Tough guys in a fight
All alone at night
Life doesn't frighten me at all.

Panthers in the park
Strangers in the dark
No, they don't frighten me at all.

That new classroom where
Boys all pull my hair
(Kissy little girls
With their hair in curls)
They don't frighten me at all.

Don't show me frogs and snakes
And listen for my scream,
If I'm afraid at all
It's only in my dreams.

I've got a magic charm
That I keep up my sleeve,
I can walk the ocean floor
And never have to breathe.

Life doesn't frighten me at all
Not at all
Not at all.
Life doesn't frighten me at all.

Things

by Eloise Greenfield

Went to the corner
Walked in the store
Bought me some candy
Ain't got it no more
Ain't got it no more

Went to the beach
Played on the shore
Built me a sandhouse
Ain't got it no more
Ain't got it no more

Went to the kitchen
Lay down on the floor
Made me a poem
Still got it
Still got it

Digging Up Words

Sometimes the words poets use sound old-fashioned because many years have gone by since the poem was written. Sometimes poets use outdated words on purpose. You remember that some poets, like Shakespeare, or even Dr. Seuss, actually invented words! Pick out some words in these or in other poems you know that sound funny or old-fashioned to you, and talk about them with your teacher or a parent.

Do you know what archaeologists do? They dig up things from the past! Why not "dig up" some of the words you find? Instead of an archaeologist's shovel, you can use a dictionary as your tool, to help you find out what the words mean and where they came from.

Afternoon on a Hill
by Edna St. Vincent Millay

I will be the gladdest thing
    Under the sun!
I will touch a hundred flowers
    And not pick one.

I will look at cliffs and clouds
    With quiet eyes,
Watch the wind bow down the grass,
    And the grass rise.

And when lights begin to show
    Up from the town,
I will mark which must be mine,
    And then start down!

Introduction
to Mythology

Many parents and teachers will greet the stories in the section on Myths from Medieval England with pleasure and familiarity. The tales of King Arthur and his Knights of the Round Table have inspired our culture's literature, music, film, and humor; think, for example, of the musical *Camelot*, or the book *The Once and Future King*, by T. H. White, or of the magician in *The Sorcerer's Apprentice*.

However, the widespread popularity of these myths was not our sole reason for including them in this form. Each book in this series attempts to build on the knowledge gained in the previous books, while having a separate coherence. World Civilization in Book Four focuses on the Middle Ages in Europe, and so we have chosen to present these myths alongside the history of the time responsible for their creation.

There are several questions we can ask ourselves and our children while reading the Arthurian myths included here. Why have people of all times been so intrigued by these stories? King Arthur and his knights or the town of Camelot may never have existed, but ever since the first telling, these stories have caught the imagination of writers all over the world, from Sir Thomas Malory to John Steinbeck. Ask children to think of places where they have seen or heard these stories before. Ask them what they like about these stories and what the stories make them think about.

Myths from Medieval England

The Legend of King Arthur and the Knights of the Round Table

Have you ever heard the tales of knights in bright armor who traveled the land in search of adventure? Of magicians who cast magic spells on anyone foolish enough to oppose them? The noble knights of medieval times followed a code of chivalry: they swore oaths to serve their king and queen, to defend the helpless, and to bring honor to their land. The most famous of these knights were the Knights of the Round Table. The king they served was King Arthur, thought to be the greatest British king of those long-ago days. To promote equality and unity, he seated his knights at an enormous round table. King Arthur was probably a real leader in the early Middle Ages in the British Isles. Although we know almost nothing about the real king, we still have many stories about the legendary King Arthur and his Knights of the Round Table. Here are just a few.

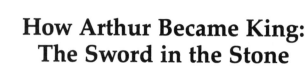

How Arthur Became King: The Sword in the Stone

In days of old, Britain had many kings. One king ruled over all the others, and his name was Uther Pendragon. The dragon was his emblem and he was a mighty warrior and a great ruler. He was not only a great man in battle, but he was wise, too, for he followed the counsel of Merlin, a great magician and seer. Merlin could cast magic spells and even turn himself into animals or other people when he wished. He was called a seer because he could see the future—for everyone, that is, except himself.

Uther Pendragon, with his emblem, the dragon, partially visible on the tunic under his cloak.

Uther Pendragon had a baby son he called Arthur, and one day when Arthur was still young Merlin had a terrifying vision. He foresaw that Uther Pendragon would soon die from a plague that was sweeping the land. And he saw that because Arthur was only a baby, many of the other kings would try to take Arthur's rightful place as the future leader of Britain. Some might even try to harm him, and war would break out. So Merlin secretly gave Arthur into the care of a noble knight, Sir Ector, who did not know he was protecting Britain's next king. Sir Ector raised Arthur along with his own son, Kay.

Just as Merlin had predicted, for years after Uther Pendragon died the other kings warred with each other. All of Britain was in strife, and threatened to fall apart. So Merlin placed a great marble stone in front of England's greatest cathedral. In the stone he placed a steel anvil, and into the stone and anvil he drove a glittering magic sword. On the stone was the inscription:

> *Whosoever pulls out this sword from this stone and anvil*
> *Is the true-born king of all Britain.*

Merlin called all the kings together to have a great feast, and afterward to see which one could pull the sword from the stone. Whoever accomplished this feat would be the king of all the kings, and bring peace to the land once more. Soon all the leaders, with their ladies and knights, assembled for the celebration. Now in those days, when there was a celebration, tournaments and contests called jousts were held in which knights proved their skill at battle. So a great tournament was held for the celebration. Arthur's step-brother, Sir Kay, was one of the knights who competed in the tournament. Arthur, still a young man, acted as his assistant, or squire.

The horses thundered toward each other, carrying the knights in their shining armor. The knights met with a tremendous crash, and Sir Kay's sword broke in the battle. He hurried to the sidelines and shouted to Arthur to fetch him another one. While making his way back to their castle, Arthur passed the front of the church and saw the sword in the stone. Unaware of the sword's magic and in a great hurry to complete his mission, he thought to borrow the sword and easily pulled it from the stone without reading the inscription. He hurried back to Sir Kay, who recognized the sword at once and took it to his father.

"Look, Father," Sir Kay said, "I have pulled the magic sword from the stone. I will be king of all Britain." His father was amazed and doubtful, because Merlin had told him it would be otherwise. He told Sir Kay to put the sword back into the stone, and then draw it out again, to prove his claim. But no matter how hard he tried, Sir Kay couldn't thrust the sword into the stone. Finally, Sir Kay admitted that it was Arthur who had pulled the sword from the stone.

Arthur easily put the sword back into the stone, and easily pulled it out again. Sir Ector and Sir Kay both fell down on their knees before him.

Arthur pulls out the magic sword as Sir Ector and Kay look on.

"Why do you kneel down before me?" cried Arthur. He felt a little frightened.

"My lord," Sir Ector said, "only one man can draw the sword from the stone, and he is the king of Britain." He told Arthur the secret of his birth. "I am not your real father," Sir Ector explained. "When you were very young, Merlin gave you to me to raise. I can see now that you are the true son of Uther Pendragon, and heir to the realm." And he kissed Arthur's hand. But Arthur was sad and began to weep.

"Why are you crying?" Sir Ector asked. "You've just gained a kingdom."

"I've gained a kingdom," Arthur said, "but I've lost a father." He put the sword back into the stone. "I'd give the kingdom back if I could have you for my father again."

"That is not your destiny," said the magician Merlin, who suddenly appeared before them. "You are our king."

The next day all the kings tried to pull the sword from the stone, but none could. Only young Arthur, barely a man, could pull the sword from the stone. The kings were reluctant to accept him because of his age, but the people cheered for their young hero. And so Arthur became king of all Britain. He made Sir Kay his right-hand man and began his reign, destined to be one of the most famous kings in all the world.

The Sword Excalibur and the Lady of the Lake

The Sword in the Stone was famous, but Arthur was to have a sword called Excalibur that was more famous still. One day in a terrible battle, the sword Arthur had pulled from the stone was broken. Arthur was rescued by Merlin, who then took him to find another sword. Merlin led him to a lake in a forest. In the center of the lake, an arm, clothed in white silk, jutted up from the surface. The hand held a gleaming sword in a jeweled scabbard.

"That is the magic sword Excalibur," Merlin said. "The Lady of the Lake will give it to you. Look! She's coming from her castle, which is carved in the rock. You must be respectful to her, and do what she tells you."

The Lady of the Lake appeared to them. "You may have the sword," she said softly, "if you give me a gift when I ask for it."

"That I shall do," said Arthur. Then he and Merlin rowed out into the lake. Arthur lifted the sword by its handle, and the arm and the hand sank under the water. Then Arthur and Merlin bid the Lady of the Lake good-bye.

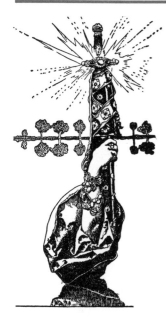

"Tell me," said Merlin as they rode along, "which do you prefer, the sword or the scabbard?"

"The sword," said Arthur, who was greatly pleased with it.

"You are a fool," said Merlin, "for the scabbard is magic too, and whoever wears it cannot lose blood, no matter how badly he is injured." Thus spoke Merlin, who could tell everyone's future but his own. He couldn't see the terrible trap the Lady of the Lake would set for him, a trap which even his magic couldn't protect him from, as you shall see in another story.

Guinevere

One day Arthur heard that a friend, King Leodegrance, was going to be attacked by an enemy, the Duke of North Umber. The Duke wanted to take King Leodegrance's lands and his daughter, the beautiful princess Guinevere. So Arthur and Merlin set off to Leodegrance's castle to help him.

Arthur had met Guinevere once before and was so struck by her that he felt foolish and could barely speak. He longed to see her again, but in such a way that she wouldn't notice him. So Merlin made a magical cap for him. When he wore it, Arthur looked like an ordinary gardener's boy, not a great king that everyone stared at. Arthur was hired to work in Guinevere's garden as a gardener's boy. And in this way he saw Guinevere every day without feeling bashful.

The lady Guinevere.

But one morning, when she looked out the window, Guinevere saw a golden knight bathing in the fountain. It was Arthur, who had taken off his cap to wash. When she hurried out to meet him, she found only the gardener's boy, for Arthur had put his cap back on. Guinevere asked where the handsome young knight had gone.

"Lady, there has been no one else here," replied Arthur, "only me."

"Really?" said Guinevere, with fire in her eyes. "And what of this?" She picked up the golden knight's collar, which Arthur had left beside the fountain, and flung it at him. "Take this and tell your knight that it is very rude to bathe in a lady's private garden."

All day Guinevere tried to figure out how the knight had suddenly vanished, leaving only the gardener's boy. So she summoned the boy to her, asking him to bring her roses. When he came into the palace, he wouldn't take his cap off. "How now," Guinevere said, "haven't they told you it's rude to leave your hat on in the presence of a lady?"

"My lady," said the gardener's boy, "I can't take my cap off—I have an ugly spot on my head."

"Then bring the roses here to me," Guinevere said. And as he handed her the roses, she snatched off his cap. Instantly he was transformed into a shining knight. All of Guinevere's maids shrieked and laughed, but Guinevere recognized the knight as the great King Arthur himself. She was awed, but she wanted to get even for the trick he had played on her. "Here," she said, and flung the cap at him laughing, "take your cap and go do your work, you gardener's boy with the ugly spot on your head!" And Arthur put on his cap, and went his way.

That very day, the Duke of Umber arrived with his army to make war on the King and take Guinevere captive. Arthur quickly borrowed some armor and rode out on his great white horse to meet him. The two horses, carrying Arthur and the duke in their shining armor, thundered toward each other. The two warriors met with a tremendous crash, and the duke's lance broke. He was hurled to the ground, and lay bleeding, but just then his army charged forward and saved him.

Arthur retreated back into the castle. He could tell that the duke would be back to fight again, so he sent for other knights to help in the fight for Princess Guinevere. When they arrived, they asked Guinevere who would lead them. She told them they must follow the gardener's boy, the one with the ugly spot on his head! They were furious until Arthur took off his cap, and showed himself in all his kingly splendor. Then the knights rejoiced and rode out with their king and conquered the Duke of Umber and all his knights.

When Guinevere saw this, she was embarrassed at how she had treated so great a king as Arthur. But Arthur declared his love for her, and asked her to become his queen. So King Arthur and Guinevere were married.

For Guinevere's dowry, King Leodegrance gave Arthur a great Round Table with fifty seats where noble knights could sit. Each time a worthy knight appeared, his name would be magically inscribed on one of the seats, and each time a knight died his name would vanish. Arthur took Guinevere and the Round Table to his home, Camelot, and so began the adventures of King Arthur and the Knights of the Round Table.

Merlin and the Lady of the Lake

Much about the powerful magician Merlin was shrouded in mystery. At any time he could vanish in a cloud, or turn into a soaring hawk. The poor beggar on the street or the stallion running free by the river might turn out to be Merlin in disguise. And so the stories about him are also shrouded in mystery, and people tell many versions. This is one story about Merlin and the Lady of the Lake.

One day as Merlin was making his way through the forest, he came upon Vivianne, the Lady of the Lake, beside her watery home. Vivianne was an enchantress, and she wove a spell of wonder on him. Merlin fell desperately in love with her. Vivianne asked Merlin to teach her all his magic arts, which were the greatest in the world, and he taught her many. But Vivianne wasn't content and looked for a way that she might keep him by her side forever. Some say this was because she was helping a wicked princess who wanted Merlin out of the way. Others say it was because Vivianne loved Merlin and wanted him never to leave her.

Whatever the reason, Vivianne asked Merlin to use his magic to make a castle, a place so strong that it could never be destroyed, where they could live together forever. Merlin agreed, but then Vivianne said: "Show me how *I* can make the castle myself, so I can make it just the way I like it." And Merlin taught Vivianne the magic to conjure up the castle. And as she conjured, out of the clouds rose bright walls of stone towering in the air, with gleaming turrets. On the front of the castle was a wrought-iron gate so strong none could break it. "Be assured," Merlin told the Lady of the Lake, "no one can come or go except as you wish." Vivianne smiled and showered Merlin with affection.

One day as they sat under a tree in the forest, Vivianne sang sweetly to Merlin and lulled him to sleep. While he slept, she circled him nine times, weaving him in her spells like a spider's silver web, until he could not escape. She brought him to the castle and bound him there forever, so that he could not leave except as she chose, while she came and went as she pleased.

So Merlin was trapped by the very magic that made him great. Some say he was happy in the castle his magic helped to build, with the woman he loved, while others say he strove to escape but couldn't. Either way, he never saw Arthur again, nor was he ever seen again at Camelot.

Sir Launcelot

As the fame of King Arthur's Knights of the Round Table spread, knights from near and far wanted to share in their glory. One day, there appeared at Camelot a young man who would later become the greatest knight of all. He was called Sir Launcelot of the Lake, because he had been raised by the Lady of the Lake.

When Launcelot arrived at Camelot, all were struck by his strong and graceful appearance—and none more so than Queen Guinevere, who felt as though her heart had been captured by the bold young knight. The charms of Guinevere made an equally strong impression on Launcelot. After a single glance, he fell deeply in love, and vowed to do many great deeds for her sake.

Launcelot served King Arthur well. He loved him like a father, and was loved by Arthur in return. But the love between Launcelot and Guinevere would eventually bring great sadness to Arthur and ruin upon Camelot. Before that happened, though, Launcelot would perform many brave feats, win many tournaments, and have many adventures.

One day, Launcelot said to his nephew, Sir Lionel, "Let us go out and seek adventures." They put on their armor, which gleamed so brightly in the sun that it would dazzle your eyes to see it. They hefted their shields, swords, and spears. Then they mounted their impatient steeds and rode forth. The sun beat down upon them and made Launcelot sleepy, so they stopped under the shade of an apple tree. Launcelot removed his helmet, lay down, and fell fast asleep.

Sir Lionel, who stayed awake, soon heard a sound like distant thunder, getting louder and louder. Then he saw three knights riding as fast as the wind. Close behind them came a knight riding even faster, a knight more powerful than any Sir Lionel had seen before. This knight overtook the other three, knocked them from their horses, and tied them up. Sir Lionel, taking care not to wake Launcelot, quietly prepared himself and then rode after the strong knight. He challenged him to fight.

The strong knight charged Sir Lionel and struck him so hard that both Sir Lionel and his horse fell to the ground. Then he tied up Sir Lionel, and took him with the other three knights to his castle, where he threw them in a deep dungeon, already crowded with many other knights he had defeated.

When Launcelot awoke, he went in search of Sir Lionel. On the road he met a damsel riding a white horse. "Fair damsel," said Sir Launcelot, "what do you know of this region?" "Sir Knight," replied the damsel, "near here lives a knight more powerful than any other. His name is Sir Turquine, and he is a sworn enemy of King Arthur. Within a mile is his castle. Near it is a tree. From that tree hang the shields of many good knights that are his prisoners. And from that tree hangs a copper basin. Strike it, and await whom you seek."

Launcelot thanked the damsel and departed. He soon found the tree and struck the basin many times. Soon he saw a huge knight approaching, with a captured knight draped across his horse. Launcelot recognized the captured knight, who appeared to be injured, as Sir Gaheris of the Round Table.

"Fair knight," Launcelot called out, "remove that wounded man from your horse. You have shamed the Knights of the Round Table. Now, prepare to defend yourself."

"If you are of the Round Table," said Sir Turquine, "I defy you and all your fellow knights." Then he held forth his spear and rushed at Launcelot. Launcelot rushed at him, and they clashed so hard that both were knocked from their horses. They drew their swords and at once the clang of their blows shook the land. Back and forth they battled until, exhausted, they paused, and Sir Turquine said, "Truly, you are the strongest man I have ever met. For your sake I will release all the prisoners that I hold, unless you should be Launcelot, the knight I hate most of all, for he slew my brother."

"I am Sir Launcelot of the Lake."

"Then," said Sir Turquine with renewed fury, "let us fight on until only one of us shall live."

For two hours they battled, exchanging blow after blow, wounding each other sorely until the ground ran red. At last, after one fierce stroke of Launcelot's sword, Sir Turquine fell lifeless to the dirt.

Sir Launcelot sent Sir Gaheris to free the knights from Sir Turquine's dungeon. Then Launcelot mounted his horse and went in search of other adventures.

As the years passed, no knight proved stronger than Launcelot, who sent many a defeated knight to Camelot, commanding each to bow down before the feet of Queen Guinevere.

Alas, the love between Launcelot and Guinevere eventually tore Camelot apart. Launcelot and Arthur fought many battles against each other though they had once been the best of friends. Their battles left the kingdom vulnerable to plunder by the evil prince Mordred and his followers.

Though the great age of Camelot ended unhappily, it stands in our minds even today as a time of peace and nobility where chivalry shone as bright as polished armor and adventure was always waiting beyond the next turn in the road.

If you would like to know more about King Arthur and his knights, you can read the following books:

Geoffrey Ashe, King Arthur in Fact and Fiction *(Thomas Nelson).*
Constance Hieatt, The Minstrel Knight *(Thomas Y. Crowell).*
Constance Hieatt, The Sword and the Grail *(Thomas Y. Crowell).*
Constance Hieatt, The Castle of Ladies *(Thomas Y. Crowell).*
Constance Hieatt, The Knight and the Lion *(Thomas Y. Crowell).*
Margaret Hodges, The Kitchen Knight *(Holiday House).*
Howard Pyle, The Story of King Arthur and His Knights *(Charles Scribner's Sons).*
James Riordan, Tales of King Arthur *(Rand McNally).*

Introduction to Language and Literature

FOR PARENTS AND TEACHERS

In the fourth grade, children should continue to identify and talk about the parts of speech, including interjections, adverbs, prepositions, and regular and irregular verbs. In addition, children learn how to look up information about favorite topics or for homework by using a bibliography, and they find out why some words are put into italics.

Experts say that our children already know more about the grammar of language than we can ever teach them. But standard written language does have special characteristics that need to be discussed with children. As with other parts of this book, the account of language conventions for fourth grade is a summary. It needs to be complemented by giving the child opportunities to read and write and to discuss reading and writing in connection with grammar and spelling.

In the classroom, grammar instruction is an essential part, but only a part, of an effective language arts program. In the fourth grade, children should also be working on vocabulary and spelling. They should enjoy a rich diet of fiction, poetry, drama, biography, and nonfiction. They should regularly be involved in the writing process: inventing topics, discovering ideas in early drafts, revising toward "publication" of polished final drafts—all with encouragement and guidance along the way. They should practice writing often and in many modes, including stories, poetry, journal entries, formal reports, dialogues, and descriptions.

Writing often is one key to writing well. Another is not to discourage children by too severe an emphasis on correctness. Still, we do our children no service if we fail to give them some knowledge of the conventions they are expected to follow in most public discourse. Children will become good writers when they know the joy and magic, as well as the rules and regulations, of language.

Learning About Language

More About Parts of Speech

Can you think of the eight parts of speech? Let's go over them: nouns, verbs, adjectives, pronouns, conjunctions, adverbs, prepositions, and interjections.

Interjections

Super!
Ouch!
Good Grief!

These are interjections. *Inter* means in and *ject* means throw. To interject something is to throw it in, like cheers or moans, to express our strong feelings or thoughts.

You can see why interjections are also called "exclamations." We exclaim them, and they are followed by exclamation marks.
Wow!

Adverbs

Adverbs often add something to the verb. They can tell us how the verb acts.

How did the butterfly come out of its cocoon?

It slipped _____ from its cocoon.
Quietly? Violently? Slowly?

Adverbs usually end in *ly*. There are some adverbs like *often* that don't end in *ly*. Can you make up a sentence with *often*?

Adverbs can also describe adjectives or even other adverbs. For instance, when you say, "I'm extremely proud of you," you use an adverb to describe the adjective *proud*. What's the difference between *proud* and *extremely proud*? When your friend asks you to "speak *more softly*," he uses the adverb *more* to describe another adverb, *softly*. If he asked you *very politely*, the adverb *very* describes the adverb *politely*.

Adverbs tell you such things as *where, when, how, how much,* or *how long*. Here's the rule to remember about adverbs: "Adverbs act on verbs, adjectives, and other adverbs."

You can often make adverbs by adding *ly* to an adjective.

great + ly	greatly
quick + ly	quickly
beautiful + ly	beautifully

Prepositions

Here are some prepositions: *in, on, under, over, about, by, with, of, before, after, through, between*. Can you figure out what all these words do? They tell you how things relate to each other. For example, let's consider John and a book.

The book can be *under* John, *with* John, or *between* John and the table. All those prepositions tell you where the book is in relation to John. Different prepositions describe other ways things are related. We mean two very different things when we say, "The book is *by* John" (he is the author) and "The book is *about* John" (gee, he must have led an interesting life). Prepositions can also describe different relations in time. (Was the book written *before* or *after* John was born?)

Prepositions relate things to other things. Let's think of some more of these relating words: *out of, without, because of, into, upon, underneath, to, from, toward, away from, along with*. Can you make up some sentences with these prepositions?

Prepositions go together with the words that come after them. Come *with* me. Step *in front of* me. The words that go together with the preposition are called a phrase. What kind of a phrase? A prepositional phrase!

Here are some prepositional phrases. Can you pick out the prepositions?

The cat lounged *around the house*.
The turtle hides *inside his shell*.
We have a family *of rabbits* living *beneath our shed*.

Regular and Irregular Verbs

Remember verbs, the action words? Most verbs are regular, which means that you form the past tense just by adding *d* or *ed*.

present tense	past tense
Today I walk.	Yesterday I walked.
We talk.	We talked.
They jump.	They jumped.
I move.	I moved.

But some verbs are irregular: if you add *d* or *ed*, you don't get the past tense, you get a mistake. Today I bring lunch. Yesterday I bringed lunch? No, I *brought* lunch.

You already know a lot of irregular verbs.

present tense	past tense
sing	sang
ring	rang
think	thought
eat	ate
take	took
rise	rose
find	found
bring	brought
buy	bought
hit	hit
sit	sat
read	read

More Punctuation Marks: Colons

A colon (:) says to a reader, "Get ready. These things are coming." Let's look at an example.

Here are the things I have to get at the grocery:
    cabbage
    chocolate pudding
    juice.

Here are some other cases in which we use colons:

—when writing time, as in 12:00.
—when naming a verse in the Bible, as in Matthew 1:3.
—when opening a formal letter, as in Dear Mr. President:

Bibliography

If you were to write a report on antelopes, there are lots of places you could go for information. Maybe you could go to the zoo. You could learn about them in a movie at the library. And you could look them up in a bibliography.

A bibliography is a list of books and magazine articles. You can find bibliographies at the end of many nonfiction books or at the end of some articles, such as those in the encyclopedia. The bibliography tells you where the writer of the book or article got his or her information.

The bibliography gives you a lot of useful information. It tells you the titles and authors of books or articles that relate to a particular subject. It tells you when or where the books or articles were published.

Say you're trying to write a report on antelopes. You're having trouble finding the information you want. But then you come across a book called *Animals of Africa*. You turn to the back, and you're in luck: there's a bibliography. You glance down the list of titles until you notice this:

Walker, Matilda. "Those Amazing Antelopes." *Wildlife World* (September 1989), 12–18.

Great! Now you go to the library and find the September 1989 issue of *Wildlife World*. You turn to page 12 and there's the article by Matilda Walker called "Those Amazing Antelopes." You read through the whole article and what do you find at the end? Another bibliography, referring you to even more books and articles about antelopes!

When you write your report on antelopes, you should put your own bibliography at the end, giving credit to the writers of the books and articles you used as sources.

Italics

Italic letters stand out because they slant to the right, *like this*. Italics are used to indicate titles of books, magazines, or newspapers: *Treasure Island, Highlights*, the *Washington Post*.

Italics are also used to indicate the title of a work of art: the *Mona Lisa;* or a movie: *Lady and the Tramp*. Books written in English will sometimes use italics to indicate words from another language, like *amigo* or *ami* (Spanish and French for "friend").

It's pretty hard to make italic letters when you write. So when you mean a word to be in italics, you can just underline it, like this:

<u>*Treasure Island*</u>

Learning About Literature

Novels, Short Stories, and Plot

Have you ever wondered why, as you get older, the books you read have more words and fewer and fewer pictures? When you read a novel or collection of short stories, you'll find that the words themselves paint the pictures.

Like many of the stories you have heard, short stories and novels are fiction or make-believe. The main difference between a short story and a novel is that one is short and the other long. They are both written in prose, and both have a plot. (Remember, the plot is the answer to the question "What happens in the story?") In adventure stories, a lot happens and the plot is very complicated. In other stories, it may seem that not much happens at all, but a character's whole life may be changed by a small event, such as meeting an inspiring person. What are the plots like in "A Voyage to Lilliput" and "The Tongue-cut Sparrow" in the Stories and Speeches section of this book?

Since novels are longer, they usually have a more complicated plot than short stories. In some novels, hundreds of characters appear. How many characters did you meet just in our retelling of *Treasure Island* in the Stories and Speeches section of this book? Most novels focus on one or two important figures called main characters, such as Jim Hawkins, Jo March, or Laura Ingalls.

The pictures you can paint in your head as you read may be even more exciting than some of the pictures in stories and books you have read before. Do you remember the pictures of Morning Star in the story called "The Sun Dance" in this book? You might read the story again and try to imagine scenes that aren't pictured, like the tepee of Sun and Moon and the coming of the cranes.

When you can imagine the pictures painted with words, novels and stories can take you anywhere—from the Little House in the Big Woods to ancient China, modern Africa, or even to another planet.

Introduction to Sayings

FOR PARENTS AND TEACHERS

Every culture has phrases and proverbs that make no sense when carried over literally into another culture. For many children, this section may not be needed; they will have picked up these sayings by hearing them at home and among their friends. But the category of sayings in the Core Knowledge Sequence has been the one most appreciated by teachers who work with children from home cultures that differ from the standard culture of literate American English.

Sayings and Phrases

Beauty is only skin deep

People use this saying to mean that you can't judge a person's character by how he or she looks.

"That new girl sure is pretty," Kim said.
"Yeah, but I wonder if she's nice, too," Carol said. "After all, beauty is only skin deep."

The bigger they are, the harder they fall

When a huge oak falls in the forest, it makes a tremendous crash. When a small sapling falls, you can barely hear it as it hits the ground. When people use this saying, they mean that the larger or more powerful something is (it could be a person, a country, or something else), the bigger the shock it will feel when a setback occurs.

Jim was the best basketball player on his team, and proud of it. He loved all the attention he got when people recognized him on the street and when kids on the bus asked for his autograph. He liked to strut down the halls at school feeling important.

Then a new player joined the basketball team. He was faster and scored more points than Jim did. That made Jim so miserable, he stopped going to basketball practice.

Finally his friend Pete talked to him. "Come on, Jim," he said, "I know how you feel, but you've got to stop sulking. You're a great player, and the team needs you."

Jim sighed. "Yeah, you're right, I miss the team, too. I've really learned a lesson from this. I guess I really got a big head and, you know, the bigger they are, the harder they fall."

Birds of a feather flock together

People say this to mean that similar types of people, or people who have similar interests, like to be with each other.

"Those guys always eat lunch together," Jenny said, nodding toward the small group of boys at the other end of the cafeteria.

"I know. They're on the same baseball team and they love to talk about mitts and bats and bases."

Jenny nodded. "Well, birds of a feather flock together!"

Don't count your chickens before they hatch

Because not every egg in a nest hatches into a baby chicken, people use this saying to mean that you may be disappointed if you count on having something before it is really yours.

"I can't wait to listen to these new tapes on the boom box I'm getting for my birthday," Nathan said.

"Are you sure someone is giving you a boom box?" Annie asked.

"Not exactly," Nathan replied.

"Well, I hope you get one," Annie said. "But don't count your chickens before they hatch."

Don't put all your eggs in one basket

What would happen if you dropped a basket full of eggs? When people use this saying, they mean that you shouldn't count on one single thing and ignore other possibilities. If you do, you could lose out.

"I called all my friends and told them to meet me at the pool tomorrow. We're going to have a pool party!" Kevin said.

"How do you know it's going to be sunny, Kevin?" asked Cybill. "Don't put all your eggs in one basket. Better make plans for an indoor party, too, just in case."

The early bird gets the worm

This saying can be used competitively, to encourage someone to win or beat out others. It implies that you can usually get ahead of others if you get going before they do. It can also be used to get someone who isn't very motivated to do what he ought to do.

Clarkson School decided to hold a raffle in order to raise money for playground equipment. Teachers, parents, and students all volunteered to sell raffle tickets over the weekend.

On Saturday morning, Billy, who wanted to sell more tickets than anyone, woke up with the sun.

"Come on, Juan!" he said, nudging his brother. "Let's sell these tickets!"

"Billy, are you crazy? Go back to sleep," muttered Juan.

"No way," said Billy. "Every other kid in this apartment building is going to be selling tickets, too. The early bird gets the worm, so let's get going!"

Half a loaf is better than none

This means that having something is better than having nothing at all, even if it's not exactly what you want. It's similar to the saying, "A bird in the hand is worth two in the bush."

By selling raffle tickets, Clarkson School raised money to buy a swing set, monkey bars, and two basketball backboards.

"But," said Billy, "I was hoping we could get one of those big spiral slides, too."

"Hey, don't complain," said Juan. "Half a loaf is better than none. Race you to the hoops!"

Haste makes waste

This saying means that when you rush you don't do as good a job as you do when you are careful and take your time.

It was Sammy's night to do the dishes. He quickly rinsed all of the dinner plates, then ran the silverware under the faucet.

"What's your hurry?" his father asked.

"I told Karl I'd meet him at the park!"

"If you aren't more careful cleaning these dishes," his father said, picking up a plate with a spot of spaghetti sauce on the rim, "you'll have to do them over again. Then you'll really be late. Haste makes waste!"

Laugh, and the world laughs with you; weep, and you weep alone

This saying means that when you are happy, people want to join in with your cheerful mood but when you are sad, people don't want to be with you.

"Come on, Tom, cheer up!" Kimiko shook Tom's shoulder. "Why are you in such a bad mood?"

"Oh, I don't know," Tom said. "Nobody likes me."

"Well what do you expect, with that big frown across your face?" Kimiko smiled. "Laugh, and the world laughs with you; weep, and you weep alone!"

Lightning never strikes in the same place twice

People use this saying to mean that if something unfortunate happens, it usually won't happen again in exactly the same way.

"Hey, Kareem, I wouldn't stand there. Remember last month when a light bulb fell and hit Mr. Vasquez right on the head?"

"Yeah, I remember, but I'm not worried. Lightning never strikes in the same place twice."

Live and let live

This saying means mind your own business and let other people mind theirs.

"You need a haircut, Daryl." Kenya put her hands on her hips. "And look at those shoes! The right one has a hole in the toe."

"I like the way my hair looks, and these are cool shoes," Daryl said. "Besides, I don't tell you how to dress. Kenya, you'd better learn to live and let live."

Make hay while the sun shines

Why do farmers harvest hay and grains like corn or wheat when the weather is fair? Because once it starts to rain, the crops can be spoiled. So people use this saying to mean that you should take advantage of your good fortune when things are working out in your favor.

Jason and Frank were watching a basketball game on television. A commercial came on with their favorite player, Michael Jordan, doing an incredible reverse slam dunk, and wearing some very fancy shoes.

"You know," said Jason, "Jordan makes a lot of money playing basketball. So why does he do commercials for shoes too?"

"Go easy on the man," said Frank. "He's just trying to make hay while the sun shines. You think he'll be able to dunk like that in ten years?"

"You're right," said Jason. "In ten years, you'll be seeing *me* on that screen, and you'll be buying 'Jason Jammers'!"

An ounce of prevention is worth a pound of cure

People use this saying to mean that it's better to take care of a possible problem before it gets worse and requires a more complicated solution. The saying "A stitch in time can save nine" may be used in much the same way.

"If you don't brush your teeth more often, you'll get cavities," Al's sister said, "and then you'll have to get fillings when you go to the dentist."

"I sure don't want that!" Al said. "You're right, an ounce of prevention is worth a pound of cure."

One picture is worth a thousand words

When people say this, they mean that, in a particular instance, a picture can explain things better than words.

"Here's a picture of Rikki after he won his diving medal." Sonia showed Mrs. Smith the photograph.

"Goodness!" Mrs. Smith said. "Wasn't he happy and proud!"

"Yes, he was," Sonia said. "Just look at his face. This picture is worth a thousand words!"

Seeing is believing

This saying means that you can't necessarily believe that something exists or is true unless you see the evidence for yourself.

"You should have seen the fish I caught," Eddie said. "It was this big!" He spread his arms as wide apart as he could.

"Yeah, right," said Daniel, shaking his head. He knew that Eddie exaggerated a lot.

"I'm not kidding!" exclaimed Eddie. He ran in the house, then staggered out holding a fish almost as big as he was.

"Wow!" said Daniel. "Seeing is believing!"

Two wrongs don't make a right

People use this saying to mean that you can't correct one wrong thing by doing something else that's wrong.

"Carl hit me, so I hit him back!" Bill said.

"What's the point of that?" Bill's big brother said. "It didn't make anything better, did it? Two wrongs don't make a right, you know."

When it rains it pours

When people say this, they mean that something that starts out as a little bit of bad luck can turn into a disaster.

Keith limped into the kitchen and plopped down on a chair.

"What happened, Keith?" his brother asked.

Keith grimaced. "What a rotten day. First I missed the bus and had to walk to school. When I got there, I got in trouble for being late. Then I messed up on my math test. I found out that I left my lunch at home this morning, I turned my ankle in gym class, and now I think I'm getting a cold. When it rains it pours."

Blow hot and cold

The wind comes from all directions, bringing warm breezes on some days and bad weather on others. So people use this saying to mean that a person or a thing is temperamental, or has frequent changes of mood.

Felicia and her mother were driving in their old station wagon.

"Jinny sure is moody lately," Felicia said. "One minute she's sweet and funny, and the next minute she's yelling at someone or sulking!"

"I know, her mother said, "that sister of yours blows hot and cold—just like this old car! Sometimes it drives like a dream, and sometimes you can't even get it started!"

You can lead a horse to water, but you can't make it drink

This saying means that you can show people what you want them to do, but you cannot force them to do it.

Vera disliked bowling. All of her friends insisted that she come with them to the bowling alley, though, because they needed an extra person on their team.

"I really don't like this game," Vera thought to herself. When it was her turn to bowl, she crossed her arms over her chest and said, "Just because you got me to come with you doesn't mean I'm going to play. You can lead a horse to water, but you can't make it drink!"

As the crow flies

If you were to drive from your house to your school, you'd have to follow the roads that were made. You couldn't drive through buildings or streams or peoples' backyards to get where you wanted to go. If you were a crow, however, you could fly above all the roads and other obstacles and follow a straight, direct, and much shorter route to your destination. When someone is trying to tell you how far away something is in a straight line, as opposed to following a system of roads, then they are describing a distance "as the crow flies."

"How far away is the Empire State Building?" Tom was tired of walking. He and his dad had been winding through the streets of New York City all day long. They could see the very top of the Empire State Building in the distance, above the other skyscrapers.

"Well," Mr. Lewis said, "the way we're going, at least a mile. As the crow flies, though, I'd say it's only half a mile away."

Break the ice

This phrase means doing something to make people who are uncomfortable more comfortable. You can also "break the ice" if you are the first person to begin speaking with someone who has not yet spoken to you.

It was the first day of camp. The four boys began to unpack their clothes and make their beds in silence. None of the boys knew each other, and no one knew what to say.

Bob couldn't stand the silence any longer. "Hey, look!" he said. The other three boys turned, and Bob did a back flip in the middle of the room. Everyone laughed, and he bowed. "Finally," he thought, "we've broken the ice!"

Bull in a china shop

People use this phrase to describe someone who is clumsy in a place where things can be upset or broken, or someone who handles a delicate situation badly.

Leroy slammed the door behind him. A painting fell off the wall and his mother's crystal vase wobbled on the dining room table. "I'm home!" he yelled, then tripped on the door mat and fell onto the floor.

"Honestly, Leroy," his mother said as she helped him up, "sometimes you are just like a bull in a china shop!"

Bury the hatchet

People use this saying to mean stop holding a grudge. This saying is very similar to the sayings "let bygones be bygones" and "forgive and forget."

"They say the McCormicks and the McVeys have been feuding for nearly fifty years. It started because old Angus McVey stole one of Dougal McCormick's chickens!"

"However it started, you'd think after all this time they'd get tired of fighting and just bury the hatchet!"

Can't hold a candle to

When one thing is much better than another, people say that the lesser thing "can't hold a candle" to the better thing. It is similar to saying that something "doesn't measure up" to something else.

"Mom, this frozen pizza is good, but it can't hold a candle to your homemade pizza!"

Etc.

Etc. is an abbreviation of "et cetera," a Latin phrase for "and the rest." It means "and so forth," or "and so on." It can also mean "and other things just like the things I have mentioned."

A few weeks before Thanksgiving, the church began collecting donations of food. Reverend Jackson made an announcement: "We would especially appreciate it if you would bring in canned foods: soups, canned juices, canned fruits, etc."

Go to pot

People use this phrase to describe what happens to something when it is not taken care of or maintained. They also use it to refer to a skill, which can be lost when it's not practiced.

"If you don't tend a garden regularly, weeds grow and the garden goes to pot."

Land of Nod

This phrase means being asleep.

"I can't sleep!" Cassie said to Anne, her big sister. Both girls had been in bed for half an hour. The room was dark and cool, and they could hear crickets chirping outside.
"Close your eyes, Cass," Anne said, "and I'll sing you a lullaby." She began to hum a tune to her little sister, and it was not long before Cassie drifted off to the Land of Nod.

Make ends meet

People use this phrase to mean doing what is necessary to have enough money to survive.

"My dad has to work overtime almost every night, and lately he works on weekends, too. He says it's what he has to do to make ends meet."

Money burning a hole in your pocket

This phrase means having money that you are very tempted to spend.

"A lot of people on my paper route gave me tips for Christmas," Luke said. "I'm rich!"

"So why don't you open a savings account and start putting your money in the bank?" Luke's big sister, Clare, asked. "Otherwise, that money's just going to burn a hole in your pocket!"

Once in a blue moon

A blue moon isn't really blue. It's the second full moon in a calendar month. They're pretty rare: there have only been two in the last five years. So people use this phrase to describe something that happens only once in a while.

Rebecca loved to sit on the beach and look out at the ocean. As she listened to the waves slap against the sand, she thought that there was nothing more wonderful than the sea. Early one morning she saw a group of dolphins come close to shore. They leaped out of the water like slippery dancers, making quick silver arcs against the horizon. "I am so lucky!" she realized. "Something like this only happens once in a blue moon!"

On the warpath

This phrase describes someone who is angry or in a bad mood and who is eager to get into a fight.

"Just because Paul lost his camera doesn't mean he can go around yelling at everybody," Roger said.

"I know," Ceil replied, "but he thinks someone stole it, and he's going to be on the warpath until that camera shows up!"

RSVP

When RSVP is written on an invitation that you have received, it means that the people who are inviting you would like you to tell them whether or not you will be able to come to their party, wedding, etc. RSVP is short for the French term *Répondez S'il Vous Plait*, which means "please reply" in English.

Helen was excited about receiving an invitation to Laura's birthday party. When she saw "RSVP" written at the bottom of the invitation, she rushed to the phone.

"Hello, Laura? It's Helen. I just called to RSVP—you bet I'm coming to your birthday party!"

Run-of-the-mill

People use this phrase when they are describing something that is very ordinary.

"How was your day, Carmen?" Mrs. Morello asked.

"Oh, nothing unusual, just run-of-the-mill," replied Carmen. "But I'm really looking forward to our field trip to the museum tomorrow."

Shipshape

This phrase means, "in perfect order."

"I'm not going to let you kids leave this room until it's shipshape," Mr. Walters said. The art classroom was littered with sheets of colored paper, small pots of paint, pans of water, and paintbrushes.

"But, Mr. Walters," Al said, "how can we make a room shipshape if we're not on a boat?"

"Very funny, Al. Now get to work and clean up this mess!"

Through thick and thin

People use this phrase to describe someone or something that remains dependable during good and bad times.

Malek and James were best friends. They stuck together and stood up for each other, knowing they could count on each other through thick and thin.

Timbuktu

Timbuktu is a town in Africa. When people use this term, however, they usually mean an imaginary place that seems exotic and far away.

Clarence had spent his whole life in the same town. He dreamed of one day visiting a magical, distant country where people were always happy, wore purple clothes, and ate mangoes and chocolate for dinner. Clarence's country was not on any map. Rather, it was his own special Timbuktu; a place of dreams that existed beyond the corners of the earth.

II.

GEOGRAPHY, WORLD CIVILIZATION, AND AMERICAN CIVILIZATION

Introduction
to Geography
FOR PARENTS AND TEACHERS

In the Geography section we continue to help children connect history, culture, and economy with the land. They will learn why waterways were important for travel and trade all over the world. They will learn how Italy's long coastline helped Germanic peoples to migrate there and take control of the land, while the high Alps slowed the progress of conquerors. Children will learn how the mountains and rivers of the American land created difficulties for settlers even as the promise of rich lands drew them westward.

We all know that the place we live gives a certain shape to our lives. But we may not think about this very much unless heavy spring rains make their way into the basement. Even then, we are probably not thinking in the broadest sense of the ways the land, with its rivers, rainfall, and vegetation, its mountains and minerals, shapes the lives of the people who live on it.

The geography and history sections of this book ask children to think about the connections between the land and people's lives, transforming the study of geography from the rote learning of lists into the living subject it should be.

We strongly recommend that children use photocopies of the maps included in Books One through Four. From their geography lessons in Books One through Three in this series, children should now be able not only to color the maps, but also to draw in major rivers and indicate continents, mountain ranges, deserts, seas, oceans, and ancient cities. These features—and terms such as peninsula, strait, gulf, channel, equator, and poles—should be reviewed.

Such basic geographical knowledge cannot be reviewed too often. Without it, historical trends make no sense, current events seem meaningless. Children will be engaged in a review of this material because they can get a real sense of scale, relationships, and their own growing competence at mapmaking.

Geography

Dividing the World into Sections

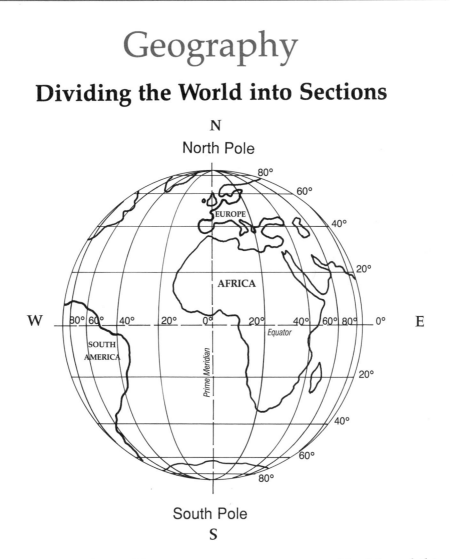

L ook at the map above. Have you ever seen your world pictured this way? You've already learned the name of the imaginary line that divides the globe around the middle. It's the equator. But what about all those lines parallel to the equator? And what about the lines that run north and south on the map? What are they for?

Mapmakers divide the world into sections in order to locate places accurately. The lines running parallel to the equator are called latitude lines, and the lines that run from pole to pole are called longitude lines. Can you see how the latitude and longitude lines intersect to make sections? Looking at the map, you can also see that each line has its own number. These numbers give every place on the globe its own unique location.

Stretched Out

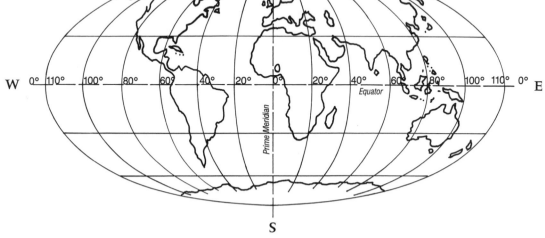

How does this map differ from the first map you looked at? The first map looks almost like a picture of a globe. But this one looks more like a globe cut open along a north-to-south seam through the Pacific Ocean and stretched flat. Mapmakers do this so you can see the whole world on one map.

The Largest Sections

Mapmakers and users sometimes need larger sections shaped something like half a grapefruit, called hemispheres (meaning half-sphere). There are two ways to make hemispheres. You can divide the world into the Northern and Southern Hemispheres or into the Eastern and Western Hemispheres.

In the stretched-out map above you can see the Northern Hemisphere north of the equator and the Southern Hemisphere south of the equator. You can also see the Eastern and Western Hemispheres. But which is which? And why is one half called "east" and the other "west"? It's really no mystery. There once was a famous observatory in Greenwich, England, built to look at the stars. Mapmakers agreed to use this location for an imaginary line around the world that is as important as the equator, but runs north and south through the poles. It is called the prime meridian.

The observatory in Greenwich, England.

You can find the prime meridian on the map by looking for the line that runs north and south through England and is marked 0°. (° is the mark for degree. We use degrees to measure distances between latitudes and between longitudes.) To the west of the prime meridian is the Western Hemisphere, and to the east is the Eastern Hemisphere. Find the Eastern and Western Hemispheres on the stretched-out map on page 88, and then on a globe.

Finding Coordinates

Now that you know about the prime meridian and the equator, you can find the coordinates for any place in the world. Let's find the coordinates for Greece to see how it's done.

To begin, you'll need to find Greece on the first map in this section. Can you find Italy's "boot"? Greece is the peninsula to the east of Italy. (A peninsula is a long strip of land extending into a body of water. You may also hear it defined as a body of land surrounded on three sides by water.) You can see that a latitude line and a longitude line intersect over Greece. Each line has a number. The latitude line is marked 40° and the longitude line is marked 20°.

So the coordinates for Greece are 40° and 20°. But when we write them, we write 40°N, 20°E because Greece is 40° north of the equator and 20° east of the prime meridian. The equator and the prime meridian divide the earth into four equal parts. Can you find 40°S, 20°E on a globe? What about 40°N, 20°W and 40°S, 20°W?

Follow Your Finger

To look at the Eastern and Western Hemispheres in more detail, you'll need a globe. Find the prime meridian by looking for a line that runs north and south through Greenwich, England. With your finger trace this line to the equator. Do you see that the prime meridian is marked 0°?

Now trace your finger along the equator moving west from the prime meridian. See how the degree numbers on the longitude lines start going up? When you get to the 180° line, you've gone exactly halfway around the world. This line is called the 180° meridian, and it's the continuation of the prime meridian on the other side of the globe. So you can say that the 180° meridian and the prime meridian divide the globe into the Eastern and Western Hemispheres.

Continue tracing your finger along the equator to the west. What hemisphere are you crossing now? What happens to the longitude degree marks as you move back toward the prime meridian?

In an atlas, find a map of the United States marked with longitude and latitude lines. Then determine the coordinates for your town or city, for the place where you, a friend, or a member of your family was born, or for a place you'd like to visit.

The Eastern Hemisphere

Look at the map of the Eastern Hemisphere on the following page. You will see the three continents—Asia, Africa, and Europe—where people first began to grow food and build cities. Perhaps the earliest great kingdom was in Africa, along the Nile, the world's longest river. Do you remember the land of Egypt and King Tut? If not, you can go back and read about him by yourself in the first book of this series or in your school library.

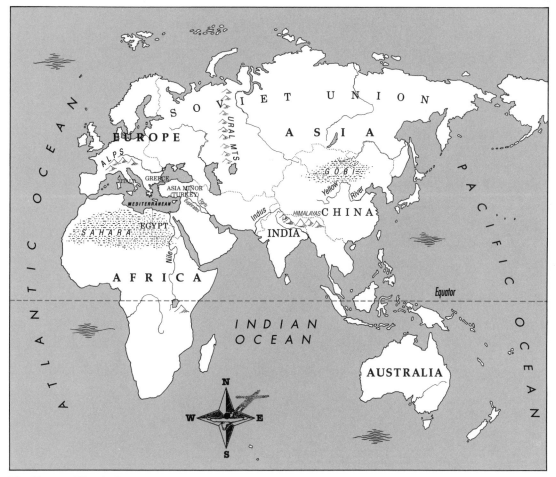

The Eastern Hemisphere.

Books One and Two in this series also told about great rivers and cities in Asia. Can you find the Tigris and Euphrates rivers? Do you remember the Babylonians and Persians? Much farther east, in India and China, kingdoms grew up around the cities along fertile rivers. What are the names of these rivers?

Look at the map again. Can you see why it was so hard to travel from India to China? The mountains between these two countries are the highest mountains in the world, the Himalayas. You will see from the map that China was also separated from other civilizations by a great desert, the Gobi, and that there are thick jungles to the south.

Dangerous Journeys

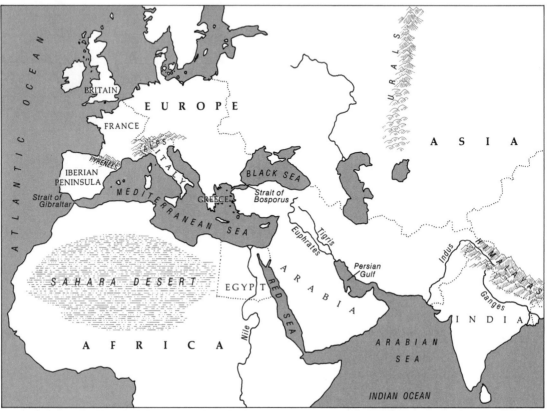

An enlargement of part of the Eastern Hemisphere.

The map on this page is an enlargement of part of the Eastern Hemisphere map. Can you see the relation between the two maps? An enlargement does what its name suggests: it takes a small area within the larger map and makes it larger. That way it includes more details of the area. In the enlargement here you will be able to trace the early voyages of Greek, Roman, and Arab travelers.

If you have read Books Two and Three of this series, you have learned about two important civilizations in Europe and around the Mediterranean Sea, the Greeks and the Romans. Some ships sailed from the Mediterranean Sea into the Atlantic Ocean through the Strait of Gibraltar (a strait is a narrow passageway connecting two large bodies of water). The ships hugged the coastline until they reached Britain. Others went into the Black Sea through the strait of the Bosporus. But most ships stayed in the Mediterranean, along the shores.

Possibly the most dangerous voyages were made by the Arabs who lived along the Red Sea and Persian Gulf and in the desert between them. The Romans had their cargoes, or goods, shipped up the Nile and carried overland to the Red Sea. Then Arab ships took on the cargoes and traded them along the east coast of Africa, around the Persian Gulf, or on to India.

Be sure to find the Arabian Sea, the Red Sea, and the Persian Gulf on the map enlargement from the Eastern Hemisphere. If you trace or make a photocopy of the map, you can make dotted lines to show where the Arab ships might sail. Since sailing ships depended on wind, the monsoons controlled sea travel to India. You can look up monsoon in the dictionary to discover why it was once so difficult and dangerous to sail to India.

That's a Relief!

Maps can show you many different things. They can show you the location of cities and the boundaries between countries. They can show you some of the natural characteristics of the land: mountains, canyons, rivers, jungles, deserts. In this book, we've added a type of map we haven't used before—a relief map. Relief maps show you elevations (high places) or depressions (low places) on the earth's surface. Look at the map enlarged from the Eastern Hemisphere and the map of Western Europe and see how many areas show relief. What are those places? Some globes are made so that you can feel the elevations and depressions with your finger.

Natural Borders

Think about the state you live in. What are its borders? Are any of these borders formed by geographical features like a river or mountain range? Why would natural barriers such as these make good borders?

Some of the main geographical features of Western Europe made the borders of the Roman Empire, as you can see from the map on page 94. But these natural barriers alone could not protect the empire from invading Germanic tribes. In the World Civilization sections of Books Three and Four of this series, you can read about how these tribes invaded the Western Roman

Empire and eventually caused its downfall. Here we will look at some of the features of the European lands where the Germanic tribes eventually settled.

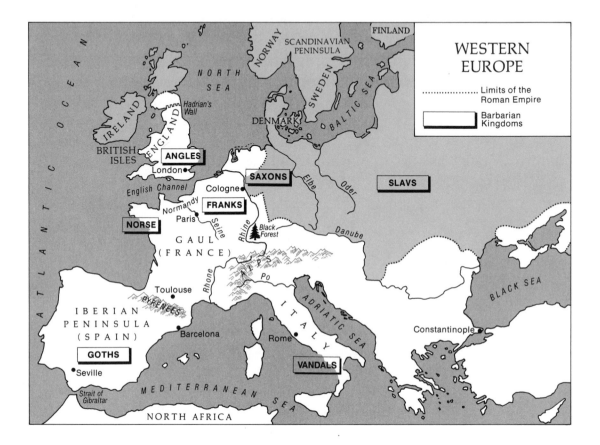

Look at the long coastline of Italy. You can see how easily it could be attacked by ships coming from North Africa or the Adriatic Sea.

North of Italy are the mountains called the Alps. You might think invaders would have a hard time getting past these mountains. But there are ways through them called passes, which are narrow gaps between mountains. In the days of the Roman Empire, some Germanic tribes settled in the valley of the fertile Po River after crossing the Alps.

Going north of the Alps, you can see three rivers that are fed by water from these mountains: the Danube, running eastward; the Rhine, running north; the Rhone, running west and south. (Why do you think rivers often begin in mountains?)

More Mountain Climbers

Southwest of the site of the Rhone River, you will see the Pyrenees mountains. They separate the country we now call France from the Iberian Peninsula, Spain and Portugal. Although very rugged, the Pyrenees also have passes that once let the Germanic tribes move southward. Do you see, too, how close the Iberian Peninsula is to North Africa? Many years after a Germanic tribe called the Goths invaded Spain, Muslim invaders from Africa crossed the Strait of Gibraltar into Spain and spread throughout southwestern Europe. Invaders first came to Spain seeking its gold and silver, and then stayed to build flourishing cities, fish, tend livestock, and grow crops, especially olives and oranges, in the warm climate.

Settling Down

A Germanic tribe called the Franks defeated the Romans and settled in fertile lands north of the Pyrenees that we call France after them. North of the Alps, another Germanic tribe settled along the fertile Rhone Valley. But most of the Germanic tribes stayed east of the Rhine and west of the Oder River, in a more thickly wooded and marshy land (along the North and Baltic seas). The Oder River separated Germanic tribes from Slavic tribes. Through the centuries, that river separated German states from Slavic countries like Poland and Russia. But of course the people mingled and married; you will read about the Franks merging with the Roman population in the World Civilization section that follows.

A New Name

Farther north still are the British Isles, separated from France by the English Channel. Once again, geography alone could not keep invaders out. When the Roman fleet in Britain withdrew to protect Italy, Britain's shores were attacked from across the Channel and the North Sea. One of the attacking tribes, the Angles, gave the fertile southern part of the island a new name, England. Later, the Northmen (Norse) or Vikings raided the northern part of the island and Ireland, and set up a kingdom in northern France (Normandy).

Top of the World

The Vikings were superb boatmen who sailed the stormy northern seas from Russia to the coast of North America. If you look at the top of the map, you will see the finger-shaped peninsula, called the Scandinavian Peninsula, from which the Vikings came. Now, that peninsula is divided between Sweden and Norway. (The Vikings also came from what is now Denmark, which is the little finger of land pointing from Europe back at Scandinavia.)

Look on a globe to see how close the North Pole is to the Scandinavian Peninsula. Do you think the Scandinavian winters are cold? Few large animals live that far north, but one very famous kind of deer does. Can you name it? Scandinavia is also famous for its beautiful fjords and rich fishing. (A fjord is a narrow inlet of the sea between steep cliffs.)

The Middle East

In the World Civilization section of this book, you can read about the Ottoman Empire. It was one of many powerful empires that grew up around the Mediterranean Sea.

The eastern region around the Mediterranean is called the Middle East. It includes the countries in southwest Asia, on or near the Mediterranean Sea. The Middle East also includes the Arabian Peninsula and countries in northeast Africa like Egypt and Sudan. (You may also hear the Middle East called the Near East; both names refer to pretty much the same area.)

The Middle East is a very important region today because it produces vast quantities of oil, needed for modern machines. It is also the birthplace of three great religions: Judaism, Christianity, and Islam, which you may have read about in previous books of this series.

Except for a few great rivers, much of this land is dry and uninviting. Look on the map for the Sahara Desert. As you know, not much will grow in a desert. And other lands in this region are high and rugged, unsuitable for farming. Now find the Atlas Mountains in northwest Africa, and the Taurus Mountains on the Anatolian Peninsula. This peninsula, also known as Asia

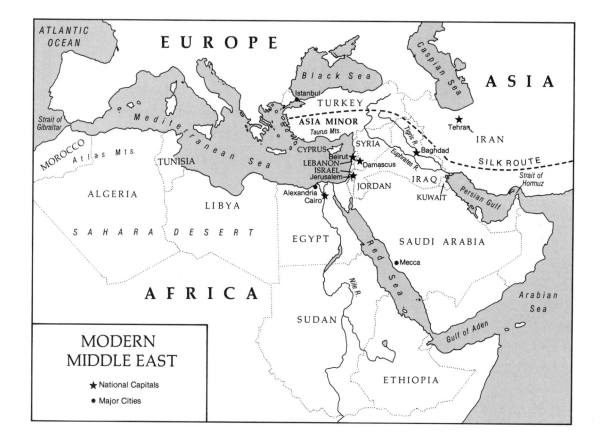

Minor, forms part of the modern-day country of Turkey. The Balkan Peninsula (Greece and northward) is rugged too.

In these dry lands there are many short, irregular rivers called wadis. For most of the year the wadis are totally dry. Then a sudden cloudburst will fill a wadi with dangerous, rushing water. In a few hours, though, it will be dry once more and perhaps will not fill again for years.

Another, more dependable source of water in these dry lands is the oasis, which is fed by water from underground. But oases are few and far between, and they may dry up for years at a time. For the nomadic peoples in these areas, who once moved with their herds of animals in search of water and food, it was a hard life.

The need for water in the Near East has led some modern-day governments to build dams that divert and store the water from some of the great rivers. Factories have been built that take salt water from the Persian Gulf and turn it into fresh water suitable for drinking and farming. But this is an expensive and complicated process, and is not yet widely used.

A wadi in Egypt.

This oasis in Egypt is a green spot in the desert.

If this region is so dry, why does it have some of the most famous cities in the world? Look at the map and find Alexandria, Cairo, Mecca, Jerusalem, Damascus, Baghdad, Tehran, and Istanbul. (Do you know the former name of Istanbul?) You'll see that most of these cities are near a river or the coasts of the Mediterranean, Black, or Red seas. These cities grew because their geographical location made them important centers of trade.

For a long time—until a sea route around the southern tip of Africa was discovered—the people of the Near East controlled trade among China, India, and Europe. Many inland cities in the Near East began as stopping places on the caravan routes of the traders. It was not an easy journey along the land route through central Asia to China. The route was called the Silk Road, not because it was smooth as silk—just the opposite, in fact! The name Silk Road came from one of the main products transported along the route, silk from

China, which was much in demand in other countries. Although this route was hard, for thousands of years there was no better way to go.

Our Land

When you look at the map of the United States, do you remember studying it before? Could you find it on a world map or a globe? Let's be sure.

Pretend the world map is a giant jigsaw puzzle, and our country, the United States, is one of the largest pieces. The first place to look, of course, is in the correct hemisphere, the Western Hemisphere. Then comes the correct continent (North America). Now it's easy, isn't it? Especially when you see the "finger" of Florida pointing southward. It is a very large peninsula. Be sure to locate the nearby Caribbean Sea.

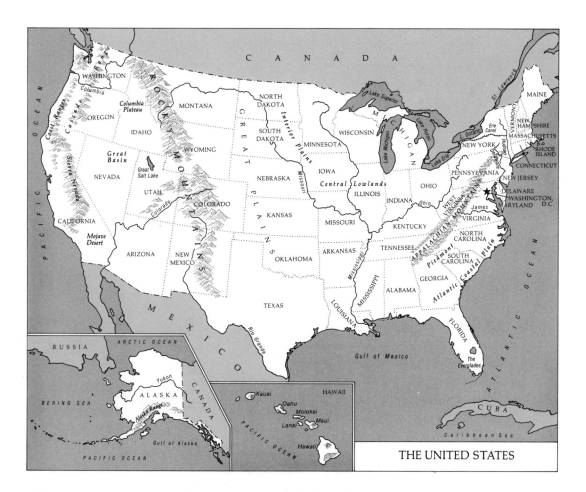

THE UNITED STATES

The position of Florida, which the Spanish discovered soon after Columbus's voyages, is important. You can see it separates the Gulf of Mexico from the Atlantic Ocean. What we can't see is an enormous current (like a river flowing within the ocean) that moves along the eastern side of Florida. This current is called the Gulf Stream, and it takes warm water from the Gulf of Mexico around Florida and all the way north and eastward through the Atlantic Ocean to the British Isles! The Gulf Stream warms Western Europe; it's the reason that Britain is not as cold as the state of Maine, which is located on roughly the same latitude. Again, as you can see, geography makes a difference in people's lives.

The geography of our land helped make us what we are today. The great bays and rivers along the Atlantic coast helped to feed the Native Americans and the first settlers from England. (Descendants of the first natives of America call themselves American Indians or Indians, but they are also called Native Americans. You will find all three names used in this book.) The settlers traveled by river to explore the new land and move westward. Later, Americans built canals connecting rivers. The Erie Canal stretched 365 miles from the Hudson River to Lake Erie and allowed barges to reach the Atlantic

In this picture you can see two common ways people once traveled and transported goods on the Erie Canal. On the right a man poles a raft; in the center a barge is being pulled by a horse on the shore.

Ocean from the Midwest. (Today the Erie Canal is part of an even longer system of canals.)

Ask Yourself

Look at your map of the United States. What other rivers allowed the settlers to move westward? What great river, one of the world's largest, allowed people

and trade to move from north to south, almost from the Great Lakes to the Gulf of Mexico?

This great river is called the Mississippi. Look carefully at the map on page 99 to see what large rivers flow into it. Rivers such as the Ohio and the Missouri were very important in the settlement of the Midwest, especially after the steamboat was invented. Without these and similar rivers, the settlers probably would not have moved west so quickly.

Steamboats were first invented in 1783, but they were not used widely until 1807, when Robert Fulton launched a steamboat he designed. Here you see goods being loaded onto a steamboat on the Mississippi River.

Mountains Old and New

If you look at your map again, you will see there are many places the early settlers could not reach by river. The Appalachian Mountains, though not terribly high, were 120 to 375 miles wide. They blocked westward movement for the 1,800 miles of their length. Of course, there were also Native Americans on the other side of the Appalachians who fought to keep out early settlers.

Down from the western side of the Appalachians and past the lowlands east and west of the broad Mississippi River, the land begins to rise gradually again. This plateau, or great expanse of flat land, is called the Great Plains. It begins in Canada and extends into Texas. (Do you remember that Canada is our northern neighbor?) The rich farm land of the Great Plains drew settlers, who almost destroyed the millions of buffalo that once thundered across the plains.

The Rocky Mountains begin even farther north than the plains, in north Alaska, and are almost twice as long as the Appalachians. The Rockies are also much "younger" and higher than the Appalachians. (Over time, erosion gradually wears away mountain rock. This is why "younger" mountain ranges are generally higher than "older" ones.)

In later books we will talk about the terrible struggle settlers had crossing the Great Plains and the Rockies. After the Rockies, they faced deserts and more mountains before they reached the Pacific coast. As you may already know, the arrival of the settlers forced Native Americans to live in some of the harshest areas of the West.

The Majestic Mountains of the World

You've already read about some of the world's mountain ranges and how they've served as natural barriers to human trade and settlement. In the following sections, we'll revisit these ranges and learn about several others that have helped shape the civilizations of the world. We'll also read about individual mountains that have inspired awe and fear and have led explorers to risk their lives climbing their high peaks.

You'll need a relief map of the world or a globe with raised sections that allows you to see and feel the elevations representing mountain ranges. You'll notice that every continent—even Antarctica—has at least one major mountain range. (As we explain in the Physical Science section of this book, there are even mountain ranges under the oceans! You might want to refer to that section to read more about how mountains form.)

A Long Backbone

Antarctica is a good place to begin our study of mountains. On your map or globe look at the portion of Antarctica that falls within the Western Hemisphere. Find the finger of land that points toward South America, and touch the mountain range that begins there. Move your finger along the mountain ranges that stretch up the west coast of South America. Notice that you could keep right on following mountain ranges, with a few skips, up through North America and all the way to Alaska!

A large collection of mountain ranges is called a cordillera (kohr-dil-YAIR-uh), a Spanish word meaning "backbone." The mountain systems you just traced are broken into two groups: the North American and South American cordilleras.

The Land of the Andes

You can see the Andes Mountains in the background of this photograph and Rio Aconcagua Valley, Chile, in the foreground.

The Andes mountains, which make up the South American cordillera, are the longest mountain chain in the world. They stretch 4,500 miles from the southern tip of the continent to the Caribbean coast of Venezuela. Can you find them on your map or globe? Their average height is 10,000 feet. At 22,834 feet, Mount Aconcagua is the highest mountain in the Western Hemisphere. Now find Aconcagua (hint: it's in Argentina).

A general rule geographers have discovered about mountains is that young mountains are high while old mountains are low. The Andes fit this pattern. Though they are about 20 million years old, they are still considered young. The Andes were created by pressure from two plates pushing against each other. (Plates are giant pieces of the earth's crust. You can read more about the earth's plates and the formation of mountains in the Physical Sciences section of this book.) The continental plate on the east side and the Pacific plate on the west were forced toward each other, and their soft sandstone and limestone rocks were easily folded upward into a long, north-south wall. Violent earthquakes and volcanoes accompanied the formation of the Andes and still occur periodically.

The Pisac Indians live in a valley of the Andes.

Today, the Andes are considered by some people to be the most valuable mountains in the world because of their incredible mineral resources. Huge deposits of gold and silver, which once motivated the Spanish to climb these mountains and conquer the native Incas, still exist today. Platinum, copper, tin, and iron are also now mined from the Andes.

A Note About Feet

Where can you look up a mountain's height? You can look in an encyclopedia, an almanac, an atlas or a geographical dictionary.

If you look up the same mountain in several sources, you may discover that the listings for its height vary. That's because measuring mountains is a complicated procedure.

The Rugged Rockies

Leaving the Andes, follow the mountain ranges of the North American cordillera. These are the Rocky Mountains, which stretch more than 3,000 miles from Mexico to Alaska. While you're looking at Alaska, find Mount

A Rocky Mountain scene: Little Matterhorn Mountain and Odessa Lake in Colorado.

McKinley, the highest mountain in North America at 20,320 feet. Native Americans call this mountain Denali, meaning "The Great One."

About 130 million years old, the Rockies are older than the Andes. They were formed when a giant upheaval of an underlying rock core forced the entire region to lift. Then they were squeezed into long folds that form the valleys and separate ranges you can see today. Rock that was too hard to fold formed sharp, rugged mountains like the Tetons in Wyoming.

Volcanic activity and cycles of uplift and erosion occurred in the Rockies for millions of years. As uplift occurred, rivers ran faster, cutting deep gorges and canyons between the mountains. Volcanic activity still occurs in some of the coastal mountains of Alaska, Oregon, and California.

The Rockies, like the Andes, are rich in mineral resources. Gold from these mountains has played an important part in shaping the history of North America. Silver, copper, lead, and other metals have also been mined. In all, the Rockies have yielded more than 34 billion dollars' worth of metals.

The Rounded, Rolling Appalachians

To the east of the Rockies, the Appalachian Mountains extend nearly 1,800 miles from Alabama north to the Gulf of St. Lawrence. Follow these mountains on your map. Because they are very old, their peaks have been greatly eroded and most are less than 6,000 feet high. That's why the Appalachians seem like mere hills if you compare them to the Rockies.

The Appalachians were formed 280 million years ago, and the uplifting, folding, and erosion of these mountains is still going on. Important mineral resources found in these mountains include iron, oil, gas, and coal deposits,

A worn peak in the Appalachian Mountains.

which have helped the United States develop as an industrial nation. In addition, the rivers flowing from the Appalachians provide waterpower to turn turbines and create electricity.

The High Peaks of the Himalayas

Let's turn our attention back to Alaska, where the Rockies come to an end. If we follow the curve of the Rockies toward the Aleutian Islands and jump over the Bering Sea, we land in Siberian Asia. With your finger, you can find the mountains of Siberia and follow them south until you reach the Pamirs, in central Asia. Turn southeast to Tibet, and follow the mountains called the Himalayas, a name meaning "the House of Snow."

This massive mountain range is so impressive, it has earned Tibet the label "rooftop of the world." The Himalayas are about 1,500 miles long, and many peaks reach over 25,000 feet. Mount Everest, at 29,028 feet, is the giant of all mountains and the highest point on the earth's surface. Find Mount Everest on your map or globe. It's on the border between Nepal and Tibet.

The Himalayas are actually made up of three parallel ridges: the Greater Himalayas, the Lesser Himalayas, and the Outer Himalayas. These ridges were formed about 20 million years ago, when a geologic "wave" in the earth rippled south from central Asia. When the wave hit a high point of land, it

Can you find the highest ridges of the Himalayas in the background?

broke, depositing most of the rock in the Greater Himalayas. Small ripples continued on and deposited their rock in the Lesser and Outer Himalayas.

The mountains benefit the people living to their north by blocking that part of Asia from the heavy rains, called monsoons, that pound into India. Copper and iron are mined from the Himalayas, but perhaps the most notable feature of this area is the grandeur of the mountains themselves. Because of their great height and beauty, the Himalayas attract many tourists, which helps provide a living for the mountain people.

The Urals: Border Between Europe and Asia

Return to the Pamirs, making a path that heads northwest and crosses the Aral Sea to the Ural Mountains. Since the days of ancient Greece, the Urals have been the accepted border between the continents of Europe and Asia. Though not very high (they average 3,500 feet), the Urals are distinctive because they run in a nearly straight line for over 1,000 miles.

The Urals are so straight because of the way they were formed. Two blocks of hard, old rock faced each other exactly, and about 280 million years ago, pressure deep inside the earth pushed them together until the Urals were forced to fold and rise in a straight line.

When they rose, some igneous rock from the earth's mantle pushed its way upward, bringing with it rich deposits of coal and petroleum, and minerals such as platinum, copper, nickel, and emerald. (You can read more about igneous rock in the Physical Sciences section of this book.)

The Alps

Return again to the Pamirs, but this time move your finger westward, scooting around the Caspian and Black seas and landing in the mountains north of Italy, the Alps.

This crescent-shaped series of mountain ranges extends 650 miles from Yugoslavia to France. Notice how the Alps dominate the European landscape. On your map or globe, locate the highest peak in Europe—15,771-foot Mont Blanc.

The Alps are a relatively young range of mountains. Geologists esti-

A view in the Italian Alps.

mate that the Alps were still forming 30 million years ago. Pressure inside the earth caused the land to buckle, fold, and fault, tilting it upward to form these mountains.

There are few mineral resources in the Alps. But waterpower from the area's rivers is harnessed to provide electricity for chemical manufacturing, textile production, and metal processing. Tourists visit these beautiful mountains year round.

The Atlas Mountains

Leave the Alps now by moving your finger from their western edge southward through Spain and into Africa. Here, the Atlas Mountains stretch for 1,500 miles along the north African coast from Morocco to Tunisia. These mountains are named for the mythical god who the Greeks believed was condemned to support the sky on his shoulders through eternity. With an average height of 11,000 feet, the Atlas Mountains block coastal rains, creating a desert known as the Sahara.

A Berber village nestled in the main ridge of the Atlas Mountains.

While you are looking at Africa, see if you can locate 19,340-foot Mount Kilimanjaro in Tanzania, west of Lake Victoria. This is the highest mountain in Africa. Amazingly, even though it is almost at the equator, it is so high that it wears a cap of ice!

The Atlas Mountains are young mountains that formed at about the same time as the Alps. However, they are not as high or rugged as the Alps. Earthquakes still occur in this region in Africa, and they can cause great tidal waves in the nearby Mediterranean Sea and Atlantic Ocean. Unlike the Alps, the Atlas Mountains have significant deposits of coal and minerals including iron ore, cobalt, and phosphate.

The Lure of Mammoth Mountain Peaks

Why do people climb a mountain? Many climbers answer this question with the words of a man who tried to scale Mount Everest: "Because it is there." Imagine spending days pushing your body to its limits, finally pulling yourself over that last ledge to stand at the peak of the highest mountain around. How would you feel?

Right now, we're going to read about the brave explorers who climbed the world's highest mountains for the first time. We'll work our way from the lowest to the highest of the high peaks of the world—mountain peaks that have inspired awe, worship, myth, and legend.

Mont Blanc: 15,771 Feet

Mont Blanc is French for "White Mountain." The highest peak in Europe, Mont Blanc used to be known as the "accursed mountain," because misfortune supposedly surrounded it. But when a prize of money was offered to anyone who found the first practical route to its summit, climbers forgot the curses of Mont Blanc and surged up its slopes. After many unsuccessful attempts by climbers, Dr. Michel-Gabriel Paccard, the village doctor of nearby Chamonix, France, and his porter, Jacques Balmat, endured hardship and frostbite and finally reached the summit on August 8, 1786. Expeditions after Paccard's lost members to avalanches and other tragedies. But in 1961 a remarkable adventurer actually made a successful parachute landing right on the summit!

Mont Blanc was the first high peak in the world to be "conquered." But it still seems incredible that anyone made it to the top of this high peak without the advanced equipment available to climbers today.

Mount Kilimanjaro: 19,340 Feet

Mount Kilimanjaro was known to local people as the "Mountain of Cold Devils" because of its snow-capped peaks. The news of a snow-capped mountain so near the equator was not believed for many years after its discovery in 1848 by two missionaries. But a little over forty years later, in 1889, the peak was first climbed by a German scientist named Dr. Hans Meyer.

Mount Kilimanjaro.

Kilimanjaro is actually the remains of an ancient volcano. Its two main peaks, Kibo and Mawenzi, are connected by a seven-mile ridge or "saddle." As legend has it, a leopard once climbed up to the saddle before he died in the snow. A famous story by the American author Ernest Hemingway called *The Snows of Kilimanjaro* uses this legend to tell the story of a man who searched and searched for something but never found it.

Mount McKinley: 20,320 Feet

It is no wonder Mount McKinley is called "The Great One" by Native Americans. Unlike some peaks in the Andes and Himalayas, Mount McKinley rises from a low, 1,500-foot elevation. It towers over the nearby Yukon Valley, and its peaks are rarely clear of cloud cover.

This imposing mountain didn't seem to frighten the four gold prospectors who attempted to reach its summit in 1910. Tom Lloyd, Charlie McGonagall, Bill Taylor, and Pete Anderson carried no special equipment with them for their climb—no instruments, heavy boots, or even a rope. On April 10, Taylor and Anderson reached the top through sheer determination and strength. They chose the northernmost of two peaks, since it looked the highest to

Mount McKinley.

them, and planted an American flag at its top. Upon returning to Fairbanks, Alaska, and celebrating, they learned they were wrong: the south peak was the higher.

That peak was conquered in 1913 by Archdeacon Hudson Stuck, an accomplished mountain climber. After a grueling climb that included hacking and clawing up a three-mile-high staircase of ice, Stuck and his party finally reached the top, leaving a cross of birch sticks to mark their triumph.

Aconcagua: 22,834 Feet

Aconcagua, the highest peak in the Western Hemisphere, is a difficult climb. Its slopes consist of broken rock and debris, and its surface has been described by climbers as "falling to pieces." But this did not stop Englishman Edward A. Fitzgerald and his companions, who set out to find a route to the top in the summer of 1896–97. (Remember, in the Southern Hemisphere, summer is from December to March.) Included in the party was Mattias Zurbriggen of Switzerland, one of the most famous climbers of the Alps.

After four unsuccessful attempts to reach the summit, all plagued by the crumbling mountainside, battering winds, and illness, Fitzgerald and the rest of the group gave up the struggle. On the fifth attempt only Zurbriggen pushed on, climbing the last 1,000 feet alone and reaching the top on January 14, 1897.

Mount Everest: 29,028 Feet

The local name of Mount Everest is Chomolungma, "Goddess of the Snows," or "Goddess Mother of the World," a fitting name for the highest peak on earth. Mount Everest is revered by followers of the Buddhist religion, and two monasteries—one in Nepal and one in Tibet—have been built facing the peak so that the monks may contemplate it.

In 1852, a British surveyor excitedly burst into the office of his supervisor and announced: "Sir, I have discovered the highest mountain in the world!" Thus the world outside the Himalayas learned of Everest's claim to fame. However, the remoteness of the peak, its "thin air," the unpredictable climate, and political and religious roadblocks delayed the first climbing expedition. It was not until 1921 that the first attempt was made to scale Everest's slopes.

Mount Everest.

This and numerous later expeditions failed, but each time, climbers got closer and closer to the summit. New equipment, including oxygen tanks to combat the thin air, helped. In 1953, a British group including a New Zealand beekeeper named Edmund Hillary and a Tibetan guide named Tenzig Norkey made an attempt. On May 29, 1953, Hillary and Norkey cut steps into the icy summit and climbed to the top of the world. They carried with them a string of flags representing Britain, India, Nepal, and the United Nations.

Introduction to World Civilization

FOR PARENTS AND TEACHERS

Following the Core Knowledge Sequence for World Civilization, in Book Four we turn first to a further look at Byzantium, and then to the Middle Ages in Europe. We will also be looking at developments in early Asian and African civilizations.

The Middle Ages are an appealing subject for several reasons. Children love the mythic lore of the time, with its stories of knights, castles, and magicians. From their interest in these myths, they readily grow to understand a real historical era very different from our own, yet one in which many of our modern ideas germinated. Your child may want to read the tales of King Arthur in the Mythology section of this volume before reading this section.

One of the central tenets of *The Core Knowledge Series* is that knowledge builds on knowledge. This study of the Middle Ages allows children to understand the period as it grew out of Rome's decline. Rather than simply memorizing what happened, children can begin to understand the clash between the Romans and the nomadic invaders, and the growing strength of the Roman Catholic church, because now they have enough context to do so. They can see the contrasts between the ways the Germanic tribes and the Romans, very different peoples, lived and thought about the world. They can make sense of the invaders' need for rich land to farm, and the Romans' fear and dislike of people they considered outsiders. They can also see that our modern-day cultural inheritance includes developments in non-European civilizations as well.

Children can learn much from contrasts. Understanding feudalism can help children appreciate what it means to be citizens in a country with senators, governors, and a president, rather than a lord or king. Children can better understand their own world, in which information and events across the globe can be known in minutes, by contrasting it with life in the Middle Ages, where the loss of a centralized government and centuries of isolation kept people from knowing what was happening in other places, and when, with a few exceptions, people lost track of knowledge that had already been attained.

Children can also be helped to understand history as a story, including some sad chapters that should make us reflect on the human capacity for destruction and cruelty. Parents and teachers should talk with children about their sense of why it is that so often one group of people is engaged in war with another, sometimes in the name of a cause that children might not associate with war (for example, the Crusades, or the Muslim "holy wars").

As always, you will find sprinkled throughout the section suggestions for activities that make these stories from history more vivid and memorable. Please feel free to supplement them with similar activities of your own devising, with the resources listed below, and with dramatic and musical activities available locally.

Books that supplement the topics covered in this chapter include:

The Time Traveller Book of Knights and Castles by Judy Hindley. (Usborne).

A Proud Taste for Scarlet and Miniver by E. L. Konigsberg. (Harper-Collins). This is a book about Eleanor of Aquitaine.

Robin Hood: His Life and Legend by Bernard Miles. (Rand McNally).

Marco Polo: His Journal by Susan L. Roth. (Doubleday).

The Invaders by Martin Windrow. (Arco).

World Civilization

Germanic Peoples on the Move

Around A.D. 200, Germanic warriors began attacking the Roman Empire. You may have read in Book Three about how tribes like the Visigoths and Vandals conquered Roman cities and eventually took over the western part of the Roman Empire (including the countries we now know as Britain, France, Spain, and Italy).

This helmet of a Frankish warrior was buried with its owner around A.D. 600.

The Germanic invasions around A.D. 200 marked the beginning of a long period during which the once mighty Roman Empire weakened—not just because of these invasions, but also because of economic problems and weak leaders within the Empire. In A.D. 476, the last Roman emperor (a boy only fourteen years old) was overthrown by a Germanic general. For this reason, people often say that Rome "fell" in 476 A.D. That's a useful date, as long as you remember that there was a long decline leading up to that fall, and that in fact only the Western Roman Empire fell, while the Eastern Roman Empire (as you'll learn in a moment) survived and even grew stronger.

The Germanic tribes who entered Roman lands sometimes arrived peacefully, establishing settlements and trading with the local peoples. But at other times they raided Roman towns and fought the Roman people.

Whether farmers or fighters, these Germanic peoples were not used to settling in one place. Peoples who move about rather than settling down are called nomadic. These nomadic tribes cleared and farmed small plots of land, built thatched wooden huts instead of sturdy stone buildings, and then moved on when the land was no longer good for raising crops.

The early Germanic peoples believed in a religion of nature gods and war gods. Some tribes even made human sacrifices. They told stories of their heroes, but these stories were never written down—these nomadic peoples usually could not write. The Germanic tribes were strong and self-reliant. The Romans admired these qualities, and in their writings described the Germanic people as large-bodied and fierce. In fact, the name given to one Germanic tribe, the Franks, means "bold" or "fierce."

Dark or Middle?

What did it mean that Germanic warriors became the new rulers of the city of Rome and its lands in Western Europe? It meant great changes, not just in the names of the people in power but in the way everyone lived from day to day.

Let's think about what makes up a civilization: planned cities, a money system, a smoothly working government, roads on which people can travel and trade, laws to make people safe, and a writing system used to communicate and to preserve knowledge. For hundreds of years after Rome fell, all these things we think of as making up civilization could not continue to develop easily because of wars and unpredictable changes in rulers.

The Germanic tribes entered Roman lands seeking a better life for themselves. Although they didn't intend it, they were also endangering some of the achievements of Roman civilization, and helping to bring on a period of hard times.

The three hundred years after Rome fell are sometimes called the Dark Ages, to suggest that these were very difficult times in the part of the world that had been the Western Roman Empire. During this period in Europe's history, fertile lands, aqueducts, and cities were often abandoned. Much of the knowledge we associate with civilization—medicine, science, law, geography, the arts and literature—was forgotten. The "light" of knowledge was temporarily turned off. Life was instead full of conflict, change, and struggle.

Today, in looking back over history, we sometimes don't speak of the Dark Ages. Not all parts of the world were experiencing the troubles and setbacks of the Western Roman Empire. Instead, we sometimes refer to the roughly one thousand years after the decline of Rome, from about A.D. 450 to 1400, as the Middle Ages. For some peoples, as we're about to see, the Middle Ages were not "dark." Instead they were years of great learning and achievement. Let's look, for example, at the Eastern Roman Empire, also called the Byzantine Empire.

The Byzantine Empire

In Book Three, you may have read how, in the western part of the Roman Empire, the once great city of Rome was wrecked by Germanic tribes. But in the Eastern Roman Empire, another great city, Constantinople, thrived. Constantinople remained "Roman" for nearly one thousand years after Rome itself fell. (Take a minute to look at a map and locate Constantinople, where the continents of Europe and Asia meet. You can see why the city was hard to attack. What are the names of the two seas on either side of the city?)

Constantinople became the center of the Byzantine Empire, as the Eastern Roman Empire came to be called. The name Byzantine comes from Byzantium, which was the city's name before the emperor Constantine renamed it Constantinople after himself. The Byzantine emperors saw themselves as carrying on the traditions of the old Roman Empire. But Byzantine civilization was in reality a mixture of various peoples and influences: Roman, Greek, Christian, Persian, Asian, and others. From about A.D. 500 to 1200, it was one of the most advanced civilizations in the world.

The city of Constantinople is now called Istanbul. This view shows the old section of the city, where the mosque of Hagia Sophia is located (it sits by the water's edge to the left in the photograph).

Justinian and the Laws

After Constantine, the most famous Byzantine emperor was named Justinian. Justinian ruled from A.D. 527 to 565. He was so powerful that he sent armies against the Germanic conquerors of the Western Roman Empire. For a while, he brought parts of North Africa, Spain, and Italy back under Roman rule. But soon these lands were lost again, and the Byzantine Empire was weakened by the fighting.

Justinian deserves credit for some lasting achievements. He ordered the building of a beautiful and famous church called Hagia Sophia. (You can read about it in the Fine Arts section of this book.)

Another of Justinian's lasting achievements was in law. As the Western Roman Empire was breaking down, Roman laws were in danger of being lost. But Justinian saved these laws by ordering scholars to gather and organize them, to improve some of them, and to write them all down in books. These laws, known as Justinian's Code, affected the way laws were made for many centuries afterward.

This coin, used as money in the Byzantine Empire, was minted during Justinian's reign and carries the stamped image of Justinian.

A Brave Empress

Justinian's wife was the empress Theodora. For an empress, she came from an unusual family. Empresses usually came from very noble or high-ranking families. But Theodora was an actress and the daughter of a bear trainer in the circus!

Even though Theodora's upbringing had not prepared her for the life of an empress, she showed great intelligence and skill in helping Justinian decide how to make laws and choose people to enforce the laws. She often showed great bravery and gave her husband the courage to make difficult decisions. Once, when angry crowds were burning parts of Constantinople and trying to make another person emperor, Justinian's advisers urged him to run for his life. But Theodora convinced Justinian to stay, face the crowds, and restore order.

(You might want to look back at the Fine Arts section of Book Three to read about Byzantine mosaics. In the Fine Arts section of this book you can see a likeness of Theodora in a Byzantine mosaic.)

The Rise of Christianity

In Book Three, we learned about how the first Byzantine emperor, Constantine, was also the first Christian emperor of the Roman Empire. In the past, Christians had been persecuted by Roman emperors. Under Constantine, however, the people of the Roman Empire were free to worship as Christians if they chose. The Christian religion attracted millions of followers who saw in it a new way of life. Christianity preached that all people had worth, although it did not preach that slavery should be abolished.

As Christianity spread, it became more influential and more complicated. The Christian religion was no longer a set of beliefs with a loose band of followers. Instead it had become a complex and powerful institution, an established organization with rules, procedures, and various leaders (who didn't always agree).

Much money went into the building of large, beautiful churches, like Hagia Sophia. As churches were built in various cities, officials were appointed to take care of the affairs of the church. High-ranking church officials were called bishops. The bishop of Rome became the leader of the Christian church for the entire Western Roman Empire. He was called the pope, from the Greek word meaning father.

As more people became Christian, they began to argue about exactly what it meant to believe in Christianity. There were quarrels about various beliefs and about who should lead the church. The leader of the church in Constantinople did not agree that the pope in Rome should be the leader of the whole Christian religion. Eventually these arguments led to a split in the Christian religion. In the Western Roman Empire, the Christian church became known as the Roman Catholic church. In the Eastern (or Byzantine) Empire, it became known as the Eastern Orthodox church.

The Germanic Tribes Become Christian

The arguments among Christians did not stop the religion from spreading. Christianity became so influential among Romans that when the Germanic tribes attacked Rome, the people looked for help not to the emperor but to the pope.

The Germanic peoples who settled in Rome often merged their ways with the ways of the local people. Many of the Germanic peoples became Christians. Since the pope was the leader of the Christian church in Rome, he became, in a way, a leader who ranked above the various Germanic chiefs who had accepted Christianity. The pope became very powerful, in some ways as powerful as the Roman emperor.

Soon, Germanic peoples outside of Italy became Christians too. When the king of the Franks took up the new religion, he brought his entire tribe into the Christian church. When a new tribe of invaders attacked Rome, the Franks saved Rome and the pope, and they gave the pope much land in the middle of Italy.

Keeping Learning Alive

Meanwhile, throughout Europe there arose places called monasteries, where men called monks lived very simple lives devoted to work, study, and Christian worship. These monks kept knowledge alive during some dark and

This picture shows medieval nuns and monks in a procession on the way to church.

difficult years. They made beautiful copies of important ancient books. In so doing, they preserved many of the "classical" writings of the ancient Greeks and Romans.

The monasteries became places that poor and sick people could go when they needed help. The monks also worked hard to spread the Christian religion. They converted many more Germanic people to Christianity.

Charles the Great

Around A.D. 800, there arose a new, strong Christian ruler, Charles the Great, known to his people as Charlemagne.

Why is someone in history called "great"? Because he or she was an especially good or brilliant person? Or because he or she made an important change that affected many people, whether in a good or bad way? Charlemagne was great for both these reasons.

Charlemagne came from a family of powerful rulers of the Franks, one of the strongest of the Germanic peoples. Charlemagne fought and won many wars. He defeated non-Christian Germanic tribes as far east as the Elbe River. He did not hesitate to force the people he conquered to accept the Christian religion.

Charlemagne conquered so many lands that much of Western Europe was reunited under a single ruler for the first time since the fall of Rome. To the pope at the time, it seemed as if the old Roman Empire was being restored. On Christmas Day in the year 800, the pope crowned Charlemagne the Holy Roman Emperor.

Charlemagne and the Spread of Learning

Charlemagne was not just a warrior. He believed in education, and he could read Latin. This was very unusual for anyone who didn't live in a monastery. Even the Frankish priests who lived among the people often didn't know the meaning of the Latin words they spoke in church services.

Charlemagne started a school in his palace at Aachen, also called Aix-la-Chapelle (see the map of Charlemagne's empire). He gathered scholars from many nations. There were no printing presses at the time, so books had to be written by hand. Like the monks, these scholars made copies in Latin of works like the Bible, and helped preserve classical learning.

Charlemagne is crowned emperor by Pope Leo III in St. Peter's church in Rome.

Charlemagne himself studied in the palace school. He learned to understand Greek. Like you, he studied mathematics. But unlike you, he began learning to write so late in life that he made little progress, although he kept a notebook under his bed pillow so he could practice.

The Holy Roman Empire

Before Charlemagne, the Western Roman Empire had been broken apart by the invasions of many Germanic tribes. But during Charlemagne's reign, it appeared that the Western Roman Empire was going to be different, and perhaps even greater, than before. It would combine the old Roman traditions, some Germanic customs, and the practices of the Roman Catholic church. It would be a Holy Roman Empire, uniting many peoples in many lands.

The *idea* of a united Holy Roman Empire was a powerful one that lived on for a thousand years. But in reality, Charlemagne's empire began to break up less than thirty years after he died in A.D. 814. In fact, as a famous French thinker said later, the Holy Roman Empire really wasn't very "Roman" or "holy," or even much of an "empire." It wasn't Roman, because it contained a large number of small kingdoms with Germanic rulers in the regions now called Germany, Austria, and northern Italy. It wasn't especially holy, because the emperors argued constantly with the popes and often fought openly with them. And it wasn't very much of an empire, because the small kingdoms didn't always obey the emperor.

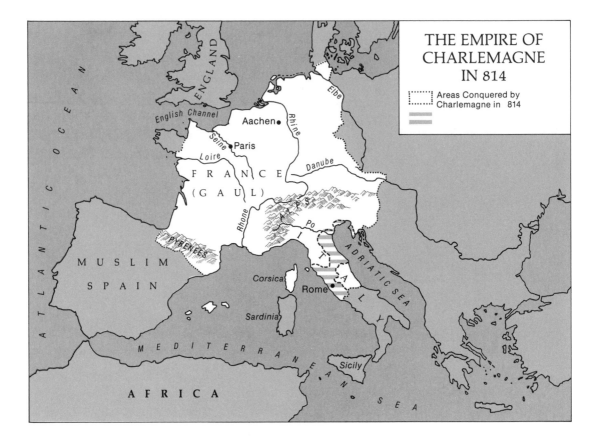

THE EMPIRE OF
CHARLEMAGNE
IN 814

Areas Conquered by
Charlemagne in 814

Year after year, the popes and emperors argued and sometimes battled for power. The Catholic church was the most powerful institution in Europe. It had laws, buildings, land, and many, many thousands of clergy (church officials). The Germanic rulers had nothing to match it. They kept trying to take some of the popes' power so they could have more control in their own lands.

One of the reasons for the church's great strength was that after Charlemagne's death, his empire broke into sections that fought against each other. The empire was also attacked by new invaders, including Muslims from the south and Vikings from the north. While the empire grew weak, Christianity grew strong. More and more people became Christians, and the church they supported grew and grew.

Feudalism

In the Middle Ages in Europe, a way of life known as feudalism developed in response to the needs of the times. Some people needed to support themselves and their families. They also needed protection from thieves or invading warriors. Other people needed workers for their lands and soldiers for their armies. To understand the system that developed to exchange protection for loyalty and labor, let's look back at the times in which feudalism began.

Let your imagination carry you back. The time is over a thousand years ago, in a village near a river in the region we now call France. One day you hear news that a village not far up the river has been burned and looted by Viking warriors. It seems as though you hear about a new attack every day, sometimes by warriors from other lands, sometimes by armies from nearby regions.

You and the other villagers know that you need some way to protect yourselves. So you ask a person who has riches and armies to help defend your village. This person, called a lord, promises to protect you if you promise to serve him loyally in return. If you promise loyalty to the lord, you become his vassal, meaning "one who serves."

You might serve the lord in different ways. You might be put in charge of some of his farmlands. If you're the son of a nobleman, you might train to become a knight—a warrior on horseback. Then it will be your duty to fight for your lord when necessary. (Young women can work in the fields or in the castle, but they cannot become knights. In general, girls and women have few rights or privileges in the Middle Ages.)

To sharpen their battle skills, knights sometimes practiced fighting each other, or "jousting," in contests called "tournaments."

By letting his vassals use his land, the lord gains their services and loyalty in exchange. Imagine that you are lucky enough to be put in charge of a good-sized piece of land. Farmers work for you, growing food on the land. You become used to having the comforts of more wealth and food than you had before you pledged your loyalty to the lord. To keep the land, you must remain loyal to your lord.

The next time invaders come, the lord leads his army against them. You must be part of that army and fight to defend your lord's lands and family, as well as your own. You might also fight the vassals of other lords if your lord tells you to.

The church tells you not to fight unarmed men on Sundays and other holy days, and not to hurt women and children. But the church also takes part in the feudal system: the church owns much of the land, so bishops are lords as well, and have many vassals loyal to them.

The Ladder of Society

In a feudal society, many people serve many others. Many farmers may serve you by working on the land you oversee. But you in turn serve your lord as his vassal. And your lord is a vassal to an even greater lord. Your lord serves the king.

You can think of feudal society as a kind of ladder. The people on the lower steps of the ladder serve the people above them. People in the Middle Ages were very aware of their position on this imaginary ladder, and of who was below or above them. And they didn't believe you could move up the ladder through hard work. The position you were born into was where you stayed.

The Middle Ages certainly didn't hold the modern American belief, expressed in the Declaration of Independence, that "all men are created equal."

The Far-Off King

In a feudal society, people give their loyalty to a king and his kingdom. But often this loyalty does not come from any great love for the king. Instead, it has to do with the ownership of land. In a way, you can think of the plot of land that you farm as being on loan from the king: he loaned it to your lord, and your lord loaned it to you. So in return you should feel loyalty to the king, who owns the land to begin with. But really, because the king is so far away and your lord so close, the word of the local lord is absolute law, and the faraway king seems only a vague idea, like somebody you've heard about in a story long ago.

What does it mean that you are more loyal to your local lord than to the far-off king? It means that even though the king is supposed to be at the head of the feudal system, the real rulers of Europe in the early Middle Ages are the lords and the church leaders.

Back on the Farm

While the lords and bishops were running the feudal governments and the vassals were fighting battles or running the lord's farms, what were other people doing?

They were doing what most people have always done until very recently. Nine out of ten of the people in Europe in the Middle Ages were farmers. Outside the church, there were no lawyers or teachers. There were few merchants or traders. With the Viking raiders in the north and the Muslims in the south, there was little opportunity to make contact with other parts of the world. The people of Europe had to grow or make what they needed right at home on their own manors.

The Manor

A manor was made up of the land and everything on the land held by a particular lord or clergyman. The manor included the farmland, woods, pastures, animal sheds, church, and everyone's dwellings, from the lord's castle to the huts of the peasants. A manor could be as big as a thousand acres.

The most important building on the manor was the lord's stronghold, the castle. There would also be a priest's house, a mill, a brewery, and perhaps a smithy. A mill is a building where grain is ground into flour. A smithy is a building where a blacksmith makes iron tools over a very hot flame. A brewery is a building where beer is made.

There was one kind of building you would see more than any other on the manor: little one-room huts with dirt floors, no windows or water, and very little heat. The people who lived in these huts often brought the farm animals inside to help them keep warm. Who were these people? They were the peasant farmers called serfs.

A serf plowing a field. This serf is using oxen to pull his plow, but during the Middle Ages people began using a new kind of plow drawn by horses. It worked better than the older plow you see here, and made it possible for people to plant more crops than they had before.

Who Were the Serfs?

The serfs did most of the work that kept the manor running. They planted and harvested crops. They milked cows, sheared sheep, made clothing and candles, built shelters, and much more. For two or three days a week, the serfs had to work very hard in the lord's fields, growing food for the lord and his household. In return, the serfs were given strips of land on which to grow their own food, and were allowed to graze their animals in the lord's pastures. The lord and his army would also protect the serfs in case of an attack.

The serfs were not exactly slaves but were much like slaves. They traded their freedom for the lord's protection. Serfs could not leave the manor unless the lord said they could. Other peasant farmers on the manor, called freedmen, also exchanged their labor and farm products for the lord's protection. But the freedmen could travel freely if they wanted to.

Fallow Fields, Unfairly Divided

On a manor, the land suitable for farming was usually divided into three fields. One of these fields was left unused, or fallow, every year. This gave the land a chance to regain its growing qualities, or its fertility, since a growing crop took away essential nutrients from the soil. Leaving a field fallow to renew itself was a great advance in farming. It changed the way people lived. Rather than move on, as the nomadic peoples did when lands wore out from overuse, people could settle down to farm and live in one place for a long time.

The manor's three fields were each divided into strips. The priest of the manor and freedmen held more strips than the serfs, and the lord held most of all. Does it seem fair that those who did the most work on the manor should hold the least land?

Work on the lord's land came first. If a big rain threatened to ruin crops ready for harvesting, then the serfs had to harvest the crops on the lord's land first, even if it meant their own crops would be ruined.

All serfs, including the women and children, worked in the fields. They were tired from constant work. They had few good things to look forward to. They were often very hungry. Their main food was soggy, sour brown bread. They had cheese in the summer and meat in the winter. They had meat in the winter because when the grass died, most of the cattle had to be killed for lack of food. But the meat went first to the lord's household in the castle, and the serfs got what was left over.

The serfs did have some days of rest on church holidays. Everyone was taught to believe in happiness in heaven as a reward for suffering on earth. Not many serfs lived to be old. It was always a hard life.

This picture shows two serfs, a man and a woman, breaking up clods of earth so that they can farm the land.

Life in the Castle

Until the later Middle Ages, the life of the lord's family and the other people in his household was almost as crude as the way the peasants lived. In a small castle with only one great hall, or room, the lord and his family would have a curtained-off section of the hall for privacy from their servants, who slept nearby on a straw-covered floor. There was little heat or light in the castle, and little knowledge of medical treatment. Men brought back to the castle who had been seriously wounded in battle usually died. Women often died in childbirth along with their babies.

When you think of a castle, you might picture a magnificent stone structure with many towers pointing toward the sky. But only the richest lords owned such castles. Most castles were smaller. The earliest ones were made of wood rather than stone. The main function of a castle was not luxury but defense against attackers. The castle might be only a small stone building surrounded by a wall. If not set on a hill, the building might be encircled by a moat, a wide, deep ditch filled with water. People could cross over the moat on a drawbridge, which could be closed up if the castle was attacked.

If the wealth of the lord grew over the years, then bit by bit the castle might grow as well. The ladies might weave large tapestries to hang on the walls. These colorful tapestries not only improved the looks of the castle, they also

Some castles were built so well that attackers could not break through the outside walls. Attackers sometimes had to "lay siege," or surround the castle and wait patiently until all the food and water inside the castle ran out and the defenders were forced to surrender.

helped keep it warm inside. Sometimes a series of tapestries would tell a story. One famous set of tapestries from fifteenth-century France tells a story about the hunt of a unicorn. (People in the Middle Ages understood that the tapestries were also telling a story with a Christian meaning hidden in it.)

Part of a famous medieval tapestry called the Unicorn Tapestry.

Chivalry

Gradually the people who lived in castles began to follow a set of formal manners. Knights, who usually rode on horses, were supposed to follow a "code of chivalry" (the word "chivalry" comes from *cheval*, the French word for horse). The code of chivalry told knights to protect the weak and to be brave, religious, honorable, and loyal. These were high ideals, and the knights didn't always live up to them.

Usually, only the sons of noblemen could become knights, and it took years of hard work. When a boy was even younger than you, about seven or eight years old, he began his training as a page. Leaving his family, he moved into his lord's castle, waited on the lord's table, and learned the proper care and use of weapons like the lance and the sword.

If a page had learned his lessons well, at the age of fifteen or sixteen he became a squire in the service of a knight. He took care of his knight's horses, weapons, and armor, and he learned how to fight. When he turned twenty, in a special ceremony he would be "dubbed": the lord would tap him on the neck or shoulder with the flat side of a sword and proclaim the young man to be a knight.

A knighting ceremony.

Legends of knights and their adventures, especially the stories of King Arthur and the Knights of the Round Table, were popular in the Middle Ages and are still popular today. You can read some of these legends in the Mythology section of this book.

William the Conqueror

Now you are going to hear the story of how, in the fateful year 1066, a lord from France became the king of England.

To understand the story of William the Conqueror, you should look at a map of France and England. The northwest region of what is now France had been conquered and settled by the warlike Vikings. The people who lived in that region became known as Normans, and the area where they lived was called Normandy. The greatest lord of this region was William, Duke of Normandy.

England at this time had been settled by two tribes, the Angles and the Saxons. That's why you may sometimes hear English people referred to as Anglo-Saxons.

In January of 1066, the king of England died. Usually, the oldest son of a king would become the new ruler, but in this case the old king left behind no sons at all. His second cousin, however, was William, Duke of Normandy, and William claimed the right to be king of England. But there was a problem—an English lord named Harold also claimed the right to be king.

William decided to fight for the crown. He gathered his vassals and many mercenaries (soldiers who could be hired to fight in any army). He also rounded up many horses, for he believed that the Norman knights, fighting on horseback, would have an advantage over the English foot soldiers.

The Battle of Hastings

In the fall of 1066, William crowded his troops and horses onto ships to cross the English Channel. The men and horses were tossed about by the rough waters of the Channel in the stormy months of autumn. William's bold decision to risk an autumn crossing took Harold by surprise. Harold had thought the Normans wouldn't attack until spring when the weather was calmer.

William and his troops landed in the south of England near the town of Hastings. They were met by Harold's army, which was tired from fighting off an attack by Norsemen in the north of England and then hurrying south to face William's army.

The English soldiers lined up with their shields and axes. At first they did well fighting off the charges of the Norman knights on horseback. But as the bloody hours went by, the Norman knights began to overpower the tired Englishmen. Later in the day, Harold, struck in the eye by an arrow, fell dead.

And so the Normans won the battle of Hastings. Their victory over the English is known as the Norman Conquest. And their leader, the former Duke of Normandy, gained two new titles: William I, King of England, and William the Conqueror.

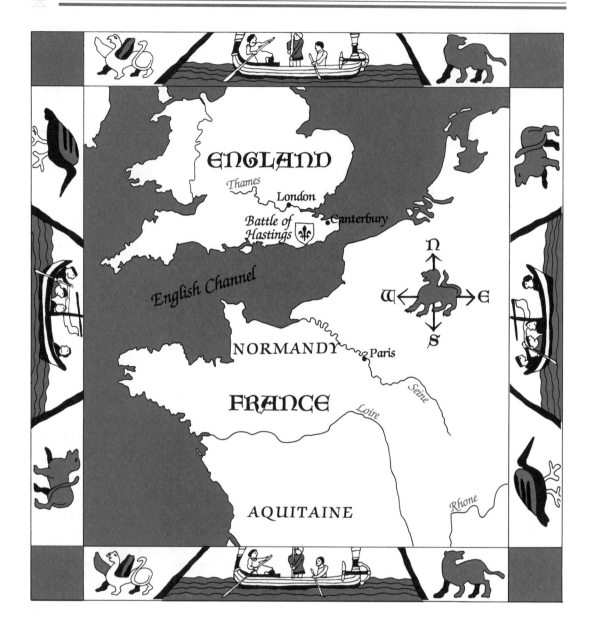

While the Norman Conquest eventually brought order and security to England, the early effect was a great deal of misery and death. After the battle, many Norman soldiers swarmed over the English countryside, robbing and killing the Anglo-Saxons.

William was a tough ruler who knew how to hold onto his power. He took lands away from the Anglo-Saxon lords and gave them to Norman lords who

This is a section of a famous weaving called the Bayeux Tapestry. *It shows the tide turning at the Battle of Hastings as the Norman soldiers break through the ranks of the Anglo-Saxons and attack Harold's bodyguards.*

had sworn to be loyal to him. Thus William brought feudalism to England. But there was a big difference from the old feudalism in France. In France, you remember, the local lords and clergymen held more *real* power than the king. But William, by keeping a great deal of land for himself, kept a great deal of power as well. And he demanded and enforced loyalty to himself as king.

Where English Comes From

One result of the Norman Conquest was the language we know as English. How did this happen?

After William's victory many Norman lords, clergymen, and their households came to England. They became the ruling class, settling in castles all across the land. They spoke an early form of the French language, very different from the Anglo-Saxon language of the people they had conquered.

For about two hundred years, the Normans ruled England. During these years, as the Normans and Anglo-Saxons lived together, their languages mixed. And so the language that we call English was born as a mixture of early French and Anglo-Saxon. That mixture has changed over time to become the English language that is spoken today.

The Growth of Towns

In the early years of feudalism, the people on a manor pretty much kept to themselves. They grew or made almost all they needed, and did not trade or communicate much with other manors. But the feudal system, and the isolation it encouraged, broke down as towns grew bigger and became important centers of activity. Let's look at how this happened.

As new techniques allowed farms to grow new and better crops, a freedman might have extra food to sell. He could take it to a nearby market, which consisted of stalls gathered at a crossroads. He might also be asked to take along his neighbor's extra food to sell. Let's say the freedman does so well selling that he decides to leave the manor and live near the crossroads, where he can sell food and other items sent to him from his old neighbors and relatives. Before you know it, the freedman has become a merchant, not a *producer* of goods but a *seller* of them.

Other merchants come and settle near the crossroads, and many buyers come to the market to purchase their goods. Soon a town begins to grow up around the marketplace. More and more people settle in the town, and they begin to rely on each other to perform different services. The merchant is too busy selling goods to bake bread, but he knows he can always buy bread from the baker. The baker spends all day baking. He has no time to farm, so he buys fruits and vegetables from the merchant's stand. The baker and the merchant have no time to make shoes, so they buy them ready-made from the shoemaker.

As civilization develops in the town, you can see that something is lost and something is gained. The townspeople lose some of their old ability to provide for all their own needs. But they gain the freedom that comes with not having to struggle constantly to provide for every necessity. From newcomers and visitors to the town, they gain knowledge of other people and their ways. In the towns, life becomes more complicated, but also, some would say, more interesting.

As the town grows, the various craftsmen—the bakers, the shoemakers, the stone masons, the carpenters, the weavers—get together in separate associations devoted to protecting the interests of their specific craft. These associations are called guilds. Each guild works to have a say in the way the town is run. The guilds also set rules concerning how someone can go about learning to become a baker, a carpenter, or master of another craft. The person learning the craft is called an apprentice. An apprentice is in some ways a

See how many things you can find going on in this picture of a busy medieval market.

student learning a skill, but in some ways he is a servant, obligated for a number of years to work in the service of the master craftsman.

The merchants of the town also have guilds that work for their interests. The merchants' guilds might find ways to improve the roads that goods are transported on (the old Roman roads were a bit worn after being used for seven hundred years!). Or they might arrange to have their caravans protected from thieves, or to have a wall built around the town, because there were still lots of fighting knights and gangs of mercenaries roaming the land.

By the year 1200, many towns operated much as towns do today. They had mayors to govern them and councils to collect taxes, which might be used to build bridges or repair the town walls. Townspeople were not vassals of any lord, so they were not part of the feudal system. They did not have to promise their loyalty and labor to a lord who would protect them. Sometimes, in fact, the townspeople joined together to protect themselves and fight against a local lord who was trying to take over the town. As towns grew in strength and size, the feudal system became weaker and weaker.

Trial by Jury

In the mid-twelfth century, a great-grandson of William the Conqueror became the king of England. This king, Henry II, established one of the most important rights England ever gave to the world, the right to a trial by jury.

Let's say that you are a knight, the vassal of a feudal lord, and you're arguing with another knight about which of you owns a magnificent horse. You know that you won the horse in a recent battle, but the other knight claims the horse is his. Before the system of trial by jury was invented, your case might be decided by the feudal lord. And what if the lord didn't happen to like you? Or what if he decided upon a trial by combat? In a trial by combat, "might makes right": what matters isn't who is right but who is stronger. How would you feel as you squeezed into your armor, lifted your heavy sword, and then glanced across the field at your opponent, who unfortunately was about two feet taller than you and had a reputation for fighting dirty?

You would probably stand a better chance under the system established by Henry II. Instead of letting feudal lords decide arguments or punish crimes, Henry gave these powers to judges who would hold royal courts throughout England. This way, you could take your case before one of these royal courts. The judge would call together a jury, usually a group of twelve local people who were your social peers (people who were as high as you on the social ladder). These people would swear to tell the truth. (The word "jury" comes from the French

A portrait of Henry II.

word *jurer,* meaning "to swear.") The judge would ask the jury questions to find out whatever he could about who should own the horse. And, if everything worked out, you'd get to keep your horse!

Juries Now

Every American citizen today is guaranteed "the right to a speedy and public trial, by an impartial jury." (These words are written in the Bill of Rights, part of the Constitution of the United States.) But juries have changed since the time of Henry II.

One big difference is that today, juries are purposefully made up of citizens who don't know the people involved in the case. If you are a member of a jury, you might be asked to decide whether a person accused of a crime is innocent or guilty. How impartial (fair) could you be if the accused person was someone you liked or disliked strongly?

Another big difference since Henry's time is the way people are asked to serve on a jury. Now, judges don't pick jury members. Instead, as a citizen of this country, when you become an adult, you may receive a letter from the government telling you to report for "jury duty." If this happens, you will go to court and listen to lawyers present evidence. Lawyers for each side of the case will try to make you believe his or her side is true. You and the other jury members will have to decide what you believe to be the truth. Determining another person's innocence or guilt is one of the greatest responsibilities you may ever have.

Murder in the Cathedral

By appointing judges to be in charge of royal courts, Henry II weakened the power of the feudal lords and strengthened his power as king. He also wanted to take

Canterbury Cathedral.

away power from the separate courts that were run by the Catholic church in England. He came up with a plan to try to make changes in the church's courts, but the plan failed. Here's what happened.

Henry wanted more power over the church's courts than the pope was willing to give up. Henry figured he could get this power by appointing someone loyal to him to a very powerful position in the church. So he appointed his good friend Thomas à Becket to be the archbishop of Canterbury. Now Henry thought he had it made: Thomas was his friend, and as archbishop he would work from the inside to weaken the church courts. But that's not what Becket did. In fact, he even worked against the king!

Henry was surprised by Becket's behavior and angry at the failure of his plans. It is said that one day Henry cried out, "Will no one free me from this turbulent priest?" Henry's men sought out Thomas à Becket and killed him, right inside Canterbury Cathedral! Becket's murder so upset people all over Europe that Henry was in danger of losing the throne.

The murder of Thomas à Becket.

Thomas à Becket was buried at Canterbury Cathedral. Soon after his death, the church declared him to be a saint. This meant that Catholics could pray to St. Thomas and ask that he help them in their affairs on earth. It also kept the heat on Henry, for people were not likely to forget the murdered archbishop. Indeed, Becket's tomb became a very popular place for people to visit. These visitors, called pilgrims, would make a journey, called a pilgrimage, to the tomb of St. Thomas or another saint. When they arrived, they would ask the saint for help, perhaps in curing an illness or forgiving a sin.

When a fire burned part of Canterbury Cathedral, donations of money from the pilgrims helped to build a new wing of the cathedral in a new architectural style, called the Gothic. You can read about the wonders of Gothic cathedrals in the Fine Arts section of this book.

Eleanor of Aquitaine

Eleanor of Aquitaine was the daughter of a powerful nobleman who owned land in the part of present-day France called Aquitaine. She inherited this land when her father died without leaving any sons. Eleanor of Aquitaine became one of the most powerful, best educated, and most independent-minded people in the Middle Ages. She had a strong talent for music and encouraged the artistic talents of others.

Almost all women in Eleanor's time were expected to obey their fathers' orders, and later, their husbands'. But to be a rich noblewoman was different, even in the Middle Ages. Eleanor was usually able to make her own decisions, and she shared the right to give orders that was usually only accorded to noblemen. Her story shows how she used her unusual freedom and rights quite powerfully throughout the entire eighty years of her life.

This statue of Queen Eleanor of Aquitane decorates her tomb. It shows Eleanor reading a book.

Eleanor's first husband was the king of France, but that marriage was annulled (canceled by the pope). Eleanor then married the king of England, Henry II, the same Henry who was Becket's one-time friend. The king of France did not like the powerful combination of Aquitaine and England and was probably quite pleased when Eleanor got angry at Henry II and set up her own household and court in Aquitaine. There, at her French court, she created an artistic and social center that attracted the best poets and writers in France. Life at Eleanor's court was a high point for culture in the Middle Ages.

When her four sons grew old enough, she encouraged them to rebel against their father. But Henry won, and he shut Eleanor in a castle for over fifteen years, allowing her few visitors. She was freed only after Henry died and her son Richard the Lion-Hearted became king. Richard was often fighting battles far from home, so for many years Eleanor was the real ruler of England. After Richard died, she helped her son John become king.

A Bad King and a Great Charter

King John was cruel and greedy. He taxed the people heavily, and even the nobles hated him. The legend of Robin Hood's robbing the rich (the Normans) to feed the poor (the Saxons) comes from John's reign.

There were other bad kings before and after King John, but he is particularly remembered today for one reason. In the year 1215, John's nobles forced him to sign a very important pledge, called in Latin the *Magna Carta*, which means "Great Charter" in English.

In signing the *Magna Carta*, King John had to promise: (1) that he could raise tax money from the nobles only if they agreed to it; (2) that he could not sell justice or deny it—that is, a rich man couldn't buy his way out of punishment for a crime he had committed; and (3) that a free man could not be imprisoned unless he was declared guilty in a trial by his equals.

Even though the nobles meant only to protect their money and freedom, the *Magna Carta* was an important step in giving liberty to the ordinary English citizen. It is important for us today, too, because England gave those same liberties to her colonies, and Americans used the *Magna Carta* to help shape the Constitution of the United States.

King John signing the Magna Carta.

Parliament

The English kings would often bring together their nobles in a meeting called a Royal Council to discuss concerns about running the kingdom. Sometimes the king and the nobles would disagree. When King John's son took the throne, one noble disagreed so strongly with him that he took a drastic step. Without consulting the king, he organized a meeting of a group of people called a Great Council, or Parliament.

This first Parliament was an important step in changing the way England was governed. It was the seed of representative government—government in which leaders respond to and work for the people's concerns and wishes. As you've seen, kings (like King John) often ruled without much concern for the people. Slowly, over hundreds of years, Parliament gained more representatives from many classes of society. Also, a custom developed that the king could not simply give orders. Instead, he had to *ask* Parliament and perhaps grant something Parliament wanted in return. With strong kings, Parliament had less say; with young or weak kings, Parliament had more say. You can see how different this idea is from the feudal system. Once power shifted to the king and Parliament, the lords and their vassals were no longer needed to maintain order.

As you've seen, people with power and privileges are generally reluctant to share them. In England it would take over seven hundred years before Parliament gave all the people a say in their government. But when rich townspeople in medieval England began participating in Parliament, the seed of representative government was planted. We call the English Parliament the "Mother of Parliaments" because from it so many countries got the idea of having people govern themselves through representatives in an assembly. Our own country inherited this idea, as well as the basis for other important laws and liberties, from England.

Fighting for a Hundred Years

One of the main reasons Parliament gained power in the fourteenth century was that for over a hundred years, the English kings needed the help of Parliament in raising money to fight in France. That's right, a hundred years! There were some years of peace and an occasional truce, but so many battles were fought for so long that we call this long, long conflict (A.D. 1337–1453) between England and France the Hundred Years' War. (What were they fighting about all this time? Mainly the ownership of lands in France.)

One result of this long war was that people began to feel even greater loyalty for something beyond their local town, and for someone beyond their local lord. They began to think of themselves as being part of something bigger—part of a distinct nation. They felt loyalty to the king of that nation. You've seen various reasons why the old feudal bonds between vassals and lords started to weaken, and here's another: feudalism grew weaker as the local loyalties of feudalism were replaced by feelings of nationalism. Nationalism is the feeling of loyalty to a nation, in this case the nations of England or France.

Nationalism is a feeling that can bring people together. But it can also keep people apart. That's because it can bring together the people within the same nation, but keep apart the people of different nations. It's something like what some people feel when they watch an exciting sporting event, like a game of basketball or football or soccer. Sometimes people get so caught up in cheering for the team they want to win that they almost start to hate the other team. The problem with nationalism is that it's not just a game. Strong feelings of nationalism have even been part of the cause for nations going to war against each other.

Joan of Arc

As the Hundred Years' War went on, the French came very close to defeat, even though their soldiers always outnumbered the English. They were saved by a remarkable young French girl named Joan of Arc. Joan was very religious. She said she had heard voices from heaven telling her to drive the English from French soil.

At first everyone laughed at Joan, but she did not give up. She wanted to restore the French king, Charles VII, to the throne, but first she had to find him, since he was hiding from the English. When she found him, she convinced

We don't know what Joan of Arc looked like, but her story inspired this picture of her triumphant entry into the city of Orléans.

him to give her an army. With it, she rescued the city of Orléans from English attack and won other battles as well. Unfortunately, some of the French nobles were jealous of her and allowed the English to capture her. Condemned as a witch, she was burned at the stake when she was about nineteen years old. But Joan's bravery had helped France win the war. Many years later the Catholic church made Joan a saint.

The Black Death

There were times during the Hundred Years' War when there was no fighting at all. One reason for this was a terrible plague (a deadly disease that spreads quickly among many people). This plague, called the Black Death, swept across the European continent in the middle of the fourteenth century. The plague was carried by rats that came to Europe on ships and in caravans.

It's hard to imagine just how many people died. In about twenty-five years, the plague killed between one third and one half of everyone living in Europe.

On feast days peasants would gather in the churchyard to dance, eat, drink, play games, and make merry, as they do in this picture. However, the skulls of victims of the Black Plague in the background remind us that even as they danced people in the Middle Ages were very aware that death could strike them down at any time.

It was a sad and terrible time, when big carts loaded with dead bodies would roll through the towns on their way to the cemeteries.

When the plague finally wore itself out, there were few workers left in the towns. Those who were still alive were very much in demand, so they could ask for and get higher wages for their labor. To keep the serfs from running away to other towns where they were now needed, the lords freed many of them and started paying them wages.

What was left of feudalism never recovered from the Black Death. When Europe's population began to grow again, most people were no longer serfs, but free.

The Crusades

While the English and French were fighting on and off in Western Europe, other battles were raging to the east. These battles were not between nations but between religions: Christianity and Islam. To understand what was going on, let's look back in history for a moment.

In Book Three, as well as earlier in this book, you read about the Emperor Constantine and about the growth of the Byzantine Empire. Constantine, you may recall, encouraged Christianity in the Roman Empire, and the religion spread rapidly. But in the seventh and eighth centuries, part of the Byzantine Empire, including most of the land on the Arabian peninsula, was conquered by nomadic Arabs. The conquerors brought their own religion, Islam.

Islam, you may remember from Book Three, was founded by Mohammed, who recorded its fundamental beliefs in a book called the Koran. Followers of Islam, called Muslims, believe in one god, whom they call Allah. Muslims pray five times a day, fast during the daytime for one month out of every year, and try to visit Mecca, the holy city of Islam, at least once in their lifetimes. The first Muslims were Arabs. They believed in fighting *jihads,* or holy wars, to spread the religion of Islam and increase the power of the Muslim peoples.

In the Middle East, the religion of Islam won over hundreds of thousands of people. Islamic armies conquered the Holy Land, where Jesus had once lived. For a while, Muslims allowed Christians to worship freely in the city of Jerusalem, especially at the Church of the Holy Sepulcher, built, it is said, upon the tomb of Jesus. It was the holiest site of the Christian religion.

Then a Muslim leader vandalized the Church of the Holy Sepulcher, and

The dome of the Church of the Holy Sepulcher.

refused to let Christians worship there. This angered Christians all over Europe. The pope called for knights and soldiers everywhere to march to the east to free Jerusalem from the Muslims. The Christians called this march a crusade, after the Latin word for "cross." The soldiers on the march carried the symbol of the cross with them to show that they were on a religious mission to free the Holy Land.

In the Islamic religion, Muslims are promised that if they die fighting in a *jihad*, they will go to heaven. Interestingly enough, at the time of the Crusades the pope promised that any Christian who died on a crusade would go straight to heaven. In some ways, the Crusades and *jihads* were much alike.

The First Crusade began in about the year 1100. For almost two hundred years there were many more crusades. Some historians count as many as nine of them.

Thousands of knights from many European countries set off on the First Crusade with the goal of recapturing Jerusalem from the Muslims. Many of the knights fell ill or died during the long journey across desert lands. When they finally reached Jerusalem, the first crusaders had an army of about twelve thousand men, less than one fourth of the number they had started out with. Still, they managed to capture the city from the Muslims.

It is sometimes hard to believe what people have done or will do in the name of their religious beliefs. When the first Crusaders captured Jerusalem, they celebrated their victory by killing their "infidel" (non-Christian) prisoners, including women and children. This kind of cruelty made relations between Christians and Muslims bitter for centuries.

Pilgrims from Europe arrive in Jerusalem.

Saladin and Richard the Lion-Hearted

Although Christians went on several more crusades, Jerusalem was later recaptured by the Muslim leader Saladin. Saladin is to this day a great hero in

the Middle East, famed for defeating the European Christians and restoring Jerusalem to Islam. When Saladin retook Jerusalem, he did not allow his army to kill the Christians there. This was just the opposite of the way the Crusaders behaved when they had captured the city.

This portrait of Saladin was painted during his lifetime. Can you figure out how old it might be?

Saladin's great opponent was Richard the Lion-Hearted. As you've learned, Richard was the son of Henry II and Eleanor of Aquitaine. When Richard the Lion-Hearted took his forces against Saladin, both sides fought well. Richard conquered several important cities that were under Muslim control. But he could not take Jerusalem. Finally, the two great warriors agreed to a truce. Richard would stop fighting Saladin, and Saladin would let Christians come to worship in Jerusalem at the Church of the Holy Sepulcher.

Saladin was a truly religious man, and a generous one. He wanted to rekindle the spirit of Mohammed in the lands he ruled from Syria to Egypt, especially by building schools to spread knowledge and Islam. Saladin paid so much attention to others and so little to himself that he died without saving enough money to buy a plot for his grave!

The Growth of Islam

In the early Middle Ages, while much of Europe was emerging from the Dark Ages, the highly cultured civilization of Islam was beginning to reach maturity. The Muslims had divided themselves into different religious groups, just as the Christians had split between Rome and Constantinople. Two main groups were called Sunni (SOON ey), and Shiite (SHE iyt).

Advances in chemistry led Muslim doctors to develop new medicines, including anesthetics that relieved much of the pain patients experienced during operations.

Although the writings of Greek and Roman civilization were nearly forgotten in Europe, many were kept alive by Muslim scholars. Islamic study of mathematics and medicine flourished. You've read earlier in this section that Europeans were isolated from the rest of the world. In contrast, adventurous Muslim merchants carried on trade with Asia and Africa, and thereby brought the Islamic religion and new knowledge to these faraway regions.

Trade and the Rise of African Empires

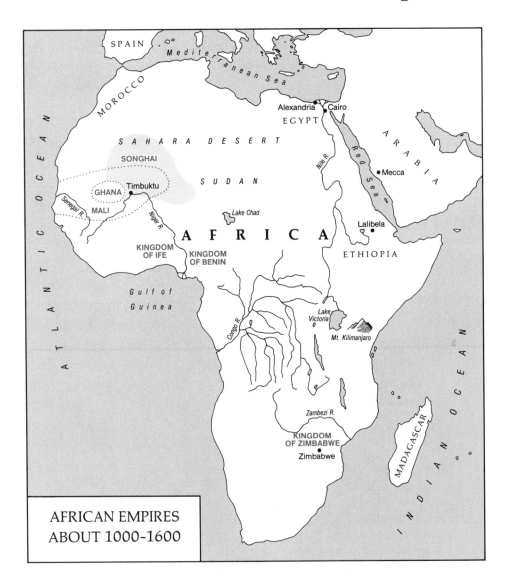

AFRICAN EMPIRES
ABOUT 1000-1600

Many Muslim merchants traveled in camel caravans across the Sahara Desert. They were headed just south of the Sahara to the grassy, sometimes wooded regions known as the Sudan. (In Arabic, Sudan means "land of the black people.") The Muslim merchants took with them cloth, spices, copper, silver, horses, and other goods. In the Sudan, they traded these goods for gold and slaves. The great demand for gold and slaves led to the rise of rich kingdoms in the Sudan, including the empires of Ghana, Mali, and Songhai.

The Slave Trade

When we look back on the development of civilization, we need to remember how often that development has been achieved at a great cost in human sweat, blood, and freedom. Every year thousands of blacks from the Sudan were sold as slaves. They were usually the prisoners captured in wars between various African peoples. Some of those who survived the terrible march across the desert to the North African ports would be resold and put to work as servants and laborers for the wealthy people in other countries. But many worked as slaves in Africa itself.

How does it make you feel that human beings could be sold as though they were nothing more than donkeys or tools? You might think that only "primitive" people a long time ago would do something as terrible as selling or keeping slaves. But the harsh truth is that slavery was accepted for many years, even in modern times. The slave trade continued to thrive in Africa until the 1800's. Many of those slaves ended up in America. (In the Stories and Speeches section of this book, you can read about one slave, Frederick Douglass, who gained his freedom and went on to write his life story.)

Islam in Africa

When people trade with each other for a long time, they exchange more than goods. Over time, they also exchange ideas and ways of life. As Muslim traders and scholars settled in towns in the Sudan, they spread the religion of Islam. Mosques were built in many towns. During the fifteenth century in the Songhai Empire, several colleges were established in the city of Timbuktu. In those colleges, Islamic professors taught about law and religion.

Among the African population, often only the leaders and merchants would become Muslims. Most other people held onto their traditional worship of spirits and ancestors. In the kingdom of Ghana, the religion of the inhabitants divided the capital city. One half, the business part, was Muslim; the other half, where the king lived, did not follow Islam but instead maintained the traditional tribal ways and beliefs.

The Splendid Reign of Mansa Musa

Mansa Musa and his wealth were so legendary that he was shown, seated and holding a nugget of gold, on the first European map of northwest Africa. The map was made in A.D. 1375.

From 1312 to 1337, the kingdom of Mali was ruled by Mansa Musa. His empire was vast and rich, mainly because of the great amount of gold found in the kingdom. A huge army of soldiers, on foot and on horseback, kept the kingdom orderly and peaceful. They also made sure that no one disobeyed Mansa Musa. No one was even allowed to sneeze when the king was around!

Mansa Musa was a Muslim, and he decided to make a pilgrimage to Mecca. It was a long trip across the Sahara Desert, so the king needed some people to go with him. If you were making that trip, how many people would you take? Some reports say that Mansa Musa took over fifty thousand! Hundreds of slaves carried heavy bars of gold, which the king spent wherever he went. Mansa Musa, with his almost unbelievable wealth and legions of followers, created a great sensation in Mecca and became famous in far-off lands.

Churches of Rock

Islam continued to spread through parts of Africa in the eighth through the sixteenth centuries. But one African kingdom remained different. This was Ethiopia, which had become Christian when monks converted the king back in the fourth century.

King Lalibela, who ruled Ethiopia from 1200 to 1230, ordered the building of eleven large churches. But the land in Ethiopia didn't provide materials for building large churches. The land was very hard; in fact, much of it was solid rock. We cannot build churches, said the king, so we will carve them. And that's what the Ethiopians did. Every part of each of these amazing "rock churches"—the windows, doors, arches, decorations—was cut out of a single huge mass of solid rock!

In St. George, Ethiopia, people still gather at one of the carved stone churches built by King Lalibela.

The Engineers of Zimbabwe

In southeastern Africa, another impressive kingdom developed in Zimbabwe. This kingdom grew wealthy through the trade of gold. The name Zimbabwe means "stone enclosure." At the ancient site called Great Zimbabwe, two huge stone walls were built that encircled the city, protecting palaces, royal tombs, places of worship, and places to store food. These walls are more than thirty feet high! (How tall are you?)

The people of Zimbabwe must have been very skilled engineers because they figured out a way to make each stone in these huge walls fit together tightly. They did such a good job that the walls are still standing today!

The Travels of Ibn Battuta

Some of what we know about these great African empires comes from the writings of a Muslim who lived in the late Middle Ages. His name was Ibn Battuta (IHB uhn bat TOO tah). He traveled east overland from his native country of Morocco all the way across northern Africa. Later he explored the Middle East. He also traveled overland to India, to the court of the sultan, who sent him to China. Just a few of the other places he visited in almost thirty years of traveling were Spain, Timbuktu, and the Niger River. His writings are still a rich source of information about the places he visited and the time in which he lived.

West Meets East

You've seen how the growth of trade between Muslim lands and Africa led to a change in cultures, resulting especially from the spread of the Islamic religion to Africa. Different cultures can affect each other whether they come together peacefully through trade or violently through war. The wars between the Christians and Muslims, the Crusades, greatly affected both Europe and Asia. It was the first contact between West and East in centuries. The knights and pilgrims who returned from the Crusades had seen an entirely new and more civilized world, and they wanted some of the luxuries the Muslims enjoyed. This included taking baths, having spices to cover up the bad taste of spoiling meat, and even wearing silk clothes. The demand for certain goods and luxuries led to trade between Europeans and the East.

Let's turn now to look at what had been going on all this time in the remarkable Asian civilization that developed the silks and other goods the Europeans so desired. We're off to China!

Civilization Under the T'ang Dynasty

In Book Two, you may have read about what was happening in China about two thousand years ago. The Chinese people at this time were ruled by the Han dynasty. (Do you recall what a dynasty is? You can refresh your memory by checking a dictionary. Do dynasties govern America today?)

Do you remember the Great Wall? It was built to keep out invaders from the north. It didn't always work, as we'll soon see. But before we look at the people who invaded China, let's look at some of the early developments that took place in China.

At about the same time as the Dark Ages in Europe, Chinese civilization was developing rapidly under the T'ang dynasty, which ruled from A.D. 618 to 907. During these years, Chinese ideas and customs spread to Japan, Korea, and an area that later became Vietnam. Under the T'ang dynasty, great cities grew in China. The capital city, now called Changan, was the biggest city in the world at that time. In the eighth and ninth centuries, almost a million people lived there. The city even had a big public park and a zoo!

In Europe during the Middle Ages, you remember, people lived on manors with little trade or communication between them. But in China during the T'ang dynasty, there was a great deal of communication between towns and cities. This was because the emperors put many people to work building roads and canals, making it easy to get goods from one place to another. Chinese merchants not only traded goods among themselves but also sold many products to India and the Middle East. These products included spices, fine silk fabrics, and beautiful dishes. We have a name for such dishes now—you guessed it—china!

This detail of a hand-painted silk scroll depicts some of the stages of silk production.

A Hard Test

Have you ever grumbled about a really hard test in school? Well, even the hardest test you've taken might seem easy compared to one that was developed in China.

This test was actually part of a very important change the T'ang dynasty made in the way government officials were selected. In earlier times and in many lands other than China, the best jobs would often be given to people related to the rulers. Say you applied for a job with the government. Even if you were highly skilled you might lose that job to someone less skilled—who just happened to be the ruler's cousin!

Things changed under the T'ang dynasty. To get a job with the government you now had to take a series of very difficult tests based on the writings of the great philosopher and teacher, Confucius. Whether you were a peasant or a noble, you were allowed to take the tests. But in reality, only wealthy people had enough money to afford the years of education necessary to prepare for the tests. Still, the tests made sure that hard-working people got the government jobs. Also, only men were allowed to take these tests for government jobs. The one exception occurred during the reign of the empress Wu Chao, who took the throne in the year 690.

How hard were these tests? Out of every hundred students who made it to the final written exam, ninety-nine failed!

The Sung Dynasty

Chinese civilization continued to develop under the Sung dynasty, which came to power in 960 and ruled for more than three hundred years. Do you remember what was going on in Europe at this time? The feudal system was spreading. William the Conqueror won the Battle of Hastings in 1066. King John signed the *Magna Carta* in 1215.

During these years, more people lived in China than in any other country. China was also perhaps the most advanced civilization of the time. During the Sung dynasty, the Chinese made important advancements in medicine and mathematics. They developed the abacus, which, like a modern-day calculator, helped them do arithmetic quickly. They invented or improved upon the recent invention of many other things we take for granted today, including the printing press, the magnetic compass, and gunpowder. They learned how to make iron and steel, and even built factories to produce iron and steel tools.

The Chinese also invented the first paper money. For a long time, merchants had to carry heavy strings of copper coins. Imagine the weight of the load if you wanted to buy something expensive! But then the Chinese established a system in which merchants could leave their coins with bankers and receive paper bank notes in exchange. To prevent people from trying to produce counterfeit (fake) paper money, each bill had a warning printed on it: "Counterfeiters will be beheaded"!

The Wrath of Genghis Khan

During the T'ang and Sung dynasties, very advanced civilizations developed in China. But despite all their knowledge and inventions, the people of the Sung period could not fight off a wave of invaders from the north. These invaders, the Mongols, were some of the most ferocious warriors of all time.

The Mongols were a nomadic people. They practically lived on their fast, hardy ponies. The ponies themselves thrived on the tough grass of the central Asian steppes (grasslands). The Mongols roamed in groups and each group had a leader, called a *khan*. The Mongols united under one fierce and powerful leader, Genghis Khan, whose name means "ruler of the world." And with the help of his armies, called "the Golden Horde," he almost lived up to the promise of his name.

In 1215, the same year that King John in England signed the *Magna Carta*, the Mongols led by Genghis Khan crashed through the Great Wall of China. Until our own century, probably no other conqueror has used terror as a weapon as often as Genghis Khan. He massacred whole towns to scare other towns into surrendering without a fight. Outside the walls of burned and looted villages, the Mongols would leave ghastly piles of the skulls of their victims.

Kublai Khan

Mongol leaders like Genghis Khan would sometimes destroy everything in their path: people, animals, churches, libraries, works of art, bridges, canals, and more. It's almost as though they hated civilization and wanted to smash it to bits.

But this was not true of one Mongol leader. This leader was Genghis Khan's grandson, and his name was Kublai Khan. He founded a dynasty that ruled China and neighboring lands from 1260 to 1368. He established a capital at the city now called Beijing. He seemed to enjoy living the luxurious life of a Chinese emperor, even though he and other Mongol rulers maintained their own language and customs separate from their Chinese subjects.

Kublai Khan.

The Adventures of Marco Polo

During the years that the Mongol dynasty established by Kublai Khan ruled China, many European travelers and merchants came to visit. The best re-membered of these travelers was from the Italian city of Venice, an important center of trade. His name was Marco Polo.

Marco was only seventeen years old when he left Venice with his father and uncle, who had been to China before. He was a good deal older when he finally reached the palace of Kublai Khan. It took the Polos almost four years to cover the vast distance over steppes, deserts, and mountains.

When they arrived, they were not disappointed. Marco found a shining palace of marble and gold. The walls of the palace ran for miles and enclosed a vast park full of animals and over two hundred kinds of birds. Marco's eyes grew wide at the sight of Kublai Khan, dressed in a long silk coat covered with jewels.

China was full of riches that Europeans were eager to buy, including silk, tea, and spices. One food that many people think came from Marco Polo's native country, Italy, actually came first from China—spaghetti!

Marco Polo quickly learned the Mongol language. Kublai Khan was im-pressed and made Marco an official of the Chinese government. (In fact, almost all high government officials at the time were foreigners like Kublai Khan himself. Kublai Khan did not trust the Chinese, whom he had con-quered, to be loyal to him.) Kublai Khan sent Marco on many important

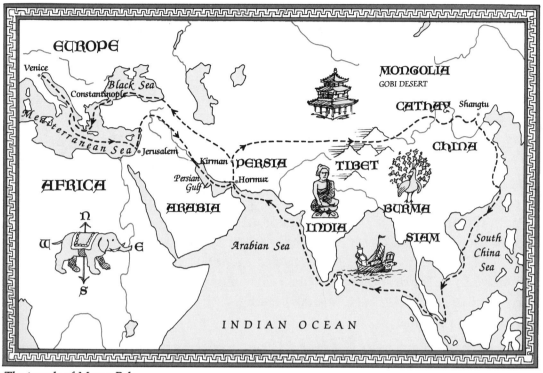

The travels of Marco Polo.

missions to distant parts of the empire, and for several years even gave him a province to govern.

When Marco was ready to return home to Venice, Kublai Khan wouldn't let him go! He thought Marco was too valuable and knew too many secrets. But a couple of years before Kublai Khan died in 1294 he changed his mind and allowed Marco to leave.

Not long after Marco Polo returned home, the city of Venice got involved in a war with another important Italian center of trade, Genoa. Marco was made a prisoner of war. While in prison, Marco told stories of the wonders he had seen in China and a fellow prisoner wrote them down. The story of Marco Polo's travels became popular all over Europe even though many people thought Marco Polo made up a lot of the wonders he described. We're still not sure today how much of Marco Polo's book is fact and how much is fiction.

One person who read Marco's book believed it all. In fact, he was so excited that he wanted to find a fast sea route to China. His name was Christopher Columbus—and you know what happened when he set off on his travels!

The Ottoman Empire and the End of Byzantium

In the early books of this series, you may have read about the civilizations that grew up around the Mediterranean Sea. The very first civilizations began in Egypt and Mesopotamia around 2500 B.C. One important empire after another ruled the lands around the eastern Mediterranean: Persian, Greek, and Roman (the Romans ruled Western Europe as well). By A.D. 700, this area had been conquered by the Arabs, spreading the religion of Islam. Eight hundred years later, another Islamic people, the Turks, conquered these lands. Their empire was called the Ottoman Empire, after the Turkish leader named Osman. Although it lost power over some areas, the Ottoman Empire lasted in Turkey and nearby lands for over three hundred years—into our own century.

In 1453, the Ottomans conquered the great city of Constantinople, which had stood for a thousand years as the Christian capital of the Eastern Roman, or Byzantine, Empire. The Ottomans changed the name of Constantinople to

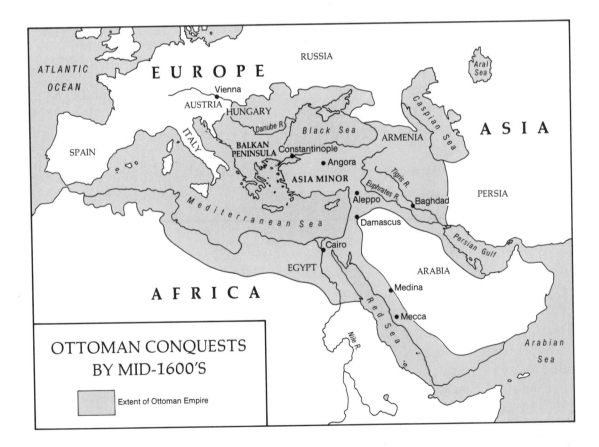

OTTOMAN CONQUESTS
BY MID-1600'S

Extent of Ottoman Empire

Istanbul. They changed the official religion of the city from Christianity to Islam. Hagia Sophia and other churches were turned into mosques.

The Ottoman Empire reached the height of its power in the sixteenth century under a leader named Suleiman, who is generally considered the greatest of all the sultans. (*Sultan* is the special title given to rulers in the Ottoman Empire. Do you remember what the Mongol leaders were called?) People in Europe were so impressed by Suleiman's power and accomplishments that they called him "Suleiman the Magnificent." In his own lands he was known as "The Lawgiver."

Islamic civilization developed greatly during the Ottoman Empire. Suleiman encouraged his people to be active in artistic creation. One man he encouraged and supported was a great architect named Sinan. Sinan designed many magnificent mosques, tombs, and other buildings. These beautiful structures have finely decorated dome ceilings, fancy stained-glass windows, and brightly colored tiles on both the inner and outer walls. One feature really catches your eye:

When Sinan was in his seventies, he designed this mosque for Suleiman's son, and it is considered one of his finest achievements.

the tall pointed towers called minarets, leaping toward the sky. Many of the buildings Sinan designed are decorated with paintings that celebrate the victories of Suleiman and his armies. These magnificent structures made Istanbul one of the most splendid cities of its time.

Greece and Rome Live On

In the years before the Ottomans conquered Constantinople, the Byzantine Empire had been trading regularly with the Italians. Over time the exchange of goods, as you've seen before, was accompanied by an exchange of ideas. The Byzantine Empire, you recall, had preserved much of what is called classical learning, the learning of ancient Greece and Rome. Byzantine scholars had moved out of Constantinople to Europe, taking with them many books and works of art preserved from the ancient world.

Soon a great interest in all this classical art and knowledge would be reborn among Europeans. The story of that great rebirth will be told in the next book of this series.

Introduction
to American Civilization

The American Civilization section of Book Four begins with an exciting time in the history of our country, the Revolutionary War and the creation of a new federal government. It ends with a discussion of important reform movements in mid-nineteenth-century America.

The ideas and events depicted here—from the writing of the Constitution to the arguments over slavery and women's rights—are central to our national identity and to any individual's idea of what it means to be a citizen of the United States.

Fourth graders, interested in their own rights and freedoms, are not too young to begin learning about the ideals, arguments, and compromises behind the framing of the Constitution and the Bill of Rights. And they are well able to understand that their own judgments of a historical figure like Andrew Jackson may not agree with the judgments of people in Jackson's own day. Early exposure to our history does more than teach ideas of government and human motives; it also provides a valuable foundation for later understanding of policy and current events.

Talk to your child about his responses to what he reads here, and whenever possible supplement his interest with outside materials. A number of titles are recommended throughout this section. Others that may prove helpful are:

Biographies in the Aladdin Books "Childhood of Famous Americans" series (including George Washington, Thomas Jefferson, Daniel Boone, Davy Crockett, Molly Pitcher, and Abraham Lincoln).

The American Reader: Words that Moved a Nation, edited by Diane Ravitch. (HarperCollins). A valuable collection of primary sources.

Johnny Tremain by Esther Forbes. (Dell). A classic novel about a boy who took part in the Revolutionary War.

Children of the Wild West by Russell Freedman. (Houghton Mifflin).

American Civilization

Looking Back

Do you remember the amazing cities of the Maya, Incas, and Aztecs? Do you remember the stories of Columbus, Pocahontas, and the first English colonies of Virginia and Massachusetts? (You can refresh your memory by looking back at the American Civilization sections of earlier books in this series, or by using an encyclopedia.)

We begin this section with the results of the American colonists' declaration of independence from Britain, and continue with our struggles as a new nation.

Fighting Words

Before we became the fifty United States, we were a much smaller group of colonies. (A colony is a region under the control of a faraway land.) In the late 1700s, the mood was tense in Britain's thirteen American colonies. The British government was demanding that Americans pay more taxes. But the Americans, who had no say in the decisions of the British government, cried out,

The signing of The Declaration of Independence.

View of *The* ATTACK *on* BUNKER'S HILL, *with the* Burning *of* CHARLES TOWN, *June 17 1775.*

"No taxation without representation!" When British soldiers fired upon a crowd in Boston and killed or wounded about a dozen colonists, the news of this "Boston Massacre" spread and made the Americans furious. More and more Americans began to agree with what Tom Paine argued in his pamphlet called *Common Sense:* it was time for America to break away from Britain.

In 1776, delegates from each of the thirteen American colonies came together in Philadelphia. At this extended meeting, called the Second Continental Congress, the delegates voted in July to accept the Declaration of Independence proposed by Thomas Jefferson. The Declaration of Independence boldly declared that America would rule itself. The delegates knew their decision meant that now the new country would have to back up its strong words. It would have to fight against Britain's well-trained, well-equipped army and navy. The Continental Congress called on the American people to join the army in the fight for independence.

But fighting had begun even before the colonists declared their independence from Britain. From Book Three of this series, you might remember the "shot heard 'round the world" that was fired in Concord, Massachusetts, and the battles between American minutemen and British redcoats at Concord and Lexington. A fierce battle took place in June of 1775 at Bunker Hill, near

Boston, Massachusetts. British troops eventually forced the Americans to retreat, but not before more than a thousand British soldiers were killed or wounded.

Were We Really Ready to Fight?

Britain had a strong army and navy. Most of the British soldiers had trained for years; they were used to taking orders and fighting according to the plans developed by their leaders. But for the Americans, it was a different story. There was no real American army. There were only small, local military units, called militia. The militia were confident and eager to fight, but they were not well disciplined. They sometimes argued about who would lead, and if they didn't like the way things were going they were free to go home at any time.

The Americans were not organized enough to put together a national effort to equip the soldiers with uniforms, arms, and other supplies. In fact, most Americans didn't even think of themselves as belonging to a big country called the United States of America. They thought of themselves more as citizens of the individual states. A person was more likely to say, "I'm a Virginian," or, "I'm from Massachusetts," than to say, "I'm an American." Within the states, not everyone agreed that America should break from Britain. People called Loyalists (or Tories) wanted the former colonies to remain loyal to Britain.

A British soldier.

Advantages and Disadvantages

You can see that a great challenge faced George Washington, the man appointed by the Second Continental Congress to be the commander in chief of the Continental army. Imagine what General Washington must have thought as he prepared to fight the British. He didn't have enough food, weapons, or soldiers, and those men he did have were not well trained or organized. The British seemed to have all the advantages.

But not quite. The Americans knew the land they were fighting on better than the British did, especially the wilderness areas where there were many trees to crouch behind and shoot from. Another American advantage was a simple fact of geography: a whole ocean, the Atlantic, separates America from England. The British had to get almost all their troops and supplies from England. As the war dragged on and the British needed more men and supplies, this distance caused them great problems.

There was another, less obvious, American advantage. Many Americans were motivated by the powerful ideas of liberty and independence. Those who

Minutemen hurrying to battle.

were willing to fight didn't have fancy uniforms or enough food or ammunition, but they did have a strong desire to make their dream of a new nation come true. You can see this spirit in the words of a letter written by a French officer that describes the American troops: "It is incredible that soldiers composed of men of every age, even of children of fifteen, of whites and blacks, almost naked, unpaid, and rather poorly fed, can march so well and withstand fire so steadfastly."

African-American men and women made an important contribution to America's struggle for independence. About five thousand black men served in the Continental army. Others joined the navy, and some did dangerous work as spies. The ideal of equal rights for all, expressed in the Declaration of Independence, made the Revolution an especially significant struggle for the African-Americans who fought in it. But almost a century would pass before they would begin to receive their civil rights.

You can read more about African-Americans who helped the American struggle for independence in Black Heroes of the Revolution by Burke Davis and Phoebe the Spy by Judith Griffin (the story of a girl who worked as a spy for General Washington).

"The Times That Try Men's Souls"

By the time America declared its independence in July of 1776, General Washington had managed to pull together about twenty thousand troops in the Continental army. The early months of the Revolution were hard on the American soldiers. Many were killed, wounded, or captured in disastrous battles in New York. Others simply left the fighting to go home. By December of 1776, Washington had barely three thousand men left. Weary and discouraged, they managed to escape into New Jersey under the cover of a sudden storm.

The end seemed near.

The Spirit of '76 has been a popular representation of the American Revolution ever since it was painted for the centennial celebrations held in 1876.

Some Americans began to wonder if it had been a mistake to break away from Britain. But others kept up hope. Thomas Paine—the author of *Common Sense,* the pamphlet that made many Americans eager to break from Britain—now wrote in another pamphlet, "These are the times that try men's souls." By "try" Paine meant "test": these dark days would test whether Americans had enough determination to keep going. As Paine said, "The summer soldier and the sunshine patriot will, in this crisis, shrink from the service of his country, but he that stands it *now* deserves the love and thanks of man and woman."

George Washington and his few remaining troops were able to stand it. Just when the Americans needed a victory most, they managed to gain one in a daring surprise attack.

Crossing the Delaware

It was Christmas night, December 25, 1776. At the town of Trenton, New Jersey, about a thousand Hessian troops were camped. (The Hessians were German soldiers who had been hired by the British.) The Hessians didn't

This famous painting shows Washington and his troops crossing the Delaware River to New Jersey on Christmas night to make a surprise raid on the Hessians.

know that in the cold darkness General Washington and his troops were crossing toward them over the icy Delaware River. Imagine the Hessians' surprise when, as they were settling down after a day of Christmas celebrations, they suddenly found themselves surrounded by American troops! The secrecy of the attack made it deadly: two thirds of the Hessians were killed or captured.

This victory and others in the months to come encouraged the Americans. Still, there were many challenges ahead. Washington needed more soldiers. To build up the army, Congress offered twenty dollars and one hundred acres of free land in the west to each new recruit. By spring, Washington had nine thousand men.

The next major battles took place in Pennsylvania, and they did not go well for Washington's troops. British troops even managed to capture Philadelphia and chase the Continental Congress out of town!

If you wanted to join the Continental army and fight the British, you had to be a man. But that didn't stop one brave woman named Deborah Sampson. You can read about her in The Secret Soldier: The Story of Deborah Sampson *by Ann McGovern and* Deborah Sampson Goes to War *by Bryna Stevens.*

Saratoga and a New Ally

Now let's find out about the battle that changed the course of the war, a battle that took place at Saratoga, New York.

The British had a plan to send thousands of troops down from Canada in order to capture all the New England states and cut the colonies in half. These troops were under the command of General John Burgoyne. While many American soldiers were ragged and half-starved, General Burgoyne came from Canada with dozens of wagons filled with his belongings, including cases of champagne and even silver plates and cups!

The march south took Burgoyne and his troops longer than they had expected. Sometimes they found the way blocked by huge trees that the Americans had cut down. As the months passed, they began to run out of food. Expected supplies and reinforcements never arrived. As Burgoyne's troops grew weaker, the Continental army in the area grew stronger; many men arrived to join the cause. A series of battles led to the defeat of Burgoyne's forces at Saratoga in October 1777. The proud British general had to surrender almost six thousand men to the Americans.

The victory at Saratoga was important because it brought the Americans a strong ally, France. France, which had been fighting England on and off for years, hoped to see the rebellious Americans embarrass the British. Early in the Revolution, the French began secretly helping the Americans by sending them supplies, especially gunpowder. But the French would not openly support the Americans. They were being cautious because early on it appeared as though the former colonies would have little chance against the mighty British army and navy.

It took the victory at Saratoga to convince the French king that the American rebels could win the war. Now the French openly supported the American struggle for independence by shipping arms, ammunition, and eventually troops overseas. By June of 1778, France and Britain were at war.

European Helpers

While France sent many soldiers to America, individual officers from other European nations also joined in the American struggle for independence.

General Bernardo de Gálvez led Spanish troops against the British in what is now the state of Florida. A Polish engineer, Thaddeus Kosciusko, offered his expert advice on how to plan battles and how to build strong forts. A Prussian general, Friedrich von Steuben, helped George Washington's troops learn professional military techniques.

One young Frenchman was so eager to join the fighting in America that he disobeyed a direct order from the French king to remain in France! The Marquis de Lafayette, an ambitious young French nobleman, wanted to gain glory by becoming a commanding officer in the American Revolution. But at the time, the French were not openly supporting America, and the French king refused to allow Lafayette to leave France. Lafayette disobeyed the king's orders. Although he was arrested, he managed to escape and sail to America. In the summer of 1777, at the age of nineteen, he met George Washington in Philadelphia.

Lafayette was given command of a division of soldiers. He served as a general in the Continental army for four years. When the war ended, he returned to France with great affection for America. He was forgiven for disobeying the king, and he went on to become active in French politics.

Valley Forge

Many Americans rejoiced upon hearing about the victory at Saratoga and news of the French alliance. But some, including General Washington and his troops, had little reason to be happy. As you've read, British troops had captured Philadelphia. When the bitter winter of 1777 set in, the British stayed warm and comfortable. But about twenty miles northwest of the city, at Valley Forge, Washington and his troops were cold, hungry, and sick.

The winter at Valley Forge was the low point of the Revolution. Many men died; others left to go home. Those who remained needed great courage to endure the suffering that was part of the struggle for liberty.

A hard winter for Washington's army at Valley Forge. The man standing next to Washington is Lafayette, a French nobleman who fought with the colonial forces.

Molly Pitcher helping the American troops in the thick of battle.

A brave woman whom we remember by her nickname, Molly Pitcher, helped General Washington and his Continental troops in a battle at Monmouth, New Jersey, in 1778. Mary McCauley earned the name of Molly Pitcher when she carried water from a nearby spring to tired and thirsty soldiers. Her husband was one of those soldiers; he was an artilleryman, loading and firing a cannon. When he fell, exhausted from the heat, Molly Pitcher stepped in and continued firing his cannon! After the battle, she received the thanks and praise of General Washington.

His Name Means Treason

For most of the Revolutionary War, General Benedict Arnold was a successful American military leader, even a hero. He led troops in some of the most important battles of the war, including the American victory at Saratoga. But in 1780 the patriots captured a British soldier. In his boot they found a letter revealing that, in exchange for money, Benedict Arnold was planning to turn the fort at West Point, New York, over to the British!

Arnold escaped to England, but his treason upset people so much that to this day we call a traitor a "Benedict Arnold."

Yorktown

The last part of the war was fought in the South. The British general Cornwallis believed that Virginia would have to be conquered in order for Britain to defeat the Americans. He and his troops marched to Yorktown, Virginia, and prepared for battle.

Yorktown, near the site of the early settlement of Jamestown, lies on a peninsula between the York and James rivers, which feed into the Chesapeake Bay. George Washington knew this area well. When he heard where Cornwallis had placed his troops, he knew that the British had made a mistake. Can you figure out what the British did wrong?

By placing his troops on a narrow peninsula, Cornwallis made it possible for the Americans to corner the British. General Washington and his troops quickly marched south from New Jersey. They were joined by thousands of French soldiers, some under the command of Lafayette. These combined forces encircled the British on land, while the French navy sailed into the Chesapeake Bay and cut off the chances of escape by sea.

American and French guns pounded away at Cornwallis's troops until Cornwallis was forced to surrender in October of 1781. When news of the

Lord Cornwallis, in the center of the picture, surrenders to George Washington at Yorktown. Can you pick out George Washington?

defeat at Yorktown reached Britain, one leader in Parliament groaned, "Oh God! It is all over." He was right: although a few more minor battles were fought here and there, the defeat of the British at Yorktown marked the end of the Revolutionary War.

Mighty Britain had lost to a young, half-united country. It seemed incredible, and Cornwallis recognized this as he ordered the British band to play an old English tune called "The World Turned Upside Down." Some accounts say that Lafayette then ordered the band to play "Yankee Doodle"!

In 1783, a peace treaty gave America the lands that reached west to the Mississippi River. Now the United States would have to make its own government. Would it do any better than the British? Was this really a New World?

Do you know what a "Yankee Doodle" is? Before the Revolution, Americans might have gotten angry if the British called them "Yankee Doodles." "Yankee" was an insulting name for a New Englander. "Doodle" meant a fool.

The song "Yankee Doodle" was well known in the colonies before the Revolution. But during the Revolution, American soldiers changed the song from an insult to a statement of pride. In the verses below, you can see how "Yankee Doodle" has become a symbol of the feisty American spirit:

Yankee Doodle went to town,
A-riding on a pony
He stuck a feather in his hat
And called it macaroni.

Yankee Doodle, keep it up,
Yankee Doodle Dandy,
Mind the music and the step,
And with the girls be handy!

Father and I went down to camp
Along with Captain Goodin'
And there we saw the men and boys
As thick as hasty puddin'.

And there was Captain Washington
Upon a slapping stallion
A-giving orders to his men,
I guess there was a million.

Yankee Doodle, keep it up,
Yankee Doodle Dandy,
Mind the music and the step,
And with the girls be handy!

Old World Ideas and New World Government

In setting out to create a government in the New World, the Americans began by borrowing ideas from the Old World. The men who wrote and signed the Declaration of Independence and those who fought for it got many of their ideas from Europe. Americans believed in the same liberties the English believed in; they decided to break from Britain only when they thought the British had denied the colonies those liberties.

The leaders of the former colonies knew the histories of Greece and Rome. They knew the rights granted in the *Magna Carta* (which you can read about in the World Civilization section of this book). They were familiar with the English Parliament, and the principle of people being represented by those who led them. They had read the writings of great English and French philosophers who believed in "natural rights."

To believe in natural rights is to believe that it is obvious, reasonable, and natural that people should have certain rights. In the Declaration of Independence, Thomas Jefferson listed three unalienable natural rights: "life, liberty, and the pursuit of happiness." What do those rights mean to you?

The Declaration of Independence also states, "We hold these truths to be self-evident, that all men are created equal." A "self-evident" truth is a clear and obvious truth, one that you really can't argue about. But in fact, especially in earlier times, many people would hardly consider it obvious that "all men are created equal." You know this already if you've read elsewhere in this series about the caste system in India, or about ancient Rome, or about feudalism during the Middle Ages in England.

In insisting that "all men are created equal," the Declaration of Independence makes it clear that *no one*—not a king, a churchman, a lord, or an emperor—can take away a person's natural rights. This is what Jefferson meant when he said that our natural rights are "unalienable"—they can't be taken away. When you think back on the history you know, can you remember the leaders of any other governments making a big deal about the "unalienable rights" of the people? What about King Tut or Kublai Khan or William the Conqueror? No way!

The idea of "natural rights" was not new to the former colonists. But it was a new idea—a *revolutionary* idea—that the purpose of a government is to respect and protect the people's natural rights. What if the government tries to take away your rights? What should you do? The Declaration of Independence tells you to change the government! As Jefferson wrote, "To secure these rights, Governments are instituted among Men . . . [and] whenever any Form of Government becomes destructive of these ends, it is the Right of the People to alter or abolish it, and to institute new Government."

Ideals and Realities

The Americans had thrown off the government of Britain. Now they had to "institute new Government." But what kind of government would do the best job of protecting the natural rights of the people? What do you think—should there be a king? What about setting up a Senate like Rome's—would that be better? Or maybe a Parliament like England's, which represents more classes of society?

It was hard to design a new government. There was no perfect model for the Americans to imitate. They had high ideals, like "life, liberty, and the pursuit of happiness." But they couldn't always agree on what those ideals meant. What does "liberty" mean to you? Does it mean you have the freedom to do anything, even if it offends or hurts people? If it doesn't mean the freedom to do anything, then how do you decide what you shouldn't be allowed to do? Obviously, the new government had to be extra careful in spelling out what "liberty" means.

Contradictions

Do you know what a contradiction is? It's when you have two statements or ideas that go against each other.

At the time of the Revolution, you could see some big contradictions in America. The Declaration of Independence said, "all men are created equal." Why, then, was there such inequality in American society? At the time of the Revolution, as in America now, some people were rich while others were poor. The existing state governments represented wealthy people more than others. And no one was suggesting that the country's wealth should be shared equally.

But there was an even bigger contradiction: some Americans at the time owned slaves. The existence of slavery contradicted the ideas expressed in the Declaration of Independence that "all men are created equal" and that all people have an "unalienable right" to liberty.

Today we probably find it very difficult to understand how people could believe in liberty and slavery at the same time. This disturbing contradiction was part of Western civilization for almost two thousand years, from the ancient Greeks (who believed in democracy) to the 19th-century British and Americans. And, unfortunately, Western civilization was not alone in practicing slavery. The terrible injustice of treating human beings as property— denying their freedom, selling them like livestock, forcing them to work against their will—has been committed by every race, and even permitted by the great religions, including Christianity, Hinduism, Islam, and Judaism.

The fact that a contradiction has existed for a long time doesn't mean we should accept it. Instead, it reminds us that contradictions continue to face Americans in the ongoing challenge of making our country live up to its high ideals of "life, liberty, and the pursuit of happiness."

Although this slave family is working together, many slave families were broken up when family members were sold to different owners.

State and Federal Governments

The founders of our nation argued a lot about how to set up the new government. Before we look back at those arguments, let's keep in mind the way our government is set up today.

In our country, each state has its own government. But there is another government that joins all the states together as a nation. This national government is called the *federal* government. The federal government is now located in our national capital, Washington, D.C. The president of the United States heads the federal government. A governor heads the government of each of the fifty states. (Do you know the names of the president of the United States and the governor of your state?)

Now, let's look back to see how we arrived at this system.

The Capitol building, Washington, D.C., where Congress meets.

The Articles of Confederation

In designing a new government, our nation's founders had to take into account what was already in place. Each state already had its own cities, boundaries, and state legislatures. Many of the states had already written their own constitutions. When the war for independence ended in 1783, there were already thirteen state governments. What kind of government could bring them together as the *United* States?

To figure out a new government for America, the Continental Congress met many times. One thing was clear: America's new government wouldn't be like England's. After all, as the Declaration of Independence charged, it was

England's strong central government under King George III that tried to take away the natural rights of the Americans. This dislike of any strong central control led to agreement that in America, the federal government should not have much power. This was the idea behind the Articles of Confederation, an agreement approved by the Continental Congress in 1777. The Articles said that state governments could rule themselves while the federal government would have little power.

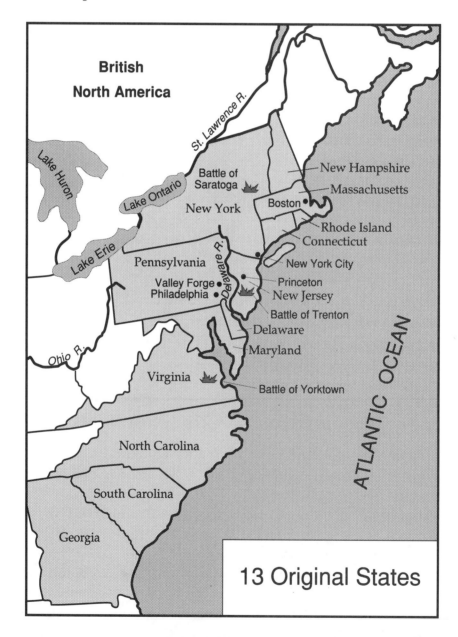

13 Original States

The Constitutional Convention

The new government under the Articles of Confederation was less than five years old when many people began calling for a better one. These were hard times for the new nation, and some people thought the weak central government was to blame. Merchants were being ruined because Britain wouldn't sign thirteen separate trade agreements with each of the thirteen states, and Congress didn't have the power to step in. Some people worried about the British soldiers who were still in forts in the Northwest Territory of Canada: would they attack and try to turn the United States into colonies again? If they did, Congress could declare war. But Congress had no power to require the states to supply soldiers, or to tax the states to raise money to pay for a war.

America needed to be able to speak and act as one nation. Clearly, the Articles of Confederation would have to be changed. To do this, fifty-five delegates from the states traveled to Philadelphia in the spring of 1787. We now call this gathering the Constitutional Convention, because after many months and many arguments the delegates produced the document that remains the highest law of our land, the Constitution of the United States.

George Washington presiding at the Constitutional Convention.

When the convention began, however, many of the delegates only intended to improve the Articles of Confederation. If they had known that they would be writing a national constitution, many of them, who still felt more loyal to their states than to the nation, probably wouldn't have come to the convention at all!

The delegates came from all thirteen states except one (Rhode Island refused to participate). There were lawyers, merchants, and farmers, many of whom had fought in the Revolution. Among them were some of the men often called our "Founding Fathers" because they played such important roles in shaping our new nation: George Washington, James Madison, and Benjamin Franklin, to name a few.

Madison's Plan

James Madison from Virginia, who is now known as the "Father of the Constitution," arrived in Philadelphia early. He had a plan. He knew from the start that the country needed to do more than tinker with the Articles of Confederation. He wrote down his ideas for a strong central government. He

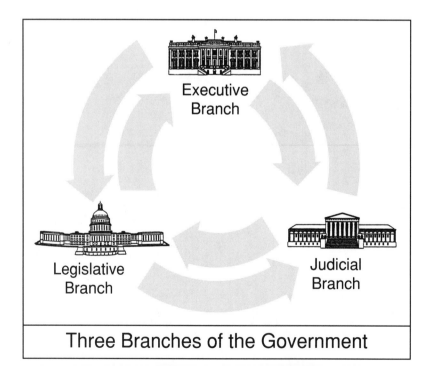

Executive Branch

Legislative Branch

Judicial Branch

Three Branches of the Government

got his friend Edmund Randolph, Virginia's popular governor, to present his plan to the delegates.

Madison's plan proposed a government with three parts, or "branches":

(1) *The executive branch.* "Executives" are leaders, the people in charge. The executive branch would be in charge of running the government.

(2) *The legislative branch.* To "legislate" means to make laws. Making laws would be the job of the legislative branch. As Madison proposed it, the legislative branch would have two parts. One part, the House of Representatives, would be composed of delegates elected by the American people. The other part would be a smaller body of lawmakers ultimately chosen by the House of Representatives. This part would be called the Senate. (Perhaps you remember this name from reading about the Roman Empire in Book Three of this series.) Together they would be called the Congress. If you hear people mention "both houses of Congress," they mean both the House of Representatives and the Senate.

(3) *The judicial branch.* If you look at the first few letters of the word "judicial" you'll see that it's related to the word "judge." Where do you find judges? In a court. The judiciary branch of government, according to Madison, would consist of a number of federal courts headed by a Supreme Court, whose job it would be to oversee the laws of the land.

Today, the Supreme Court has nine judges, called justices. The head judge is called the chief justice. The justices are appointed by the president of the United States, but they also have to be approved by the Senate. Until recently, only men have served as Supreme Court justices. But in 1981, the first woman justice was appointed. Her name is Sandra Day O'Connor.

Who Needs a President?

After the delegates heard Madison's plan, the arguments began. Tempers flared as the delegates argued through the hot summer months of 1787.

One heated argument was about the executive branch. Today, we call the chief executive of our government the president. But in 1787 some delegates didn't believe the country needed a president at all. Bad experience with King George III of England made them suspicious of any single leader with a lot of power.

But other delegates pointed out that America under the Articles of Confederation was weak because it had no strong executive. And wouldn't it be a good idea to have a strong president to deal with the leaders of other countries, and to command the armed forces?

Finally, the delegates agreed on the need for a president. They also thought of ways to limit the president's power. Unlike a king, a president wouldn't rule for as long as he lived. He would serve a term of four years. And if he was a bad president, the legislative branch would have the power to remove him from office. The delegates also agreed that the president should have the help of a vice president, who would take the president's place if anything happened to him.

Taxation with Representation

Think back: what does the legislative branch do? What are the two houses of Congress?

The delegates to the Constitutional Convention decided to give Congress certain powers. They gave Congress the power to raise tax money directly from the citizens of the country. Raise taxes? Now wait a minute—isn't that what made the colonists angry enough to shout "No taxation without representation!" and dump British tea in Boston Harbor? Yes—but since Congress would consist of representatives elected by the American people, this would be taxation *with* representation (which didn't mean people would be happy to pay taxes).

Before the Constitutional Convention, people paid taxes only to their own states. But the nation as a whole needed money. Federal taxes were needed, for example, to pay for something else that Congress was given the power to establish: a national army and navy. The national armed forces would need equipment, weapons, and, of course, money to pay the soldiers and sailors.

Today, Americans still pay taxes to the federal government. The tax money is still used for such purposes as making sure we have a strong army and navy. It's also used to help pay for many other things: building and maintaining highways and bridges, medical care for older people, sending astronauts to outer space, and loans to help people pay for college, to name just a few.

Big States versus Little States

The delegates to the Constitutional Convention agreed to give Congress the power to tax. But they couldn't agree on how many representatives from each state should be in the Congress.

Under Madison's plan, states with more people in them would have more representatives. That way, the bigger states would have more say in making important decisions. "Not fair!" cried the delegates from the small states with fewer people. These delegates wanted each state, big or small, to have the same number of representatives in Congress. "Not fair!" cried the representatives from the big states. Why should a little state have as much say as a big state?

You've probably been in an argument in which you and a friend go back and forth saying, "Is not!" "Is too!" "Is not!" "Is too!" That's just about what happened at the Constitutional Convention. It got so bad that the delegates from the small states threatened to leave.

Fortunately, all the delegates finally agreed to a compromise: each side would gain a little and lose a little. They decided the House of Representatives would reflect the population of each state: the bigger states would have more representatives than the smaller states. But in the Senate, each state would have exactly the same number of members—big or small, each state would have two senators. And before any law could be passed, both the House of Representatives and the Senate would have to agree on it.

That's still the way it is today. How many representatives to Congress does your state have? And (trick question, watch out!) how many senators? One change you should know about is that the House of Representatives no longer elects senators. Since 1913, the senators have been directly elected by the people. When you turn eighteen, you'll have the power to cast a vote for the people you think would make the best senators and representatives from your state. Who knows, you might even run for office yourself!

Checks and Balances

The Founding Fathers were not perfect. But we can be proud of them for working hard to solve problems that had puzzled people for hundreds of years. The new government they constructed was far more fair than any before.

Like you, the Founding Fathers knew the history of Rome and Europe; they knew about emperors and kings and generals who did terrible things to gain power. That's why the Founding Fathers were careful to invent a system to make sure that none of the three branches of our government became too powerful. We call this system "checks and balances."

You know one meaning of the word "check"; when your teacher asks you to "check your spelling," you make sure it's correct. But did you know that "to check" can also mean "to stop"? The Founding Fathers gave each of the three branches of government—executive, legislative, and judicial—the power to check, or stop, the other branches if they went beyond what the Constitution said they could do. That would keep power balanced among the three branches.

Here's an example of how checks and balances work. Let's say Congress passes a law. If the president doesn't like it, he can refuse to approve it. When the president does this, we say he *vetoes* it, which means the law will not take effect. But Congress can override the president's veto. If two thirds of the members of both houses of Congress vote to pass the law, then the law takes effect whether the president likes it or not.

Do you know of a problem in your state, or in the nation, or in the whole world, that you would like to see solved? Maybe the president, the senators, or the members of Congress who represent you can do something about it—but you have to let them know what the problem is and that you care about it! Here are their addresses:

The Honorable [name of Congress member]
House Office Building
1409 Longworth
Washington, DC 20515

The Honorable [name of Senate Member]
Senate Office Building
493 Russell
Washington, D.C. 20510

The President of the United States
The White House
1600 Pennsylvania Avenue NW
Washington, DC 20500

We the People

The Constitution.

The delegates came to the Constitutional Convention in May of 1787, but not until September did they come up with a written document they could agree on and sign their names to. They had finally designed the system of government that would turn a loose confederation of states into "a more perfect Union."

Those words come from the opening, or preamble, to the Constitution of the United States. Here is the preamble. Read it aloud, and talk with an older person about the words and ideas you may not understand at first. And notice the first three words, "We the People," which announce that the Constitution was meant to speak for all Americans, not just a few.

> We the People of the United States, in Order to form a more perfect Union, establish Justice, insure domestic Tranquility, provide for the common defense, promote the general Welfare, and secure the Blessings of Liberty to ourselves and our Posterity, do ordain and establish this Constitution for the United States of America.

The Constitution Criticized

John Adams, who would become our second president, wrote in a letter to his friend Thomas Jefferson that the new Constitution meant good-bye to the Old World.

But not everyone was so pleased with the Constitution. Before it could become the law of our land, the people in the states had to vote to ratify (approve) it. And if you think the arguments were heated among the delegates during the Convention, you should have heard what went on in the states!

Those who were for the Constitution were called Federalists. Some, like Alexander Hamilton of New York, wrote many newspaper articles explaining how the Constitution worked and urging people to ratify it. Besides Hamilton, James Madison and John Jay also wrote many articles supporting the Constitution. These writings are known as *The Federalist Papers*.

People who disagreed with Hamilton, Madison, and Jay were called Anti-Federalists. Many Anti-Federalists were afraid that the Constitution created a central government so strong that it could endanger the rights of "life, liberty, and the pursuit of happiness" that thousands of Americans had so recently fought and died for.

The arguments between Federalists and Anti-Federalists went on for years. Once again, a compromise was necessary. The Constitution was changed by having sections added to it, as the Anti-Federalists desired. These additions were called amendments. The amendments persuaded most people to ratify the Constitution.

There are now twenty-six amendments to the Constitution, but it started out with ten. These first ten amendments to the Constitution are known as the Bill of Rights, because they clearly state the rights of all Americans. Here are some of your rights and freedoms protected by the Bill of Rights:

◆ *Freedom of speech.* You have the freedom to express yourself and your beliefs. This freedom is denied to people in some countries even today; in China, for example, in 1989 government soldiers shot and imprisoned members of a crowd of young people who had gathered to express their belief in democracy.

In America, people sometimes disagree over whether "freedom of speech" means you are free to express yourself even in ways that may offend or insult other people. The difficult question is, if you begin taking away the freedom of speech in some cases, where do you stop?

◆ *Freedom of the press.* Newspapers and other publications are free to print almost anything they want, including articles that criticize the government.

◆ *Freedom of religion.* You can worship as you choose. That may seem obvious today, when no American is required by law to hold any specific religious beliefs. But think back to the time of the Puritans in the Massachusetts Bay Colony, where you could be punished for not following the required religion. That was why people like Roger Williams and Anne Hutchinson left the colony to be free to practice their own religious beliefs.

What About Slavery?

Slaves being sold at an auction.

The Bill of Rights did not apply to the many thousands of African-American slaves. They had no rights or freedoms. The word "slavery" was never mentioned in the Constitution at this time. Some delegates to the Constitutional Convention were opposed to slavery, but they didn't insist that the Constitution make slavery unlawful. Perhaps they feared there would be no Constitution at all if they attempted to pass a national law that would anger the delegates from Southern states where thousands of slaves worked on plantations.

A delegate from Connecticut probably spoke for most when he said, "The morality or wisdom of slavery are considerations belonging to the states themselves." This solution worked long enough to get the Constitution written and approved. But the existence of slavery would soon tear apart the country that the Constitution was meant to hold together.

The Father of Our Country

Our first president was George Washington. He was elected by a great majority because he was trusted and admired by the people. He had helped win the Revolutionary War for Independence, and he played an important role at the Constitutional Convention. As president, he governed fairly. He did not try to gain the powers of a king for himself.

Washington did not find it easy to be president. At the end of his four-year term, he accepted a second term only to help unite a quarreling country. He refused a third term, which set a tradition of limiting presidents to two four-year terms in office. (The tradition became law when the twenty-second amendment to the Constitution was adopted in 1951.)

George Washington died only two years after the end of his second term. He is often called "the Father of Our Country" because he dedicated so much of his life to serving

The famous painting of George Washington by Gilbert Stuart.

the United States when it was still young and in need of wise guidance. After Washington died, a congressman from Virginia spoke words that expressed the general admiration for our first president: he was "first in war, first in peace, and first in the hearts of his countrymen."

There are many good books on the life of George Washington. Check your library or bookstore for these: Meet George Washington *by Joan Heilbroner;* George Washington Wasn't Always Old *by Alice Fleming;* If You Grew Up with George Washington *by Ruth Gross.*

Arguments and Parties

When George Washington was president, he put a number of men in charge of running different parts of the government. We call these government officials the president's cabinet. Two of Washington's cabinet members were Thomas Jefferson and Alexander Hamilton.

Jefferson and Hamilton couldn't agree on much of anything. They held very different views about human nature, about who should rule the country, and about what kind of country the United States should be.

In the Declaration of Independence, Jefferson wrote that "all men are created equal." But Hamilton was not a big believer in equality. History, he said, showed that a strong, wealthy minority had always dominated a weak majority of people. Jefferson put his faith in hard-working, educated people. But Hamilton once shouted at Jefferson, "Your people, sir, is a great beast!"

Hamilton wanted a very strong federal government. He wanted to help businessmen by establishing a national bank and taxing imported goods. But Jefferson was suspicious of the power of big financial institutions. It would be dangerous, he thought, to have so much money under the control of one big bank.

When Hamilton looked to the future of America, he saw a wealthy nation of prosperous businessmen, big cities, and a strong federal government. When Jefferson looked ahead, he saw a republic of independent, hard-working farmers. Jefferson thought strong state governments were necessary to prevent tyranny by the federal government. He feared that Hamilton's policies would create a wealthy ruling class with control over a poor, ignorant working class.

Many people agreed with Hamilton. Just as many people agreed with Jefferson. To support the leader they agreed with, people joined together in political parties. Political parties, and the disagreements between them, are a continuing part of democracy in America. The names of the major political parties in America have changed over the years. Today we have two main political parties, the Republicans and the Democrats. They often disagree about the way our government should be run. You might think all this disagreement

Alexander Hamilton: he believed in a strong federal government.

would make it hard to get things done, and sometimes it does. But it's better than having everything done according to the will of a single, all-powerful ruler nobody dares to disagree with!

A New Capital City

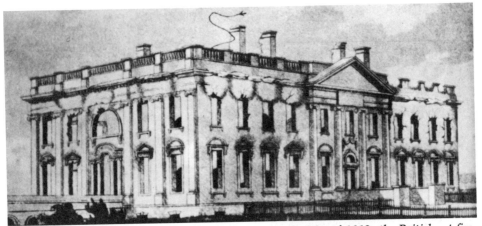

This is how the White House looked in 1814. During the War of 1812, the British set fire to the White House. Can you see the smoke marks above the windows?

The new country of the United States needed a new city as its capital. A place midway between the North and the South was chosen. Benjamin Banneker, an African-American inventor, astronomer, mathematician, and mapmaker, served on the commission that surveyed and planned the new city. You know who the new city was named after—it was called Washington, the District of Columbia (which we abbreviate as Washington, D.C.).

Builders worked all through the 1790s on a building where Congress could meet, called the Capitol, and on a house for the president. We now call the president's house the White House. When our second president, John Adams, moved in with his wife Abigail in 1800, there was no stairway to the second floor, and many of the walls were still unfinished.

At this time, Washington was only a muddy town with what one person described as a lot of "miserable huts." One foreign ambassador found a two-foot-long snake in his house!

The city is very different today. It has many huge, stone office buildings for the government. It has magnificent museums and a great library, the Library of Congress, where you can find just about any book you could want. Perhaps you have visited Washington, D.C., and seen the great monuments built to honor three of our great leaders: Washington, Jefferson, and Lincoln.

Thomas Jefferson

Thomas Jefferson was only thirty-three years old when he wrote the Declaration of Independence. As you've read, he served in President Washington's cabinet. And in 1801 he was elected the third president of our country. (You may have read in Book One of this series how our country doubled in size because of the great bargain President Jefferson got in the Louisiana Purchase.)

Thomas Jefferson: when he was only thirty-three he wrote the Declaration of Independence.

Thomas Jefferson was a man of many talents. He could read many different languages. He studied mathematics, science, geography, and music. He believed strongly in the value of a good education; he wanted to be remembered for founding the University of Virginia.

Jefferson also studied architecture and designed his own house, called Monticello. You might have a picture of Jefferson and Monticello in your pocket! Look on the front and back of a nickel.

Jefferson died on July 4, 1826—the fiftieth anniversary of American independence, which he did so much to make possible.

Monticello sits on a hill outside Charlottesville, Virginia. Jefferson's architectural designs for Monticello and other buildings set the style for much of American architecture until the Civil War.

To learn more about the life of our third president, you can read Thomas Jefferson: Man on a Mountain *by Natalie Bober or* Meet Thomas Jefferson *by Marvin Barrett. Teachers can order materials and lesson plans on a variety of topics from the Monticello Education Department, P.O. Box 316, Charlottesville, VA 22902. Materials are available on the architecture of Monticello; plantation life; the life of Isaac Jefferson, one of Thomas Jefferson's slaves; Jefferson's family life; and Jefferson's travels.*

Madison's Troubles: The War of 1812

The Father of the Constitution, James Madison, had his hands full as our fourth president. Many of his troubles resulted from continuing quarrels between the United States and Britain.

In the West, Americans were angry because of a false rumor that the British were encouraging Native American tribes led by Tecumseh to attack the settlers. On the seas, matters were more complicated. Britain was again at war with France. Both Britain and France were interfering with American merchant ships. But the British made Americans especially angry by pulling American sailors off their ships and forcing them to help the British in their fight against France.

Tecumseh (1768–1813), a Shawnee chief, called for all Indians "to unite in claiming a common and equal right in the land, as it was at first and should be yet. For it never was divided, but belongs to all, for the use of each. The white people," he said, "have no right to take the land from the Indians who had it first; it is theirs."

You might think that after the war for independence, Americans would be tired of fighting. But a group of angry congressmen demanded that America go to war *again* with Britain. The "War Hawks," as they were called, pushed President Madison to declare war in 1812. The War Hawks had one other motive: they hoped to take over Canada, the vast British-owned territory north of the United States.

The United States was not ready for the War of 1812. The country lacked soldiers and supplies. Although Congress was willing to talk a lot about battling Britain, it was not willing to tax the American people to pay for the war. American troops lost many battles in the north and the west of the country, and it quickly became clear that it was useless for America even to think about taking Canada from the British.

In sea battles, Americans did better. The battleship *Constitution* was nicknamed "Old Ironsides" because it survived so many battles.

But despite these victories at sea, the war went poorly for the Americans. The British attacked Washington, D.C., and set fire to the White House. (You may have read in Book Two of this series how the president's wife, Dolley Madison, saved a portrait of George Washington just before the British arrived with their torches. You might also recall the story of our national anthem, "The Star-Spangled Banner," which was written during the War of 1812 by Francis Scott Key.)

The War of 1812 was a war that America never should have gotten into at all. The fighting dragged on. Neither side was winning. Finally, the two tired countries signed a peace treaty on Christmas Eve in the year 1814. America and Britain would never go to war against each other again. In fact, in later wars, the two countries would fight as allies.

One of the biggest battles of the War of 1812 was fought a few weeks *after* the peace treaty was signed. News traveled slowly in those days; word of the treaty had not yet reached the city of New Orleans, in the deep South. American troops, led by General Andrew Jackson, were in a well-protected position when the British troops advanced. The Americans fired their rifles, and kept on firing. The British, marching in the open, didn't have a chance. Many died in the Battle of New Orleans, even though the war was officially over.

"Old Ironsides," the battleship Constitution.

The Monroe Doctrine

The United States was not the only country in the New World to struggle for independence from the Old World. Not long after the United States broke away from Britain, Spain's colonies in Latin America began fighting—and winning—their independence. (From Book Two, you might remember Simón Bolívar, a great liberator of Latin America.)

Because Americans had so recently fought for their own independence, they sympathized with their Latin American neighbors. Our fifth president, James Monroe, sent a message to the European countries that had once held so many colonies in the New World: Don't even *think* about trying to start any more colonies in North or South America! This policy, called the Monroe Doctrine, told the great powers of the Old World not to interfere in the affairs of the New World—a pretty confident demand for a young country to make! At the same time, the Monroe Doctrine said that America would not get involved in European wars or politics.

General Jackson

The overwhelming American victory in the Battle of New Orleans made General Andrew Jackson a hero in the eyes of many Americans.

A year before the Battle of New Orleans, General Jackson led his troops into present-day Alabama against the Creek Indians. He forced the Creek Indians to give up 23 million acres of land they had claimed as their own, thus opening much of the South for new settlement.

In 1818, Jackson was fighting the American Indians again, this time in Florida, which was still a colony of Spain. Some Americans were angry at the Seminole Indians in Florida, because they gave refuge to slaves who had run away from American settlers. General Jackson scattered the Seminoles and burned their villages.

But Jackson went beyond his orders to fight the Seminoles. He led his American troops well into Florida, and there they stayed put. The government of Spain objected to the presence of American troops in a Spanish colony. But Spain was weak from years of fighting its Latin American colonies that wanted independence. The American government took advantage of this weakness and put pressure on Spain. Without much resistance, Spain agreed to sell Florida to the United States for five million dollars.

Andrew Jackson, President

Andrew Jackson may have been a headstrong, stubborn general, and cruel to Native Americans, but he was very popular with the American people. His great popularity helped get him elected president in 1828.

President Jackson brought his rough, frontier ways to Washington, D.C. He had grown up in the Carolina backwoods and had lived much of his life as a soldier. Many people saw him as a "self-made man" who had succeeded because of his own toughness and efforts, not because he was born rich or with any special advantages. This made him popular, although some people were horrified to hear Jackson's supporters claim, "Any man is good enough to hold office."

Andrew Jackson during his presidency.

At the celebration when Jackson became president, huge crowds of farmers came from as far away as western Pennsylvania and Tennessee to cheer their hero. Many of these "backwoodsmen" pushed their way into a reception at the White House. Senators and their wives, who were used to more polite conduct, were shocked to see farmers in muddy boots standing on the satin-covered cushions of beautiful chairs, trying to catch a glimpse of the president.

One People's Dream, Another People's Nightmare

During the time that Andrew Jackson was a soldier and, later, our president, the dream of many Americans was to expand this country, to create a nation that stretched "from sea to shining sea." One of the reasons Jackson was so popular in his time was that he helped make this dream come true. But the American dream of expanding westward across the continent was a nightmare for the Native Americans who already lived there.

Jackson shared the view of many white Americans at the time that the American Indians were uncivilized savages. The first question that occurred to Jackson and others was not, "How can we understand these peoples and their ways of life, which are different from ours?" but, "How can we get these people off the land we want?"

Jackson's answer was to force the Native Americans from their lands. In 1830 he urged Congress to pass the Indian Removal Bill. Not all white Americans approved of Jackson's harsh plan: almost half of the House of Representatives voted against the bill. But the bill passed, and the American government began its official campaign to force the Native American tribes to move, sometimes more than a thousand miles, from their lands and homes. Most were moved to what was called the "Indian Territory," now the state of Oklahoma.

One southeastern tribe, the Cherokee, refused to go. American soldiers were sent in. With rifles and bayonets, they herded the Cherokee men, women, and children into steamboats and railroad cars. Then the Cherokee were forced to walk the last eight hundred miles of their journey—a path now called the Trail of Tears. It is estimated that almost one fourth of the Cherokee died on this terrible journey.

In Florida, the Seminoles, under their strong warrior leader, Osceola, also fought against being moved from their homes. The fighting had gone on for two years when Osceola agreed to meet with an American general to discuss a peace treaty. But the meeting was a trap: Osceola was captured. The Seminoles kept fighting, but soon they lost. Osceola died in prison.

Along the Trail of Tears.

President Jackson's policies helped clear the way for land-hungry Americans moving west. At the time many Americans supported Jackson's policies. But today many Americans look back on that period with mixed feelings. They feel pride in the creation of a country committed to the great democratic principle of "liberty and justice for all." But they feel regret for the people who were denied liberty and justice. They feel sad, sometimes angry, that the creation of this country was achieved at the cost of the destruction of the lives and ways of life of so many Native Americans. And they feel determined to ensure that, despite the mistakes of the past, Americans of all races and classes can work together, now and in the future, to achieve liberty and justice for all.

"Manifest Destiny" and the Mexican War

Throughout the 1830's and 1840's, more and more Americans moved westward. (To get a sense of what life was like for these pioneers, you can read Laura Ingalls Wilder's books about growing up on the western frontier. You'll find a selection from one of these books in the Stories and Speeches section of this book.) The pioneers kept expanding into lands that were not officially part of America. Some were American Indian lands, some were claimed by Britain, some were part of what was then Mexico.

Many Americans believed in an idea that a magazine editor called "manifest destiny." "Manifest" means clear and obvious; "destiny" means what will happen. Many people believed that what was obviously meant to happen was that the United States would expand until it covered the continent. There was also something religious about the idea of manifest destiny: people believed that God wanted Americans to keep moving west and raising families until the United States reached from the Atlantic Ocean to the Pacific Ocean.

This idea made many Americans enthusiastic when the United States entered a war against Mexico in 1846. The war was sparked when Texas became a state. Texas had already been an independent republic for nine years. (You might remember reading in Book Two about how Texans broke off from Mexico, and about the Texans who fought and died at the Alamo.) Now, as the United States prepared to accept Texas as a new state, the American government claimed that Texas would include a vast stretch of land north of the Rio Grande River. But Mexico claimed this land as its own.

One American general, Zachary Taylor, became a popular hero during this war. He was nicknamed "Old Rough and Ready." To encourage his soldiers in one battle, he sat calmly on his horse, Old Whitey, while bullets whizzed about them. Taylor was such a hero when he returned home that people pulled all the hairs out of poor Old Whitey's tail for souvenirs! (Taylor was later elected our twelfth president.)

Zachary Taylor, "Old Rough and Ready," at the Battle of Palo Alto in 1846.

Although many people supported the Mexican War, others spoke strongly against it. In February 1847, a senator from Ohio, Thomas Corwin, made a stirring speech. He predicted that the Mexican War would lead to dangerous disagreements over whether to allow slavery in the territories America would gain from the war. The result of the Mexican War, he said, would be "to force us at once upon a civil conflict"— a war in which Americans would fight against each other. He also accused America of acting like a big, bullying country. Here is some of what he said:

> *What is the territory, Mr. President, which you propose to wrest [grab] from Mexico? . . . [America] says to poor, weak Mexico, "Give up your territory, you are unworthy to possess it; I have got one half already, and all I ask of you is to give up the other!" England might as well . . . have come and demanded of us, "Give up the Atlantic slope—give up this trifling territory from the Allegheny Mountains to the sea. . . ."*

The Americans thought the war against Mexico would be over quickly, but it wasn't. The Americans had better weapons, and the Mexicans lost many battles, but still Mexico would not surrender.

The war ended when American troops defeated Mexican soldiers commanded by General Antonio López de Santa Anna. General Santa Anna was trying to keep the Americans from reaching Mexico City. But the Americans broke through, and the war was soon over.

As a result of the war, Mexico lost more than the stretch of land north of the Rio Grande. The United States gained about a half-million square miles of territory, including the present-day states of California, Nevada, and Utah, and parts of Colorado, New Mexico, and Arizona. In one violent leap, the country had come much closer to the "manifest destiny" in which many believed.

The Spirit of Reform

When you see something wrong, what do you do about it? You can ignore it or you can try to make it right. In the 1820's and 1830's, many people saw things wrong with American society, and worked to reform them—to make them right. Some reformers worked for better schools and better care for the mentally ill. Others tried to change people's behavior and morals: for example, reformers in the temperance movement wanted people to stop drinking alcoholic beverages.

The most obvious thing wrong in America at this time was the existence of slavery. Many reformers in the North wanted to abolish slavery. They were called abolitionists. In the 1830s, abolitionists formed the Anti-Slavery Society, which wanted to outlaw slavery. Many dedicated women and men devoted their efforts to the abolitionist cause. We'll learn more about some of the women shortly. (In the Language Arts section of this book, you can read about an abolitionist who was once a slave. See the selection from the *Narrative of the Life of Frederick Douglass*.)

Dorothea Dix Helps the Mentally Ill

At the age of fourteen, Dorothea Dix became a schoolteacher in Massachusetts. (How old are most American students today when they graduate from high school?) She taught for many years, and wrote books for children. But we remember her now because of her great efforts to help the mentally ill. It all started almost by chance.

In 1841, Dorothea Dix volunteered to go to a Massachusetts jail to teach a Sunday school class. She was horrified by what she saw there. Locked up with the criminals were people who had committed no crimes. They were mentally ill. They were confined in rooms without heat. They were treated little better than animals.

This chance observation turned into Dorothea Dix's great cause: getting better treatment for the mentally ill. For the next two years she traveled throughout Massachusetts, visiting jails and houses for the poor. In a report that she wrote for the Massachusetts government, she described how she found mentally ill people locked in "cages, closets, cellars, stalls, pens."

Dorothea Dix.

Because of Dorothea Dix's efforts, many states built new hospitals, or fixed up old ones, to take care of the mentally ill. She was a true reformer: she found something wrong, and she did not rest until it was made right.

Horace Mann and the Public Schools

Horace Mann was a reformer devoted to improving education. In America in the early 1800s, there was much to improve. There were some good private schools for the children of parents who could afford to pay. But most schools were small one-room buildings, with very few books. Teachers received very little pay; many were not trained to teach.

A nineteenth-century classroom. What does your schoolroom look like?

Most children went to school for only a few years. And during each year, they were only in school for about three or four months. Why did they spend so little time in school? Because their families needed them to help with farm work. When would children be most needed to help on the farm? In summer, the growing season. That's the reason why many of *you* don't go to school in the summer!

Horace Mann believed in "universal education"—that *all* children should learn to read and write and become good citizens. As the leader of the first state board of education in Massachusetts, he worked hard to achieve his goals. Because of his efforts, more schools were built. The school year was lengthened to a minimum of six months. (How many months are you in school?) Teachers got better pay. And the state of Massachusetts established the first college for training teachers.

Horace Mann wrote, "Education creates . . . new treasures—treasures not before possessed or dreamed of by any one."

Women's Rights

If people from mid-nineteenth century America could see our country today, many things would surprise them. They might be most surprised to see women as doctors, soldiers, managers, astronauts, construction workers, members of Congress, and judges (a woman Supreme Court justice might make them faint!). In the 1800s, women were not expected to take an active role in society. But some women, and men, disagreed strongly. These people were called feminists: they believed (as many people do today) that women should have equal rights and opportunities with men.

Margaret Fuller was an important feminist writer. In Boston, she held classes in which women could learn and talk about topics that had nothing to do with housekeeping duties: Greek mythology, for example, or the fine arts. In her book called *Woman in the Nineteenth Century*, Margaret Fuller claimed, "If you ask me what offices [jobs] they [women] may fill, I reply—any. . . . Let them be sea-captains, if you will."

Women at this time had few rights. They couldn't vote. They couldn't attend most colleges. They couldn't hold most jobs. Women did hold some jobs—as factory workers, teachers, and office helpers, for example—but in general they could not be the managers or bosses. If they were married, all the property and money in the family belonged to the husband, even if the wife worked to bring in some money.

Seneca Falls

The movement to abolish slavery was one cause in which women did play an active role. But their efforts were not always appreciated. For example, consider what happened in 1840 at an important antislavery meeting held in London. Two American abolitionists, Lucretia Mott and Elizabeth Cady Stanton, had made the long trip across the Atlantic in order to take part in the meeting and speak their beliefs. But they were not allowed to participate. They were told to sit quietly while the men did all the talking!

Later, Mott, Stanton, and others organized a gathering of people to take a stand on the issue of women's rights. In July of 1848, about a hundred people, women and men, met in the town of Seneca Falls, New York, where Stanton lived. Calling for a meeting in which women would speak their minds was a dramatic step: "nice" women weren't supposed to speak in public. Among the people who attended were two former slaves who had become great abolitionists, Frederick Douglass and Sojourner Truth. (You can read a speech by Sojourner Truth in the Language Arts section of this book.)

The people who gathered at Seneca Falls put their beliefs about women's rights into a document called the Declaration of Sentiments and Resolutions, modeled after the Declaration of Independence. The Seneca Falls Declaration announced, "We hold these truths to be self-evident: that all men and women are created equal." In strong words, it went on to claim, "The history of mankind is a history of repeated injuries . . . on the part of man toward woman." The declaration accused men of desiring "the establishment of an absolute tyranny" over women.

The declaration also attacked the promise a woman traditionally made when getting married: to "love, honor, *and obey*" her husband. This promise seemed like a kind of slavery to the people at Seneca Falls. The

The Seneca Falls Convention. It took courage for women to meet and to talk publicly about their political and social rights during the 1840s and 1850s.

One woman who attended the Seneca Falls convention also later called for reforms in the way women dressed. Amelia Bloomer urged that women should not be confined in layers of tight girdles and frilly petticoats. Instead, they should be free to wear clothes more suitable to an active life: loose-fitting, comfortable pants, which came to be called "bloomers," under a short skirt. Bloomer was also the founder and editor of The Lily, perhaps the first American monthly journal for women written mostly by women. It dealt with many of the important reform issues of the time, including temperance, education, and women's rights.

Amelia Bloomer in the pants she championed. Such outfits were considered scandalous by those who believed that women should keep their ankles covered.

declaration charged that a woman "is compelled [forced] to promise obedience to her husband, he becoming, to all intents and purposes, her master."

For many people, the most shocking part of the declaration was the demand that women be given the right to vote. The idea of women voting upset some newspaper writers so much that they called it "monstrous," "ridiculous," and "evil." The struggle for a woman's right to vote would go on for more than seventy years.

A Divided Country

While people were working to reform American society in many ways, American society was growing increasingly divided over the issue of slavery. The division would go beyond arguments. In the next book in this series, you will read about how our country was torn in half—the North against the South—in the bloodiest war in our history, the Civil War.

III.

FINE ARTS

Introduction
to the Fine Arts

FOR PARENTS AND TEACHERS

In this chapter on Fine Arts, we treat harmony in Music and Gothic art and architecture in Visual Arts. These sections can stand on their own, but using a keyboard instrument will further a child's understanding of harmony, and reading the World Civilization section of this book will enhance his appreciation of the Gothic style.

Harmony is the third element of music, after rhythm and melody, and is generally the most difficult element to teach. Using the keyboard, we cover the major scale, intervals, basic chords, and chord progression, keeping all of these in the key of C major for simplicity.

Harmony is a basic part of music that often goes unnoticed by listeners. Yet simple harmony can be learned with relative ease from a book and a keyboard. Just knowing the difference between major and minor chords or being familiar with the most common chords and chord progressions can add greatly to people's understanding and enjoyment of music.

The discussion of music should be complemented by having the child play, sing, and listen to songs, and, if possible, follow along with printed music. It will help her learning and enjoyment if her parent or teacher can play the piano, guitar, or other instrument, but we have tried to write this section in such a way that parents and teachers who are not musically trained can learn along with their children.

Resources for music include the following books:

Meet the Orchestra by Ann Hayes. (Harcourt Brace Jovanovich).

A Very Young Musician by Jill Krementz. (Simon & Schuster).

The Philharmonic Gets Dressed by Karla Kuskin. (HarperCollins).

Go In and Out the Window: An Illustrated Songbook for Children by Metropolitan Museum of Art Staff. (Metropolitan Museum of Art).

The Orchestra by Mark Rubin. (Firefly).

You can also find musical works that young people enjoy listed in activity boxes throughout the Music section in this book.

In the Visual Arts section, we have tried to enhance children's appreciation of Gothic art by describing what inspired the Gothic style and how people felt about cathedrals. The history of Gothic cathedrals is an especially good example of how art forms develop. We hope that our narrative approach will engage and inform adults and children alike.

We also hope you and your child continue to experience and appreciate art by making your own artworks, listening to and seeing art, and reading more about it. The following resources may be helpful for your ongoing exploration:

Cathedrals: Stone Upon Stone by Brigette Gandindice-Coppin, published by *Young Discovery Library,* is a good general guide to Gothic cathedrals for ages five and up.

Many children will enjoy David Macauley's book *Cathedral,* published by Houghton Mifflin, which does a fine job of illustrating the construction of a Gothic cathedral. *Cathedral* also shows some of the mechanical innovations (tools, scaffolding, and buttressing) that permitted people in the Middle Ages to build these amazing structures.

The Education Department of Washington National Cathedral in Washington, D.C., is in the process of preparing a for-loan social studies education packet, written for children, on the Middle Ages and the Gothic style. A teacher's packet is currently available either for loan (for a $5.00 handling and postage fee) or for sale ($35 plus handling and postage). The packet is designed to help teachers prepare fifth through seventh graders for an onsite tour of Washington National Cathedral, but it also has a bibliography of resources to be found across the United States that will be useful for any parent or teacher who wants to get more material on the Gothic style. Contact Educational Programs, Washington National Cathedral, Massachusetts and Wisconsin Avenues, N.W., Washington, DC 20016-5098, or call (202) 537-2930.

Music

Harmony

You may have already learned about melody and rhythm in previous volumes of this series. Now we're going to tell you about the third part of music: harmony. When you play or sing more than one note at the same time, that is harmony. For example, when you hit several notes on the piano at the same time and they sound good together, that is harmony. Or when a choir sings many different notes at the same time, that is also harmony.

The Major Scale

Much of our harmony is based on the major scale, which is a very commonly used scale. If you have read Book Two of this series, you may have already learned a little about this scale. Do you remember how the song "Do Re Mi" helped us learn about the scale? Let's look again.

The notes of the C major scale are often called by sounds instead of letters, like this:

do	re	mi	fa	so	la	ti	do
C	D	E	F	G	A	B	C

The song "Do Re Me" can help you learn the scale because it turns the sounds "do," "re," "mi" into phrases you can remember.

Do Re Mi

Doe—a deer, a female deer,
Ray—a drop of golden sun,
Me—a name I call myself,
Far—a long, long way to run,
Sew—a needle pulling thread,
La—a note to follow sew,
Tea—to drink with jam and bread,
That will bring us back to Do, Do, Do . . .
                (repeat)

The first words of each line—Doe, Ray, Me, Far, Sew, La, and Tea—are the notes of the scale. (The song spells them that way to help you remember them, but you usually see the spelling as we have it above.) Sing "Do Re Mi" and listen especially to the first sound in each line. Now sing just these notes—do, re, mi, fa, so, la, ti, do—in a row. When you sing them in order, one after the other, you are singing the scale. You can sing them backward, too: "do, ti, la, so, fa, mi, re, do."

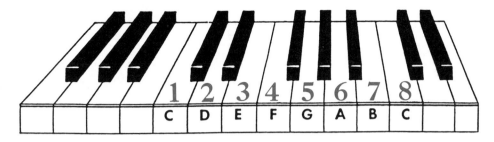

In addition to singing the scale, you can play the scale on a keyboard by hitting just the white keys. You will learn about the black keys later, but for now we will use only the white keys. Begin with the white key marked 1 in our illustration, and hit each note, all the way up to 8. The picture below shows how these notes are written going up a set of lines called the staff:

NOTE TO PARENTS AND TEACHERS: *In this section we often refer to the keyboard to illustrate harmony. Some of the exercises in this book may be done effectively without a keyboard if an adult who is familiar with music can guide the child. However, the keyboard remains the easiest way to teach the elements of harmonic theory, as notes can easily be sounded together and related spatially. A piano or synthesizer is frequently used for these purposes (most synthesizers also feature ready-made chords). Good alternatives are instruments such as bells or xylophones, whose layouts are like the keyboard. These are all durable instruments that allow the child to play exuberantly.*

Now play the scale again while singing "Do Re Mi" at the same time. Move up a note as you start each new phrase. Can you hear that the notes you're singing and playing are the same?

You already know the scale you've been using here is the C major scale. We call it that because it begins with the note we call the letter C. We can also call the notes of our scale by numbers, beginning with the number 1, and going to 8. C is the 1 note, D is the 2 note, and so on.

The scale has a total of eight notes in it. When we use letters for the scale, the last note, 8, has the same letter (C or "Do") as the first note, 1. That is because it is the same note, only higher. How can something sound the same, only higher? It's a wonderful mystery, but when you sing the scale, you will hear that it's true. The 8 note is called the octave. Once you reach the octave, you begin the scale all over again!

The 1 Note, or C

The 1 note is the most important note of the scale. The scale is named for the 1 note. (Our 1 note is called C, so we are playing the C scale. We also say we are playing in the key of C.) You can think of this note as "home." Most songs will go on a journey, but they will always want to come back to their home eventually. So most songs end on 1. Or they end on the 8 note, the octave, which, as you now know, is a higher version of the 1 note. So you can see how important the 1 note is! Both "Row, Row, Row Your Boat" and "Frère Jacques" begin *and* end on 1, for example. The words are on pages 220 and 221, so you can try them and see.

Let's Sing

Playing or singing notes together creates harmony. There is an easy harmony you can sing using the song "Do Re Mi." The first note of each line in the song makes a harmony with the last note of that line. If one person holds the note for the word "doe" while another person sings "a deer, a female deer," then the notes for "doe" and "deer" will make a harmonious sound. Try the same thing with the next two lines of the song. "Ray" and "sun" will make a harmony when sounded together. So will "me" and "self." The song was written this way on purpose, so people could enjoy the harmony you can make with it.

Harmony: Thirds

When you were singing "Do Re Mi," you were making a special kind of harmony. Sing the first line of "Do Re Mi" again and listen to the sounds of "Doe" and "deer." They are the 1 note and the 3 note on the scale. Try hitting them together on a keyboard. This sound is called a third, because you sing or play the third note along with the first note.

Any two notes played together, skipping one note in between, make a third. (Remember, we're not using the black keys yet, so you're skipping a white note to make a third.) For example, hitting the 2 and 4 notes together is also called a third. Try going up and down the keyboard, hitting thirds. People think that thirds sound very sweet together. The composer Mozart, for example, loved the sound of thirds.

Now try hitting the 1 and 4 notes together (called a fourth), and the 1 and 5 notes (a fifth), and so on. Which sounds do you like best?

Chords

Hitting *three* notes at the same time gives you a chord. Chords may have even more notes, but basic chords have three notes. Chords are often played on instruments like the guitar and piano while someone sings the melody (the main tune). Different people can also sing the notes of a chord together as harmony. Chords give a song a rich, full sound.

The 1 Chord, or Tonic

The most important chord is the 1 chord, which comes from the 1 note. An easy way to make a chord is to start with a note, and make a triple-decker sandwich on it. To make the 1 chord, *you hit the 1 note*, skip a note, *hit the 3 note*, skip a note, and *hit the 5 note*, which is the top slice of your triple decker sandwich. Like this:

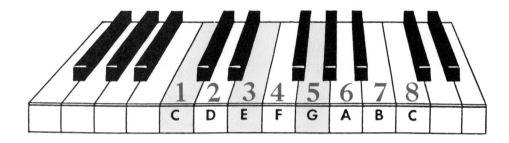

Now hit your three notes at the same time. That's a chord! Our chord can also be called by its letter name, the C chord, because it's based on the C note. We can hit the notes with the letter names C, E, G anywhere on the keyboard to make the chord. We can go up an octave and start our sandwich over again, or we can go to the octave below the 1 note and build a sandwich eight notes lower.

The 1 chord is the most important chord in most songs. The 1 chord is called the tonic, because it sets the tone for the song. The tonic is the home

---

*I*t's fun to sing a chord, with people singing the different notes at the same *time. Try singing "1," "3," and "5," to make the 1 chord. Try singing the same notes with "do, mi, so," and just the sound "ahh." It's fun to go up the notes of a chord and then go down them. Play them on the keyboard and then sing: 1,3,5,3,1. Do, mi, so, mi, do. C, E, G, E, C. La, la, la, la, la. Singers often do this to warm up, or exercise, their voices. "The Star-Spangled Banner" starts with these same three notes, but the other way around, going* down *and then* up*:*

> 5   3   1   3   5   and   8
> *oh—oh say can you   see*

So you see, the melody of our national anthem begins with the notes that *make up the 1 chord. If different people sing the notes of "Oh, say can you see" all at the same time, then they will make the 1 chord! Have each person sing and hold one note in the phrase. You'll be surprised how nice it sounds.*

chord. Many songs begin on the home chord and end on the home chord. This is one of the things that makes us feel that a song has a beginning and an end. (Some songs use *only* the 1 chord: "Row, Row, Row Your Boat" and "Frère Jacques" for example.)

The 5 Chord, or Dominant

You can make other chords by starting your triple-decker sandwich from other notes in the scale. The second most important chord in harmony is the 5 chord. You can form the 5 chord by starting your triple-decker sandwich from the 5 note. The chord beginning at the 5 note is called the dominant chord. Sometimes, to make chords like the dominant chord, you may use notes outside the octave. To play the 5 chord, hit the 5, 7, and 9 notes. Sounds nice, don't you think? But that gets you up very, very high if you're singing along, doesn't it? So there is another way to form the 5 chord. We can hit the notes with the same letter names, G, B, D, lower down on the keyboard, if we like. For example, hit the 5, 7—and 2 note down below! It's the same chord, but easier to sing. You can call the 5 chord by its letter name, too, the G chord.

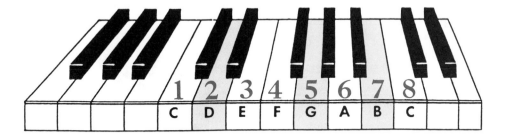

The 5 chord is very important. It is like the 1 chord's best friend. Try playing the 1 chord and then the 5 chord, and then go back to the 1 chord again. Do it several times. Many songs work this way. Moving from chord to chord like this is called a chord progression when it is part of a musical plan or composition. Mozart liked to write melodies with the 1-5-1 chord progression you've been playing here. This progression can give music a sense of balance and symmetry.

Now let's sing and play some songs that use the 1 and 5 chords, and you'll hear what we mean. The best way to learn about chords is to hear them a lot. Listen for the difference between the two chords as you sing these songs. You may be familiar with the first song: "Down in the Valley."

Down in the Valley

(1 chord) C --------------------------(5 chord) G
Down in the valley, the valley so low,

(5 chord) G --------------------------------(1 chord) C
Hang your head over, hear the wind blow.

(1 chord) C------------------------------------- (5 chord) G
Hear the wind blow, dear, hear the wind blow,

(5 chord) G-------------------------------- (1 chord) C
Hang your head over, hear the wind blow.

Can you hear how the music starts with the 1 chord and goes till "low," where it hits the 5 chord, and then goes home to the 1 chord at the last word, "blow"? Sing it again and listen.

Here is another favorite song that uses the same 1 and 5 chords, the tonic and dominant. Listen to how the melody goes back and forth between them in the same way as "Down in the Valley."

Hush Little Baby

(1)C-------------------------------- (5)G
Hush little baby, don't say a word,

(5)G--------------------------(1)C
Papa's gonna buy you a mocking bird.

(1)C--------------------- (5)G
And if that mocking bird don't sing,

(5)G------------------------(1)C
Papa's gonna buy you a diamond ring.

The two songs you've just sung are very different, but both of them use the 1 and 5 chords. As you learn more about music, you will find these important chords used in many kinds of songs.

Here are two other familiar songs that use the 1 and 5 chords. They often use a special version of the 5 or the G chord called the G^7 chord, which adds one extra note, the F note, to the G chord. We'll tell you more about seventh chords like the G^7 in a later book. You can play either the G chord or the G^7 chord in these two songs. Listen to see if you can hear when the chords change from the C chord to the G chord and back again in each song.

Clementine

    (1)C   (5)G^7
In a cavern in a canyon, excavating for a mine,

            (1)C   (5)G^7 (1)C
Dwelt a miner forty-niner, and his daughter Clementine.

(Chorus)

     (1)C   (5)G^7
Oh, my darling, oh, my darling, oh, my darling Clementine!

     (5)G^7 (1)C   (5)G^7 (1)C
Thou art lost and gone forever, dreadful sorry, Clementine.

The Yellow Rose of Texas

       (1)C
There's a yellow rose of Texas that I am going to see,

       (5)G^7
No other fellow knows her, no fellow, only me;

   (1)C
She cried so when I left her, it like to broke my heart,

   (5)G^7 (1)C (5)G^7 (1)C (5)G^7 (1)C
And if I ever find her we never more will part.

Harmony: A Review

So now you have learned about the third part of music: harmony. Chords, which change as a song goes along, make harmony. Chords are made up of three or more notes. The easiest way to make a chord is to make a triple-decker sandwich of notes around the base note. The most important chord is the 1 chord, or tonic. It's like home base—most songs start and end on the 1 chord. Another important chord is the 5 chord, or dominant. We also learned about the major scale, which is played on only the white keys of the keyboard.

There are many other chords besides the tonic and dominant, and we'll learn some of the important ones in later books of this series. There is even another set of notes to learn about—the black keys of the keyboard. As our system of harmony has developed, it has become more and more complex, as we'll see. That makes the music even more interesting.

This system of harmony that we use in our music developed in Europe around the time we call the Renaissance (about A.D. 1400–1600). One famous song from the Renaissance is called "Greensleeves," which has a beautiful, haunting melody. Let's sing it now.

Greensleeves

Alas, my love, you do me wrong,
To cast me off discourteously,
For I have loved you so long,
Delighting in your company.

Greensleeves was all my joy,
Greensleeves was my delight,
Greensleeves was my heart of gold,
And who but my lady Greensleeves.

Other Scales

Now you have learned about one system of notes and the harmony you can make with it. This musical system, with its eight-tone (octaval) scale, is the one used most often in the United States and in Western Europe, where it *originated. But did you know there are other kinds of scales? There are also different systems of music. For example, India has its own, very complicated, system of music. Asian music and Native American music are also based on different systems. If you want to listen to the wonderful music produced by many different peoples, here are some records and tapes to get you started:*

The Nonesuch Explorer Series, Nonesuch label (Note: there are sixty titles in this series.)

American Indian Songs & Chants, Bala Sinem Choir, cassette recording (available from the catalogue, Music for Little People, *Box 1460, Redway, CA 95560, for $9.98. This catalogue features many sound recordings, books, etc., for children.)*

Classical Music

Some of the greatest composers we know created works that we call classical music. Loosely defined, classical music is the music played by orchestras in great concert halls, and by smaller groups like string quartets. Two of the most important instruments in classical music are the violin and the piano. Operas, which are like plays that people sing, are another kind of classical music. Classical music began in Europe around 1600, and is now played throughout our country and many others around the world, including countries as far apart in culture as Japan and Israel. Sometimes you might find it difficult to listen to because it can be very complicated, but many people think it is some of the most beautiful music in the world.

Bach

One of the first great classical composers was a German musician named Johann Sebastian Bach. Bach (1685–1750) helped develop the art of harmony, which you read about earlier in this section. He wrote beautiful church hymns, in which many voices harmonize with the main melodies. He loved to play two or more melodies at the same time, and make them sound good

Bach and his family enjoying music.

together. A great example of this is his hymn called *Jesu, Joy of Man's Desiring*. While people are singing the words, the instruments in the background are playing another very beautiful melody. In fact, people like this second melody so much, they often remember it as the main melody of the song! When you listen to the song, try to hear both melodies at the same time. Which one do you like better?

Fugues Are Like Rounds

Bach also liked to write music where the voices sing the same melody, but at different times. They're like rounds you may have sung, in which people start singing the same song at different times. First one group begins, then another, and another. Let's sing a famous round now, in four groups. New voices begin the song when the group that goes before them reaches the italicized words.

Row, Row, Row Your Boat

Row, Row, row your boat
Gently down the stream,
Merrily, merrily, merrily, merrily,
Life is but a dream.

It's fun to try to listen to the others singing their parts while you're singing yours, and hear how they all fit together. Here is a famous round from France. The lyrics repeat: "Brother John, are you sleeping? The morning bells are ringing. Ding dang dong."

Frère Jacques

Frère Jacques, Frère Jacques,
Dormez-vous, dormez-vous?
Sonnez les matines, sonnez les matines,
Ding, dang, dong. Ding, dang, dong.

Bach's rounds are often played on instruments and called fugues. One famous piece is his *Fugue in C minor.* When you hear it, listen to how the different parts follow each other with the same melody, just as in the rounds you've sung.

Four-Part Harmony

Remember how we told you a basic chord is like a triple-decker sandwich? Four-part harmony is like adding this triple-decker sandwich on top of the melody, to create a great musical feast. So while one voice is singing the melody, three other voices are singing other notes that harmonize with it. Bach loved to write hymns, called chorales, which use this four-part harmony.

Four-part harmony is used in many other kinds of music, too. You find it in barbershop quartets, for example. Country singing groups like the Oak Ridge Boys and soul groups like the Four Tops feature four-part harmony. Many gospel music groups have four singers who sing a rich harmony. Many popular singers have three back-up singers, and create their own kind of four-part harmony. It's also used in string quartets, in which each part is played by a violin or other stringed instrument.

The Orchestra

Like most classical composers, Bach wrote music for the orchestra. During his time, orchestras were just beginning to take shape. Today the orchestra is made up of four basic types of instruments: strings, woodwinds, brass, and

percussion. The stringed instruments are the heart of the orchestra; they include the violin, viola, cello, and bass. These four instruments are like brothers and sisters from the same family. In the order listed here, each stringed instrument is slightly bigger and plays slightly lower than the one before, but they all have a similar

The violin, a stringed instrument.

The clarinet, a woodwind instrument.

sound. An orchestra can make a very wide variety of musical sounds when all the instruments in each "family" play together.

Many musical instruments, like the violin and the piano, were still being invented or improved upon during the time that Bach wrote his music. Some of Bach's most famous works for orchestra are *The Brandenburg Concertos*. A concerto is played by an orchestra, just as a symphony is, but in a concerto one instrument is featured and plays much more than all the others. Notice how skillfully Bach makes the parts fit together when you listen to *The Brandenburg Concertos*.

The french horn, a brass instrument.

The kettledrum, a percussion instrument.

Vivaldi

Vivaldi and Handel were two other great composers who wrote around the same time as Bach. Antonio Vivaldi (about 1677–1741), an Italian priest with flaming red hair, was nicknamed the Red Priest. He played and taught music at a school for orphan girls in Venice. He could compose music very fast—sometimes faster than it could be copied down! Much of his music has a bouncy feel in the bright parts, and a sad, haunting sound in the slow parts.

Vivaldi's most popular work is a series of concertos called *The Four Seasons*. It captures in music the feeling of the seasons: spring, summer, autumn, and winter. When you listen to it, try to feel each of the times of the year. Does the *Winter* concerto remind you of winter? Why? In the great *Spring* concerto, Vivaldi gave the violas the sounds of "a barking dog," and the violins the sound of spring's "sweet rustling of leaves." Can you hear them?

Handel

George Frederick Handel (1685–1759) wrote such wonderful music that the king and queen of England paid him an annual salary for life just so that he could compose and direct music. They say that the kings and queens of England have always stood up during the rousing Hallelujah Chorus of Handel's famous work *The Messiah*. You may stand up, too, when you hear it. It's hard to resist.

A portrait of Handel.

Classical Music: Recordings and Books

If you want to listen to the composers you read about in this section, you can try any of many fine recordings of these works:
Bach, The Brandenburg Concertos; Suites for Orchestra
Handel, The Messiah; Water Music
Vivaldi, The Four Seasons

These works are fun, and they can teach you about the orchestra:
Britten, A Young Person's Guide to the Orchestra
Prokofiev, Peter and the Wolf
Saint-Saëns, Carnival of the Animals
Leopold Mozart, The Toy Symphony

And these books will tell you about musical instruments:
Eyewitness: Musical Instruments *by Neil Ardry. (Alfred A. Knopf)*.
An Introduction to the Instruments of the Orchestra *by Jane Bunche. (Golden Press)*.

Visual Arts

Design in Art

In Book Three we talked about how the different elements of art relate to show emotion, tell a story, give us new ways to look and see, or please our senses. The mosaics at Ravenna, which make pictures out of thousands of tiny colored pieces of glass and precious metals and stones, showed us a lot about the way an artist can repeat shapes to help our eyes move in certain ways around the artwork.

Let's look more closely at the shapes in these mosaics. Are your eyes first drawn to the shape of the border, the fountain, or the people? Many people notice the figures first because the artist has used a bold black outline to help us see them. Because the repeating shapes are so much the same, you may find that the rhythm they create slows down the movement of your eyes. Your eyes tend to look for long periods at one figure at a time, rather than follow the variations from shape to shape.

It makes sense that the artist created a design that slows down the movement of our eyes because the mosaics at Ravenna were placed on the wall of a church. The design is meant to help people slow down and spend time concentrating on the things of heaven. But the artists who designed the mosaics were creating many other effects at the same time, and in this section we will learn about some of them.

A Church of Great Domes

The mosaic you have been looking at is of the Byzantine Empress Theodora and her attendants. Her husband, Justinian, who ruled from A.D. 527–565, is pictured in other mosaics in Ravenna. The artist who made the mosaics wanted to commemorate Justinian and Theodora because they were important people in Byzantium, and because they built many churches so that people would have places to worship. This picture shows a church built by Justinian that is famous throughout the world. It is called Hagia Sophia (HAH jah so FEE ah). In Greek, *hagia* means holy and *sophia* means wisdom. So Hagia Sophia is the "Church of Holy Wisdom."

There was already a smaller church called Hagia Sophia in Constantinople when Justinian became emperor. But during Justinian's reign, riots broke out in Constantinople, and vandals burned most of the old Hagia Sophia. After Justinian calmed the crowds and restored order, he rebuilt the church so that it would be even more splendid than before. (The four pointed towers, called minarets, were added by Islamic rulers hundreds of years after Justinian finished rebuilding Hagia Sophia.)

Look at the roof of Hagia Sophia. Its round shape is called a dome. Justinian's architects made the dome rise as much as 180 feet into the air. Here is one way to imagine how high that is: if forty-five people your age stood on one another's shoulders they would reach about as high as the tallest dome of Hagia Sophia!

Suspended from Heaven

The height and size of Hagia Sophia's main dome help make the outside of the church awe-inspiring, but the truly special effects of the dome are best seen from the inside. Think of a building with the highest ceiling and largest open space you know. Is it a sports stadium? a school gym? a church? an ice-skating rink? Imagine that you are standing in the middle of the floor of this building and think of the shape of the space that the walls and ceilings make around you. How would you describe it?

Hagia Sophia is now used as a mosque. That's why you see Arabic writing on the round medallions hanging from the walls.

Now look at the picture of the inside of Hagia Sophia and imagine you are standing in the middle of its floor. Notice the shape of the space that the walls and ceiling create. How does it compare with the shape made by the building you know?

The inside of Hagia Sophia is a complicated shape. The floor of the main part of the building is basically square. But two sides of the square open and extend out into a half-circle that makes the entire floor seem as though it were a rectangle with a round bulge at either end. Each of the two half-circle floors also opens onto other half-circle floors, so that the floor seems to keep expanding farther out every time you look at it.

Look up at the ceiling formed by the main dome and the several smaller domes. Can you think what kinds of shapes the ceiling makes? The ceiling forms the rounded shapes of upside-down bowls—half-domes. Because the half-domes touch one another, the ceiling also seems to keep expanding out and up through more and more domes.

Are there any other rounded shapes in this church? Look at the many arches and windows. Their semicircular shapes may make you feel as though round shapes march across the floor and up to the ceiling. The shapes piled up all around make many people feel surrounded by rounded space.

Notice, too, how the light pours down from the windows at the base of the big dome overhead. Because there are so many windows all around the base of the dome, people often feel as though the dome is not attached to the rest of the building at all, but floats in a mysterious fashion *above* the building. When Hagia Sophia was finished, one man was heard to exclaim that it was "a golden dome suspended from heaven."

Imagine standing in a huge building where the floor and ceiling seem to swell and billow away from you, and where light streams in everywhere from many windows. Do you think you would feel very large or very tiny in such a space? Would you notice more how powerful the foundation and walls were in order to hold up the massive roof, or would you notice how light and airy the building felt to you?

Hagia Sophia is a remarkable building because of its special use of space and light, and because of other arts used to decorate the interior (such as mosaics). No other church has been built exactly like Hagia Sophia, but most Byzantine churches copied its use of domes to create an open and rounded inside space. You could almost say that Hagia Sophia set the standard for the Byzantine style of architecture through the 1400's.

Abbot Suger's Fiery Vision

To make a work of art, an artist needs many things. He needs materials, imagination, and time to put materials and imagination together. And he needs inspiration. Have you ever had the feeling that your whole mind has suddenly come alive because you realized something for the first time? Or have you ever been so excited by a new idea or a new fact that you could not wait to write something down or make something? Then you have had the feeling of inspiration.

Artists can be inspired by many different things. Throughout the history of art, religious beliefs have had a strong effect on lots of artists, as we have already seen by learning about Hagia Sophia. In Western Europe, the Christian religion in particular was a very important inspiration for many artists, especially during the Middle Ages. One man who lived in France during the early 1100's, Abbot Suger (SUE-zhay), was powerfully affected by a certain idea of God. This led to the style of architecture that we call Gothic.

Abbot Suger believed that you could think of God as acting like fire. Just as fire gives warmth and light to the human body, God gives warmth and light to the human spirit. Abbot Suger thought that, just as fire changes the materials it burns, God transforms the human spirit. As flames reach toward the heavens, God carries the human spirit to heaven. Abbot Suger was so inspired by this idea of God that he wanted others to share his excitement and feel the same way too. He wanted to build a church that could give people this feeling when they worshiped.

Gothic Cathedrals

Churches in Western Europe in Abbot Suger's day had heavy, thick walls and low ceilings, and were often very dark inside. Abbot Suger wanted to build a church that would instead be filled with light and soar toward heaven like the flames of his vision of God.

In addition, Abbot Suger had heard of the wonderful light and space in Hagia Sophia. He wanted to build a church close to home that was different from Hagia Sophia, but one that could impress people as Hagia Sophia impressed people. He wanted people to feel surrounded by lots of space, as though they had entered heaven itself when they walked into his church.

Abbot Suger was not an architect. He did not draw the design or create the architecture of his new church himself. But he found someone who could listen to his ideas about God and figure out a way to make a building that would let in lots of light, have a high ceiling, and give a feeling of spaciousness. The church he built outside Paris, Saint Denis (SAN duh NEE), was considered a marvel in its time.

Soon this new style of architecture spread across France, and then across all of Europe. Look closely at the photographs on page 229 of three famous large churches, or cathedrals. Would you agree that, as time went on, the outsides of some cathedrals looked more and more like the leaping flames of Abbot Suger's vision?

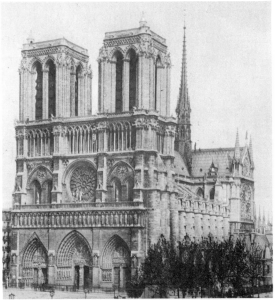

Notre Dame cathedral in Paris, France.

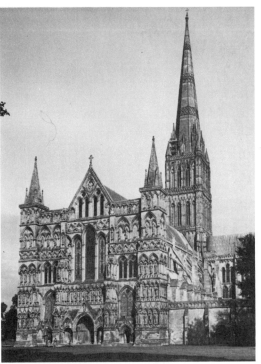

Cathedral at Salisbury, England.

Cathedral at Cologne, Germany.

The picture you see above is another example of Gothic architecture. This is the inside of a famous Gothic church in Paris, France, called Sainte-Chapelle (SAN shah PEL). If you were at Sainte-Chapelle, your head would probably not even reach halfway up the doorway! Imagine you are standing in the middle of the room pictured here, with a friend who is blind. How would you describe it to your friend? How would you compare it to Hagia Sophia? Notice how the arches made by the tall windows are pointed, not rounded as they are in Hagia Sophia. Pointed arches like these are one of the things that make the Gothic style.

You have just learned that knowing what inspired an artist can often help you understand the artwork. Look back at the mosaics at Ravenna and try to imagine what might have inspired this artwork.

An Age of Faith

People in the Middle Ages often cared deeply about the cathedrals where they worshiped. When a cathedral was being built, a whole town would help by giving money, materials, fine sculpture, and stained glass. People thought it was an honor to work on the cathedral, even though they might not be alive when the building was actually finished (Gothic cathedrals sometimes took as long as a hundred years or more to complete). When the cathedral at Chartres, France, was being built, many people showed their devotion to the cathedral by taking the place of the oxen and horses that pulled carts full of building materials and supplies!

Why did people love the cathedrals? They knew that the building would be a place that the whole community could use as a school, a theater, or gathering place. The cathedrals were full of riches that everyone, not just the nobles, could look at and enjoy. Many people lived crowded together in tiny cottages, but in a cathedral anyone, even a peasant, could enjoy lots of space, quiet, and privacy.

But most important, the people thought of the cathedral as being an image of heaven itself, almost like a little heaven on earth. By putting the cathedral right in the middle of their town, they meant to show that God was the center of their lives. The people believed that their devotion to the cathedral was a sign of their faith in God. This devotion to God not only inspired Gothic art, but also is one reason why the Middle Ages is sometimes called the "Age of Faith."

Rose Windows

The picture on page 232 is of a special kind of window, called a rose window, which is often found in Gothic cathedrals. Rose windows, like most cathedral windows, are made out of bits of brightly colored glass, called stained glass. Light that comes through a transparent window usually does not make special colors, but light passing through stained-glass windows makes many vivid colors.

To put color into the glass, an artist would put colored material between sheets of glass, and then bake the layers until they sealed together into one piece. This big piece of colored glass was then cooled and cut into little bits that could be put together, almost like a mosaic, to make pictures. Sometimes the artist also painted smaller details, like the features of a face, directly onto the glass.

Notice the circular shape of the rose window. Many times, the artists of the Middle Ages showed Jesus standing in the center of a sun-shaped wheel. You can think of the rose windows as a kind of sun wheel built into the wall of the

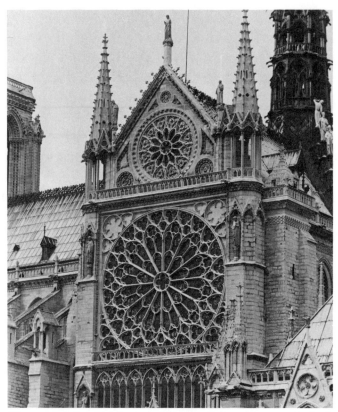

The rose window on the north facade of Notre Dame cathedral in Paris, France.

cathedral. In most rose windows you can see either the figure of Jesus or his mother Mary standing in the center of the window, surrounded by pictures in stained glass that tell the story of their lives.

Make a small rose window. Cut a large circle out of black construction paper and fold the paper in half two times so that your paper looks like a quarter of a pie. Use your imagination and cut many little shapes out of your quarter pie. When you are done cutting out shapes, unfold the construction paper. You have made the frame for the rose window. Now glue or tape small pieces of colored tissue paper over the holes on one side of the construction paper. Turn the frame over and hang or tape your rose window onto a window in your house. Look at it glow as light comes through it!

The Importance of Windows

Windows were very important in the construction of Gothic cathedrals because they allowed more light into a church, and because the scenes in the glass told stories of the Christian faith. But they were also important because, by putting in more windows, the architects could take out parts of the stone. Stone is still part of a rose window, but see how little there is compared to the amount of space taken up by glass? The thin stone that runs from the center of the window to the edges of the circle like spokes of a wheel is called tracery.

The tracery does have a job to do—it helps hold the glass in place. But by making the stone so thin, the artist has made stone more like a decoration than a support. Compare a stone with a piece of glass. Which one looks more solid and massive? Which looks more airy and open? Many people would say that stone looks more solid and massive, while glass looks more airy and open. By replacing stone with glass in a wall and supporting the glass with delicate tracery, the architects could make the whole building look more airy and open.

The rose window of the cathedral at Amiens, France.

Statues Standing Freely in Space

Look back at the photographs of the three cathedrals. They may not look equally fancy, but they all have lots of statues. Can you see the row of figures above the doors of Notre Dame cathedral in Paris? Even though these figures

Dover Publications produces inexpensive coloring books that are designed to produce stained-glass effects. You may order these books from Dover Publications, 31 East Second Street, Mineola, NY 11501.

look small in the photograph, if you were standing next to one of these statues, you would find that it was as tall as your mother or father! The statues were placed there to remind everyone who looked at the cathedral of people who showed their great faith in God through their deeds.

The photograph you see on the next page is a close-up of some statues decorating a Gothic cathedral. During the early Middle Ages, artists in Europe for the most part made statues that were not completely separate from the stone they were carved from. These kinds of statues are called reliefs. (Do you remember reading about relief maps in the Geography section of this book? The idea of relief statues is the same.) As time went on, artists began to separate sculptures completely from the surrounding stone. If you go to a Gothic cathedral, you may notice that some statues are in relief, while others stand apart from the surrounding stone.

Notice how each freestanding statue in this picture has its own ledge to stand on. You can also just see the canopy that hangs over each statue. You can think of each ledge and canopy as being like a frame for each sculpture. Have you noticed how a frame seems to outline a painting? By clearly separating the painting from the wall with an outline, a frame helps us concentrate on the painting itself. In the sculptures shown here, the ledge and canopy form a niche, a special, separate space for each statue. The niche works the way a frame does, making us concentrate on what's inside it.

We usually think of a statue as something made of hard materials. But a niche helps us see that space is as much part of a sculpture as the stone it's made of. Compare each of the figures in the picture. Even though they are given about the same amount of room to occupy, does the space around each figure look the same? The space is as important as the figure itself because the way the space looks helps us pay attention to the differences in each figure.

Statues flanking a door of the cathedral at Strasbourg, France.

A Little Personality

The figures' differences make each one seem to have personality. Look at the faces on the figures and the way the figures are standing. Notice how, even though each statue is separated from the others by its own space, its head and shoulders are tilted toward the side edge of each niche. Some of the figures seem to be trying to turn to one another, as though they were just starting to speak.

If they were alive, do you think these people would be cheerful or sad, lively or quiet? Do you think they would like one another? What do you think they would say? Remember the mosaics of Ravenna. Would you say that Empress Theodora and her attendants look as though they are trying to talk to one another? The artists who made statues for Gothic cathedrals often wanted people to see how joyous and full of life the faithful were.

Even though these freestanding statues were primarily meant to remind ordinary people of saints, they also helped change the way the walls of the cathedrals look. The statues are part of the cathedral wall, and the niche for each sculpture creates open space on the cathedral wall. Like the stained-glass windows, the freestanding statues on Gothic cathedrals make the walls look more open and airy.

The Beauty of the Natural World

The artists of the Middle Ages were keenly interested in the beauty of the earthly world as well as of the heavenly world. This picture shows carvings of leaves from the hawthorn, maple, and buttercup trees that were commonly found in the area around this cathedral. Notice how carefully the artist carved these so that it would be easy to recognize the leaves. See if you can find some carvings of leaves in the picture of the free-standing statues.

Carvings on the exterior of the cathedral at Southwell, England.

This photograph shows a statue of an imaginary demon, which was intended both to remind people of bad spirits and to scare those spirits away! The drain-spouts of Gothic cathedrals, called gargoyles, were so often decorated with strange, sculpted creatures like this one that we have come to call the statues gargoyles, too.

A famous gargoyle on the cathedral of Notre Dame, Paris, France.

A Feast for the Eyes

Look at the photograph below of Cologne cathedral. In art, the part of an art-work that we can see is called a visual field. In this photograph, the visual field is mostly made up of the face, or facade, of the cathedral. So far we have been looking at and reading about details of Gothic cathedrals such as stained-glass windows and tracery, freestanding sculptures, and carvings of the natural world. Now let's see how all the details relate on the facade of the cathedral.

Do you see a lot of flat wall space or hardly any? Are there lots of the kinds of details we have been looking at, or few? In this cathedral, there are many different shapes packed together.

How do you feel when you try to notice all the details there are to look at? If looking at the cathedral wall was like sitting down to eat a meal, would you be eating a simple meal of soup and bread, or a feast of many different foods? Many people feel that looking at this cathedral is like a feast for the eyes because there is something to study everywhere you look, and because there is much variety in the details. You may also get a feeling of activity because your eyes have to roam around the facade in order to observe the variety of details.

The architect of Cologne cathedral helped create a feeling of richness and activity by packing the front of the cathedral with many details. Most people in the Middle Ages hardly ever left the place they were born. But the cathedral gave the people of Cologne so much to look at, enjoy, and learn about, that, though they would see the cathedral every day of their lives, it always had more to offer them.

Cathedral at Cologne, Germany.

Stretching to the Sky

The many details of the cathedral's facade not only give us a great deal to look at, they also help make the cathedral look especially tall. Let's see how the architect did this. If you trace around every part of the building except the towers, you will see that the shape of the cathedral is basically a rectangle.

Now look closely at the long, strong piers that run up the building. It is easy to see the vertical lines made by the piers. Can you find any horizontal lines in the face of the building? It is harder to see the horizontal lines because large decorations stand in front of them and block your view. Because vertical lines are easy to see and horizontal lines are harder to see, we say that the architect has emphasized vertical lines in his design.

Notice the shape of the windows. The decorations over the doors and windows make a triangle shape. Look at the shape of the towers (towers that end in a point like these are called spires). Where do all the shapes seem to point? They point up!

This cathedral was built to be tall, but the architect has made it seem to stretch even higher by giving the cathedral a long rectangular shape, by emphasizing vertical lines, and by using decorations that reach toward the clouds. All of these things help move our gaze up toward the top of the cathedral and beyond it. Why would the architect do this? In the Middle Ages, heaven was often shown as being in the sky, high above the clouds. The design of the building is meant to remind people of God by pointing toward heaven.

What Makes Gothic Buildings Possible?

You have learned in this section that Gothic cathedrals were built to let in lots of light and to stretch up toward heaven. But in the Middle Ages it was a difficult task to make a building both tall and full of windows. Why? The taller a wall gets, the heavier it gets, and the stronger it has to be to hold up its own weight and the weight of the roof. In a cathedral it is even harder for the walls to hold up the roof when big sections are made of glass windows instead of sturdy stone. Walls alone aren't enough to support cathedrals.

There are several parts of the cathedral that work together to give more support to the whole building. The picture on the facing page shows one of the parts, called a flying buttress. A buttress helps hold something up by

jutting, or projecting, outward. The winglike shape of these particular buttresses led them to be called "flying." The flying buttresses look like piers with
bridges leading to the cathedral wall.

*Some of the flying
buttresses of the
cathedral of Notre Dame,
Paris, France.*

It is easy to feel how flying buttresses support a Gothic cathedral. Stand
with your feet wider than your shoulders. Try to lift one foot off the ground
without moving your hips and chest. Can you feel your body falling over as
you take away the support of your foot? Now put a chair by your side and hold
it as you stand with your feet apart. Lift the foot nearest the chair. Can you feel
lots of energy going down your arm to the chair? Your arm and the chair have
made a flying buttress so that your body can stand straight even when it is
missing the support of one foot.

Vertical Lines in African Arts

The people of Europe in the Middle Ages were not the only ones who used
vertical lines in great buildings to create the effect of even greater height. Long
ago the people of the country of Mali in Africa used vertical lines in some of
their buildings, too. The picture on p. 240 shows the Great Mosque in the
town of Djenné (JEH neh). A mosque is a building that Muslims worship in.

The original mosque was built by the Mali people sometime between A.D.
1100–1300, when most of the leaders of Mali became Muslims and Djenné
became a center of Islamic learning. Legend has it that when the leader at that
time, Konboro, converted to Islam he asked a holy man, "How may I please
God?" One of the things the holy man said was, "Build a mosque. The people
who pray in it will bless your name for centuries." So Konboro turned his own

palace into a mosque. The building was later destroyed, and this
one was built in 1906 to take its
place. A man named Ismalila
Traore made the design based on
the area's traditional style for
mosques.

The Djenné mosque is built
entirely out of mud bricks treated
with oil or butter to make them
waterproof. Just as Gothic cathedrals were centers for the entire
community, the Great Mosque at
Djenné is very important for the
people who live around it. Every
spring the people of Djenné repair any damage caused by wind
or rain. The repair takes place as a contest between each half of the town to see
who can repair their half of the mosque the faster. The replastering begins
very late at night, with a large group of men racing to the mud sites with
baskets to fetch mud, crowds of women balancing buckets of water on their
heads as they walk back from the river, and town elders looking on from their
seats on the terrace walls. Musicians play flutes and drums to cheer the
workers in their task, and children are allowed to play in the mud. Everybody
works carefully, according to the old traditions. Repairing the mosque is fun
for the whole town, but it is also a very important job because without this
kind of regular attention, the building would quickly melt away in the rains.

Even though the shape of the building is a very broad rectangle, we tend to
notice how tall the mosque looks because the long lines of the pointed piers
and the pointed towers emphasize its height rather than its width. The piers
are a characteristic feature of this kind of mosque, and they act as buttresses.
But, as you can see, these buttresses, unlike the Gothic ones, are completely
connected to the building.

Notice the palmwood rods, called *toron*, sticking out from the sides of the
building. They are an important part of the style of this kind of African
mosque and are there not just for decoration, but also to give the people who
plaster the building something to stand on.

Gothic in Modern Times

Even though the Gothic style of architecture was created very long ago, it can still be seen today. Many universities in Europe and the United States are Gothic in style, and paintings sometimes borrow from the Gothic style, too.

This picture, called *American Gothic*, was painted by the modern artist Grant Wood. At first you may not see elements of the Gothic style. Perhaps the stern expression on the couple's faces attracts your attention. Perhaps you notice the neat, clean appearance of the couple and their farmyard. But look at the painting again. Remember that some of the architectural elements that help us recognize the Gothic style are pointed arches and vertical lines. Can you find pointed arches and vertical lines in the farmhouse? Are there other vertical lines in the painting? Notice the prongs in the farmer's pitchfork. See how the three lines of the prongs are repeated in the lines of his overalls?

What Have You Learned?

Think of all the things you have learned in this section. You have learned how important inspiration is for artists. You have seen how looking at the elements of art can help viewers understand an artist's vision. You have learned how space and light are used in buildings to create certain effects. You have learned how architects use windows, spires, sculptures, and decoration to help make buildings look and feel heavy or airy. And you have learned some of the architectural elements that help us recognize the Byzantine style (many domes) and the Gothic style (vertical lines, pointed arches, and flying buttresses).

IV.

MATHEMATICS

Introduction to Mathematics, Grades One through Six

FOR PARENTS AND TEACHERS

Americans do not pay enough attention to mathematics in the early grades. As a proportion of total class time, we spend less time on mathematics and more time on language arts than other countries do. Yet those other countries outshine us not only in math, but also in language arts. Their children's reading and writing levels are as high as or higher than ours by seventh grade. Do they know something we don't?

Because of our poor math showing in international comparisons, discussion about the teaching of math in the United States is in ferment. Experts are debating whether we should burden young children with mental computation, or encourage the use of calculators to relieve children of drudgery and free their minds to understand math concepts. The experts we consulted may disagree about the best techniques for teaching math, but they do agree that we must define with great clarity the outcomes we want to achieve in each grade. The main purpose of the math chapters in this series is to describe these outcomes with clarity and specificity. Achieving these clearly delineated goals will require expert teaching and, of course, many more exercises and problems than we have room to include.

We have arrived at our summary of outcomes by consulting the goals that have been promulgated by the National Research Council and the National Council of Teachers of Mathematics. We have, in addition, coordinated the recommendations of these bodies with the math standards of the nations that produce top results in math achievement at the elementary level—especially France and Japan.

Every successful program for teaching math to young people follows these three cardinal rules of early mathematics education: 1) practice, 2) practice, and 3) practice. Not mindless, repetitive practice, but thoughtful and varied practice. Problems need to be approached from a variety of angles, and where possible connected with physical intuitions and facility at quickly estimating correct results.

Math is potentially great fun, and math skill yields a sense of mastery and self-esteem. The destroyer of joy in mathematics is not practice but anxiety—anxiety that one is mathematically stupid, that one does not have that special numerical talent. But math talent is no more rare than language talent. The number of great mathematicians and the number of great poets per million of population are roughly the same. Yet people experience math anxiety to a much greater degree than language anxiety. Why? Because their early training has denied them systematic familiarity with the vocabulary, grammar, and spelling of mathematics. Those of us adults who experience math anxiety must resolve not to let this same educational wound be inflicted upon our children.

Since intelligent practice and problem-solving activities are essential to learning math, we must stress again that the math section of this book must be regarded as a supplement, not as a sufficient vehicle for teaching mathematics. The section is, in effect, a detailed *summary* of the math that should be mastered in this grade. We have thought it important in this series to include these detailed summaries to help parents and teachers ascertain that children have in fact learned the math they should know in each grade. The math sections should be used in conjunction with problems and activities taken from workbooks, from standard math texts, or from the imaginations of teachers and parents.

Introduction to Fourth-Grade Mathematics

FOR PARENTS AND TEACHERS

In mathematics, fourth grade is a transitional year between the basic work done in earlier grades and the more sophisticated concepts taught in fifth and sixth grades. Students should learn to multiply and divide by several-digit numbers, and they should also solidify their understanding of these operations in a number of ways: through mental arithmetic (particularly exercises involving place value), and through estimation and checking exercises. Their work in geometry should be quite extensive, and should include informal constructions of the various kinds of quadrilaterals as well as area and perimeter problems. Students should also practice converting an amount from one unit of measurement to another, begin working with decimals, and continue simple work with fractions.

Some of the approaches we take to this material are more demanding than is customary in fourth grade in the United States. Emphasis is put, for example, on writing the answer to a division problem as a multiplication and an addition, or on checking multiplication by finding a range in which the product must fall. It is particularly important that these kinds of exercises be expected of all students: students need to have a flexible and secure understanding of these operations for their later work in mathematics. With consistent effort and practice, all students can acquire this secure understanding. In countries that teach mathematics more successfully than we do, the mathematics taught to fourth, fifth, and sixth graders becomes markedly more demanding and sophisticated at each level and leads naturally to algebra and geometry. Students are thus well prepared for algebra and the rest of high school math; whereas in this country, the demands of algebra too often come as a sudden change for which students are not well prepared.

With much and regular practice on the types of problems in this curriculum, students will be well prepared for mathematics in the fifth grade and beyond.

Fourth-Grade Mathematics

Numbers Through Millions

Place Value

10 hundred thousands equal 1 million. We write the number one million in digits as 1,000,000.

A group of three digits is called a period. Beginning at the right, the first three digits are the ones' period, the next three digits are the thousands' period, and the next three digits are the millions' period. Each period is separated by a comma.

millions				thousands				ones		
hundreds	tens	ones		hundreds	tens	ones		hundreds	tens	ones
		4 ,		3	1	5 ,		8	2	5
4	6	2 ,		9	7	7 ,		0	0	3

   millions' period   thousands' period   ones' period

In each period, the pattern of ones, tens, and hundreds repeats itself. Beginning at the right, the values of the places are: ones, tens, hundreds; thousands, ten thousands, hundred thousands; millions, ten millions, hundred millions. Each place has a value 10 times greater than the place to its right. This system of writing numbers is called the decimal system.

"Decimal" means having to do with ten. In the decimal system, the place values are based on groups of 10. You've already been learning how this works, but let's review the basic ideas. In the decimal system, whenever we have 10 of a certain place value, we write it as 1 in the next highest place value. For example, there are *10* tens in *1* hundred. There are *10* hundreds in *1* thousand. How many hundred thousands in 1 million?

When you read a number, always begin with the largest place value. The commas let you know the value of the largest place.

4,315,825

The four is one digit to the left of the millions' comma. It is in the millions' place. 4,315,825 is read, "four million, three hundred fifteen thousand, eight hundred twenty-five."

462,977,003

The four is 3 digits to the left of the millions' comma. It is in the hundred millions' place. 462,977,003 is read, "four hundred sixty-two million, nine hundred seventy-seven thousand, three."

Notice that you write each period separately, using a comma to set them apart:

38,436,509
thirty-eight million,   (millions' period)
four hundred thirty-six thousand, (thousands' period)
five hundred nine   (ones' period)

The Value of Digits

By practicing with numbers in the millions, you can learn to name what place a digit is in and what its value is. For example, in the number

936,455,171

the underlined three is in the millions' period and the ten millions' place. Its value is 30,000,000—thirty million. The underlined four is in the thousands' period and the hundred thousands' place. Its value is 400,000—four hundred thousand.

Another very useful way to look at place value is to see how many of a certain place value a number has. For example, the number 43,289 has 432 hundreds. You can write the number in terms of how many ten thousands, thousands, hundreds, tens, or ones it has. Here is another example: 3,567,859 has 3,567 thousands; it has 3 millions; it has 356,785 tens. Learning to use place value in this way is very useful in both subtraction and division.

Standard Form and Expanded Form

The standard way to write a number is to express it as a single number with digits. For example, we say that 8,532,706 is in standard form. There are two ways to write this number in its expanded form. You can write 8,532,706 = 8,000,000 + 500,000 + 30,000 + 2,000 + 700 + 6. Or, you can multiply each digit by its place value, like this: 8,532,706 = (8 × 1,000,000) + (5 × 100,000) + (3 × 10,000) + (2 × 1,000) + (7 × 100) + (6 × 1).

Can you make up six numbers in the millions and write them in both their standard and expanded forms?

Commas and Place Value

You can write the numbers from 1000 to 9999 with a comma or without a comma. You can write 9,672 or 9672. Either form is correct. However, whenever you write numbers ten thousand or greater, always write them with commas, to mark off each period.

Always 10,403 Never 10403

Comparing Numbers

When you practice comparing numbers in the hundred thousands and millions with the signs >, <, and =, always begin comparing numbers with their largest place values. For example, to compare 286,563 and 97,800, you begin at the left, with the largest places.

Think:

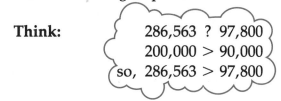

286,563 ? 97,800
200,000 > 90,000
so, 286,563 > 97,800

Remember that the statement "286,563 > 97,800" is called an inequality because it shows how the numbers are *not* equal.

Another way to practice comparing numbers is to first write a double inequality: find a number that fits between the two numbers in order to compare them. 286,563 is greater than 200,000. 200,000 is greater than 97,800.

You write: 286,563 > 200,000 > 97,800
and 286,563 > 97,800

In the first method, you can compare the numbers in your head, and you only need to write a single inequality as an answer. In the second method, you should first write a double inequality, and then the answer.

Rounding

Remember that sometimes you do not need to know an exact value for a number. In these cases you can round numbers. You have learned to round numbers to tens, hundreds, and thousands. Now you can learn to round a number to any place value.

When rounding a number to a certain place value, you must always think: should I round down, to the value of the digit that is in this place, or round up, to the value of the next highest digit?

As an example, we'll round 543,417 to the nearest hundred thousand. When you look in the hundred thousands' place, you see 5 hundred thousands. So your two choices are to round the number down to 500,000, or up to 600,000.

$$500,000 < 5\underline{4}3,417 < 600,000$$

To decide which way to round, always look at the place just to the right of the one to which you are rounding. If the digit to the right is 4 or less, you round down, because the number is closer to the lower round number. If the digit to the right is 5 or greater, you round up because the number is halfway, or more than halfway, between the two round numbers. When a number is exactly halfway between two numbers, you always round up.

In 543,417, the digit to the right of the hundred thousands' place is a 4. You know that 543,417 is closer to 500,000 than it is to 600,000. So you round 543,417 down to 500,000.

Let's round 675,802 to the nearest ten thousand. The digit to the right of the ten thousands' place is a 5. So you know that 675,802 is at least halfway between 670,000 and 680,000. You round 675,802 up to 680,000.

Now you can practice rounding large numbers to the nearest hundred thousand, ten thousand, and thousand in this way. Here are some numbers to start with: 6,734,111; 238,446; 7,052,919. Notice that when you round a number to a certain place value, all the digits to the *right* of that place become zero.

Large Sums and Differences

You add and subtract large numbers using the same addition and subtraction methods you have already learned.

The table shows the populations of some cities in California from the 1980 U.S. Census.

City	Population
Berkeley	103,328
Fresno	217,491
Los Angeles	2,968,528
Sacramento	275,741
San Francisco	678,974

What is the population of all the cities in the table except for Los Angeles? You add those four numbers to find out.

Add from right to left. Regroup as you need to. (Did you know you can regroup in your head? Try it. Remember to check the problem by adding the numbers up.)

$$
\begin{array}{r}
1 \quad 1\,2\,2 \quad 2\,1 \\
1\,0\,3,\,3\,2\,8 \\
2\,1\,7,\,4\,9\,1 \\
2\,7\,5,\,7\,4\,1 \\
+\ 6\,7\,8,\,9\,7\,4 \\
\hline
1,\,2\,7\,5,\,5\,3\,4
\end{array}
$$

The total population of all the cities in the table except Los Angeles is 1,275,534.

How many more people does Los Angeles have than all the other cities combined? You subtract the total you already found for the other cities from the population of Los Angeles.

```
      8 16 7  14 12                 Check:
   2, 9́ 6́ 8́, 5́  2́ 8            1, 6 9 2, 9 9 4
 − 1, 2 7 5, 5  3 4            + 1, 2 7 5, 5 3 4
 ─────────────────            ─────────────────
   1, 6 9 2,  9 9 4             2, 9 6 8, 5 2 8 ✔
```

Los Angeles has 1,692,994 more people than all the other cities combined. Notice how you regroup with ten thousands, hundred thousands, and millions in the same way you have always regrouped. Make sure to check each sum or difference.

---

*S*ince you will often need to find information from tables, here's a table and *some questions you can use for practice:*

Temple Hill Elementary School Lunchroom Supplies	
Apples	523,313
Cartons of milk	2,467,235
Pizzas	755,992
Oatmeal cookies	1,874,005
Juice boxes	983,767
Loaves of bread	81,398

1. *How many more milk cartons than juice boxes does Temple Hill Elementary have?*
2. *Add together all of the food items except for the cookies. How many items does your answer have?*
3. *If you add together the apples and the pizzas, do you have more than the number of oatmeal cookies?*

Mental Addition and Subtraction

Can you think of reasons you might need to be able to add or subtract a pair of two-digit numbers in your head? If you are buying something in a store, for example, it's good to be able to make sure you have received the correct amount of change. There are several techniques that can help you. Let's say you need to add 47 and 28. One way is to add 47 and 30, then subtract 2, instead of adding 47 and 28:

$$47 + 28 = (47 + 30) - 2 = 77 - 2 = 75$$

Or you can break 47 and 28 down into tens and ones and add the tens and ones separately:

$$47 + 28 = (40 + 20) + (7 + 8) = 60 + 15 = 75$$

Now let's look at an example with subtraction: $46 - 27$. You can first subtract the tens in 27 in your head, then subtract the ones.

$$46 - 27 = (46 - 20) - 7 = 26 - 7 = 19$$

Or instead of subtracting 27, you can subtract 30, then add 3:

$$46 - 27 = (46 - 30) + 3 = 16 + 3 = 19$$

Geometry, Part One—Lines and Angles

Planes and Rays

A plane is a flat surface that keeps on going forever in all directions. It has no thickness. The flat figures you have learned about in Books One, Two, and Three—circles and rectangles, for example—are called plane figures because they are part of a plane. Plane figures have definite boundaries that give them their shape, while a plane has no boundaries.

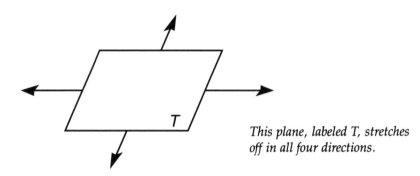

This plane, labeled T, stretches off in all four directions.

Do you remember from Book Two that a line goes on forever in two directions? A ray is part of a line. It has one end point, and continues forever in only *one* direction—away from its end point. You name a ray beginning with its end point. This is ray EF.

Angles

An angle is formed by two rays that have the same end point. The end point is called the vertex of the angle. Here is angle WXY.

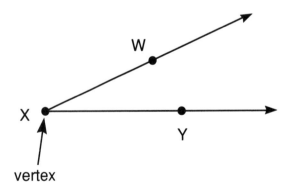

Point X is the vertex of angle WXY. When you name an angle, you always put the vertex in the middle. You can begin by naming either of the other two points, so this angle can also be called angle YXW. The word "angle" is sometimes abbreviated with the sign ∠ like this: ∠YXW.

Types of Angles

There are three kinds of angles: right angles, acute angles, and obtuse angles. Here's what they look like:

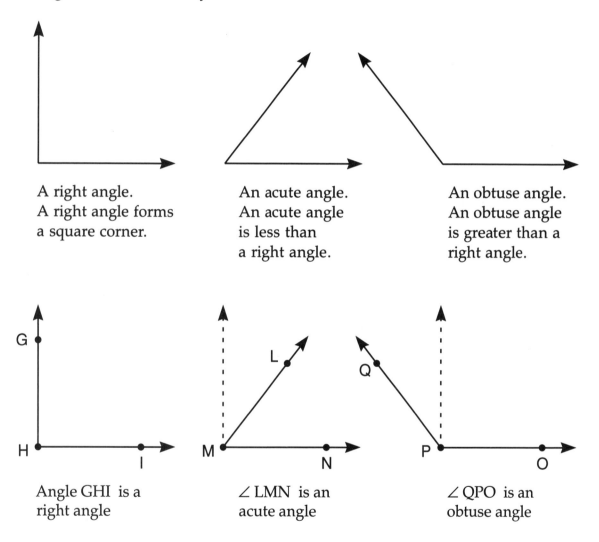

A right angle.
A right angle forms
a square corner.

An acute angle.
An acute angle
is less than
a right angle.

An obtuse angle.
An obtuse angle
is greater than a
right angle.

Angle GHI is a
right angle

∠ LMN is an
acute angle

∠ QPO is an
obtuse angle

With practice, you can learn to identify whether an angle is acute, right, or obtuse. Look around you for angles. What kind of angles do the hands of the clock, the corner of a windowpane, and the shape of a pie slice form?

Perpendicular Lines

When two lines meet, we say they intersect. Here are two intersecting lines.

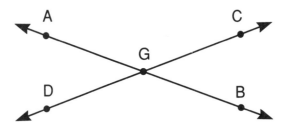

Lines DC and AB intersect at point G. When two lines intersect to form right angles, we say that they are perpendicular.

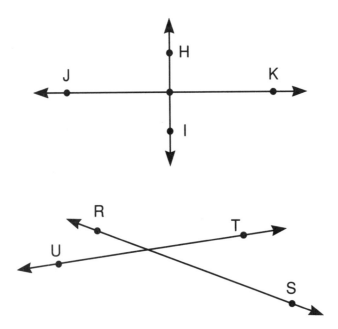

Lines HI and JK are perpendicular. Where they meet, they form 4 right angles. $\overleftrightarrow{RS}$ and $\overleftrightarrow{UT}$ are not perpendicular.

Practice drawing a line perpendicular to another line. You can use an instrument like this triangle that has a right angle. Walk around your house looking for right angles. Can you find 20 right angles?

Parallel Lines

Parallel lines are lines that never intersect. $\overleftrightarrow{BE}$ and $\overleftrightarrow{GH}$ are parallel lines.

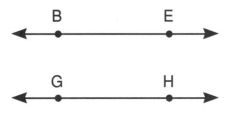

Here is one way to draw a line parallel to another line.

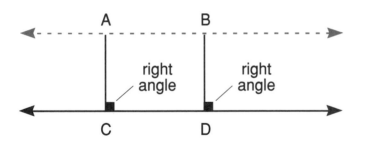

$\overline{AC}$ and $\overline{BD}$ have the same length.

Using a triangle, draw a horizontal line CD. Draw a line segment AC perpendicular to $\overleftrightarrow{CD}$. Draw another line segment BD perpendicular to $\overleftrightarrow{CD}$ and on the same side of the line as $\overline{AC}$. Make sure $\overline{BD}$ is the same length as $\overline{AC}$. Then, draw a second line AB through the end points of $\overline{AC}$ and $\overline{BD}$. Line AB will be parallel to line CD.

Multiplication

Multiplication Review

Remember that multiplication is a quick way of adding the same number over and over again. You can solve $3624 + 3624 + 3624 + 3624 + 3624$ in two ways. You can write the numbers in a column and add them, or you can multiply 3624×5. Last year you learned how to do a multiplication problem like 3624×5: first you multiply $5 \times$ the ones, then $5 \times$ the tens, then $5 \times$ the hundreds, then $5 \times$ the thousands. Then you add those numbers together.

$$
\begin{array}{r}
3\ 6\ 2\ 4 \\
\times\ 5 \\
\hline
\end{array}
\qquad
\begin{array}{r}
3\ 1\ 2 \\
3\ 6\ 2\ 4 \\
\times\ 5 \\
\hline
1\ 8{,}1\ 2\ 0
\end{array}
$$

When you regroup in a multiplication problem, you do not need to write down the numbers you are carrying to the next column. You can remember them. You can write 5×3624 like this:

$$
\begin{array}{r}
3\ 6\ 2\ 4 \\
\times\ 5 \\
\hline
1\ 8{,}1\ 2\ 0
\end{array}
$$

Think: $5 \times 4 = 20$ or 2 tens, 0 ones. Write 0 ones in the ones' place and *remember the 2 tens*. 5×2 tens $= 10$ tens $+ 2$ tens $= 12$ tens. Write 2 in the tens' place and remember the 1 hundred for the hundreds' column. Continue to multiply and add in this way.

A Property of Multiplication

Remember that you can find a product by first multiplying with one part of a number and then multiplying with the rest. Then you add the two partial products together, to find the whole product. Here is an example with 9×4.

$$9 \times 4 = (6+3) \times 4 = (6 \times 4) + (3 \times 4) = 24 + 12 = 36$$
$$9 \times 4 = 36$$

Because of this property of multiplication, there is an easy way to multiply numbers of more than one digit in your head. You can multiply the value in each digit separately, and then add to find the whole product. Practice finding the product of one-digit times two-digit numbers in your head in this way.

Here's an example: $3 \times 27 = \_\_$? You can break this problem down in your head like this:

$$3 \times 27 = (3 \times 20) + (3 \times 7)$$
$$= \quad 60 \quad + \quad 21$$
$$= \quad\quad 81$$

Multiples

24 is a multiple of 6, because $6 \times 4 = 24$. A multiple of a number is the product of that number and any whole number. 36 is also a multiple of 6 because $6 \times 6 = 36$.

Here are some multiples of 6:   6, 12, 18, 24, 30 . . .
Here are some multiples of 7:   7, 14, 21, 28, 35 . . .
Here are some multiples of 10:   10, 20, 30, 40, 50 . . .

Notice that all multiples of 10 end in zero. All whole numbers that end in zero are multiples of 10.

Here are some multiples of 2:   2, 4, 6, 8, 10, 12, 14 . . .

Notice that all the multiples of 2 are even. You can define even numbers this way—even numbers are numbers that are multiples of 2.

Multiplying by Tens

Whenever you multiply a number by ten, you make it ten times as large. In the decimal system, you make a whole number ten times as large just by adding an extra zero to it. So it is easy to multiply by ten—just add an extra zero to the number you're multiplying by ten.

$$
\begin{array}{r} 4 \\ \times\ 1\ 0 \\ \hline 4\ 0 \end{array}
\qquad
\begin{array}{r} 5\ 4 \\ \times\ 1\ 0 \\ \hline 5\ 4\ 0 \end{array}
\qquad
\begin{array}{r} 1\ 8\ 4 \\ \times\ 1\ 0 \\ \hline 1\ 8\ 4\ 0 \end{array}
$$

When you multiply by ten, 4 becomes 40, 54 becomes 540, and 184 becomes 1840.

You can use this knowledge to multiply easily by any multiple of ten. Remember that these are the numbers 10, 20, 30, and so on, up to 90.

You know how to solve 23×6. Now think about 23×60.

$$23 \times 60 = 23 \times (6 \times 10) = (23 \times 6) \times 10$$

So the product of 23×60 is the product of 23×6 times ten:

Write a zero in the ones' place because you are multiplying by tens.

Multiply 6 tens × 23.

$$
\begin{array}{r} 2\ 3 \\ \times\ 6 \\ \hline 1\ 3\ 8 \end{array}
\qquad
\begin{array}{r} 2\ 3 \\ \times\ 6\ 0 \\ \hline 0 \end{array}
\qquad
\begin{array}{r} 2\ 3 \\ \times\ 6\ 0 \\ \hline 1\ 3\ 8\ 0 \end{array}
$$

You can multiply by any multiple of ten in the same way.

Multiplying by Two-Digit Numbers

Once you know how to multiply by tens, you can multiply by any two-digit number. You just break the problem down into two parts: First you multiply by ones, and then you multiply by tens. After this, you add.

Think: 23×58 is $(20 \times 58) + (3 \times 58)$

Multiply 58 by 3 ones.

$$\begin{array}{r} 5\ 8 \\ \times\ 2\ 3 \\ \hline 1\ 7\ 4 \end{array}$$

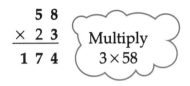
Multiply 3×58

Multiply 58 by 2 tens. Make sure to write a zero in the ones' place.

$$\begin{array}{r} 5\ 8 \\ \times\ 2\ 3 \\ \hline 1\ 7\ 4 \\ 1\ 1\ 6\ 0 \end{array}$$

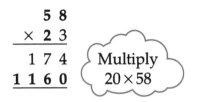
Multiply 20×58

Add.

$$\begin{array}{r} 5\ 8 \\ \times\ 2\ 3 \\ \hline 1\ 7\ 4 \\ 1\ 1\ 6\ 0 \\ \hline 1\ 3\ 3\ 4 \end{array}$$

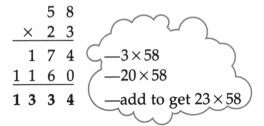
—3×58
—20×58
—add to get 23×58

You can multiply larger numbers by two-digit numbers in the same way. Here are two examples.

$48 \times 372 = (40 + 8) \times 372$
$\qquad = (40 \times 372) + (8 \times 372)$

$$\begin{array}{r} 3\ 7\ 2 \\ \times\ 4\ 8 \\ \hline 2\ 9\ 7\ 6 \\ 1\ 4\ 8\ 8\ 0 \\ \hline 1\ 7{,}8\ 5\ 6 \end{array}$$

— 8×372
— 40×372
— 48×372

$64 \times 2034 = (60 + 4) \times 2034$
$\qquad = (60 \times 2034) + (4 \times 2034)$

$$\begin{array}{r} 2\ 0\ 3\ 4 \\ \times\ 6\ 4 \\ \hline 8\ 1\ 3\ 6 \\ 1\ 2\ 2\ 0\ 4\ 0 \\ \hline 1\ 3\ 0{,}1\ 7\ 6 \end{array}$$

— 4×2034
— 60×2034
— 64×2034

Checking Multiplication

There are two different ways of checking multiplication. In Book Three you learned how to check multiplication by estimation. Estimation lets you know if your answer is "about right"—for example, if the product you came up with has the right place value. You can also check multiplication by changing the order of the factors and multiplying again.

To check this problem,   reverse the order of the factors and multiply.

$$
\begin{array}{r}
6\ 8 \\
\times\ 3\ 7 \\
\hline
4\ 7\ 6 \\
2\ 0\ 4\ 0 \\
\hline
2\ 5\ 1\ 6
\end{array}
\qquad
\begin{array}{r}
3\ 7 \\
\times\ 6\ 8 \\
\hline
2\ 9\ 6 \\
2\ 2\ 2\ 0 \\
\hline
2\ 5\ 1\ 6\ \checkmark
\end{array}
$$

If your answer is correct, the product will be the same both times.

To check a multiplication problem by estimation, round each factor to its greatest place value (you do not need to round one-digit factors). First round each factor down and multiply. Then round each factor up and multiply. The original product should fall between the two estimated products.

To check this problem:
$$
\begin{array}{r}
2\ 5\ 5 \\
\times\ 4\ 9 \\
\hline
2\ 2\ 9\ 5 \\
1\ 0\ 2\ 0\ 0 \\
\hline
1\ 2{,}4\ 9\ 5
\end{array}
$$

Round both factors down and multiply them.

$$
\begin{array}{rcr}
2\ 5\ 5 & \longrightarrow & 2\ 0\ 0 \\
\times\ 4\ 9 & \longrightarrow & \times\ 4\ 0 \\
\hline
& & 8\ 0\ 0\ 0
\end{array}
$$

Round both factors up and multiply them.

$$
\begin{array}{rcr}
2\ 5\ 5 & \longrightarrow & 3\ 0\ 0 \\
\times\ 4\ 9 & \longrightarrow & \times\ 5\ 0 \\
\hline
& & 1\ 5{,}0\ 0\ 0
\end{array}
$$

See if the original product falls between the estimated products:

$$8000 < 12{,}495 < 15{,}000 \checkmark$$

Multiplying Money

You multiply dollars and cents the same way you multiply other numbers. Make sure to put the cents' point and the dollar sign in your answer when you are done.

$$
\begin{array}{r}
\$\ 5.6\ 2 \\
\times\ 8\ 6 \\
\hline
3\ 3\ 7\ 2 \\
4\ 4\ 9\ 6\ 0 \\
\hline
\$\ 4\ 8\ 3.3\ 2
\end{array}
\qquad
\begin{array}{r}
\$\ 6.7\ 0 \\
\times\ \ \ \ 9 \\
\hline
\$\ 6\ 0.3\ 0
\end{array}
$$

When you multiply dollars and cents, the product is always in dollars and cents.

$$
\begin{array}{r}
\$\ 5\ 7 \\
\times\ 4 \\
\hline
\$\ 2\ 2\ 8
\end{array}
$$

In this problem, there are only dollars in the factor. So there are only dollars in the product—no cents.

Multiplying by Hundreds

When you multiply a whole number by ten, you add *one* zero to it. When you multiply a whole number by one hundred, you add *two* zeros to it. Multiplying by one hundred is like multiplying by ten twice.

$$100 \times 6 = (10 \times 10) \times 6 = 10 \times (10 \times 6) = 10 \times 60 = 600$$

6	8 7	9 4 2
× 1 0 0	× 1 0 0	× 1 0 0
6 0 0	8 7 0 0	9 4,2 0 0

To multiply by any hundred, write zeros in the ones' place and the tens' place of the product, because you are multiplying by a hundred. Then multiply. Here is an example.

Write zeros in the ones' place   Multiply.
and the tens' place.

4 8 7	4 8 7
× 3 0 0	× 3 0 0
0 0	1 4 6,1 0 0

Multiplying by Three-Digit Numbers

Once you know how to multiply by hundreds, it is easy to multiply by three-digit numbers. First multiply by the ones, then by the tens, then by the hundreds. Then add. Here is an example.

Multiply by 4 ones.   Multiply by 9 tens.   Multiply by 3 hundreds.

5 6 5	5 6 5	5 6 5
× 3 9 4	× 3 9 4	×3 9 4
2 2 6 0 —4 × 565	2 2 6 0	2 2 6 0
	5 0 8 5 0 —90 × 565	5 0,8 5 0
		1 6 9,5 0 0 —300 × 565
		2 2 2,6 1 0 —add to get
		394 × 565

Practicing Multiplication, Multiplying with Zeros

Often you need to multiply numbers that end in several zeros—for example, when you are checking a multiplication problem by estimation. There is a shortcut for multiplying numbers that end in zeros.

Let's say you want to check this multiplication problem:

$$394 \times 565 = 222{,}610$$
$$300 \times 500 < 222{,}610 < 400 \times 600?$$

You can multiply 300×500 as you would normally. Write two zeros in the product. Multiply 500 by 3.

$$
\begin{array}{r}
5\ 0\ 0 \\
\times\ 3\ 0\ 0 \\
\hline
0\ 0
\end{array}
\qquad
\begin{array}{r}
5\ 0\ 0 \\
\times\ \ 3\ 0\ 0 \\
\hline
1\ 5\ 0{,}0\ 0\ 0
\end{array}
$$

Or you can take a shortcut. You can rule off the zeros at the ends of the numbers, and write *all four* of the zeros in the product right away. Then multiply 5 by 3.

$$
\begin{array}{r}
5|0\ 0 \\
\times\ \ 3|0\ 0 \\
\hline
|0\ 0\ 0\ 0
\end{array}
\qquad
\begin{array}{r}
5|0\ 0 \\
\times\ 3|0\ 0 \\
\hline
15|0{,}0\ 0\ 0
\end{array}
$$

Now multiply 400×600 the short way.

$$
\begin{array}{r}
6|0\ 0 \\
\times\ \ 4|0\ 0 \\
\hline
2\ 4|0{,}0\ 0\ 0
\end{array}
$$

The problem checks:

$$150{,}000 < 222{,}610 < 240{,}000 \checkmark$$

Here is another multiplication problem which can be done easily by ruling off the zeros. Multiply 2000×360.

$$
\begin{array}{r}
3\ 6|0 \\
\times\ \ 2|0\ 0\ 0 \\
\hline
7\ 2|0{,}0\ 0\ 0
\end{array}
$$

Practice setting up multiplication problems in vertical columns when they are given to you horizontally. Since you can multiply in any order, you can choose which number you are going to multiply by to make your work easier.

Multiply 678 × 209. You can multiply these factors in any order. But it is a little easier to multiply 678 by 209, rather than 209 by 678, because 209 has no tens, and you will be able to do this problem in two steps.

Two steps	Three steps
6 7 8	2 0 9
× 2 0 9	× 6 7 8
6 1 0 2	1 6 7 2
1 3 5,6 0 0	1 4 6 3 0
1 4 1,7 0 2	1 2 5,4 0 0
	1 4 1,7 0 2

When one of the digits in the number you are multiplying by is zero, you can skip multiplying by that place because the product of any number and 0 is 0.

Make sure to practice multiplying three-digit numbers times four-digit numbers. For example, multiply 456 × 3084, 2301 × 695, and 443 × 7936. Check each multiplication problem by estimating or by changing the order of the factors.

Mental Multiplication with Zeros

Multiplying in your head with numbers that end in zeros can help you get a good understanding of how multiplication and the decimal system work. When you multiply a whole number by a thousand, you add 3 zeros to it.

Practice solving in your head.

40 × 4 = _____ (160)	4 × _____ = 4000 (1000)
600 × 70 = _____ (42,000)	8 × _____ = 480 (60)
8000 × 8 = _____ (64,000)	_____ × 5 = 1500 (300)

Multiplying Three Numbers

Remember that when you multiply three numbers you can multiply them in any order, but one particular order may be easiest.

Look at $879 \times 5 \times 6$, for example:

$(5 \times 6) \times 879$ is easier than $(879 \times 5) \times 6$.

In this problem, you save time if you multiply 5×6 in your head to get 30, and then multiply 30×879.

Practice multiplying three numbers, choosing an easy way to multiply the numbers if there is one: multiply $3 \times 194 \times 8$ and $73 \times 63 \times 14$.

Would you get a different answer if you multiplied $(16 \times 28) \times 33$ or $(28 \times 33) \times 16$? Find the products to check your answer.

Geometry, Part Two—Kinds of Polygons, Circles

Triangles

Polygons that have three sides are called triangles. The prefix "tri" means three. All triangles have three angles and three sides. They also have three vertices, or points where the sides of the triangle meet.

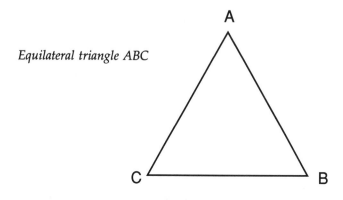

Equilateral triangle ABC

The vertices of triangle ABC are points A, B, and C. Remember that you name polygons by their vertices. Triangles that have three sides of the same length are called equilateral triangles. Because their sides are all of equal length, their angles will have the same measure, too. Triangle ABC is an equilateral triangle.

Triangles that have a right angle are called right triangles. Triangle RPS is a right triangle.

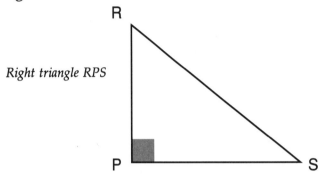

Right triangle RPS

Practice drawing different triangles that have right angles.

Quadrilaterals and Diagonals

The prefix "quadri-" means four and "lateral" means side, so quadrilaterals are polygons with four sides.

Rectangles and squares are quadrilaterals. The figures below are also quadrilaterals.

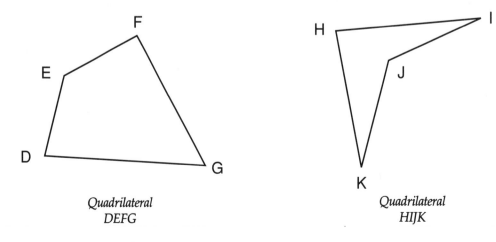

*Quadrilateral
DEFG*

*Quadrilateral
HIJK*

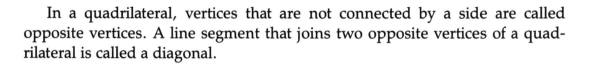

In a quadrilateral, vertices that are not connected by a side are called opposite vertices. A line segment that joins two opposite vertices of a quadrilateral is called a diagonal.

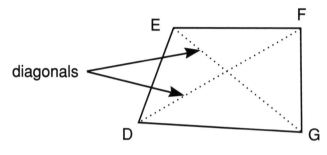

D and F are opposite vertices.
G and E are also opposite vertices.

Segments DF and EG are the diagonals of quadrilateral DEFG.

Kinds of Quadrilaterals

A quadrilateral with only *one* pair of parallel sides is called a trapezoid.

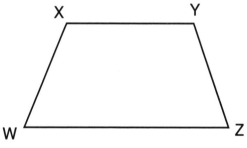

This quadrilateral is a trapezoid.

Quadrilateral WXYZ is a trapezoid. $\overline{XY}$ and $\overline{WZ}$ are parallel.

A quadrilateral with *two* pairs of parallel sides is a parallelogram.

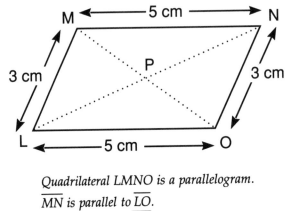

Quadrilateral LMNO is a parallelogram.
$\overline{MN}$ *is parallel to* $\overline{LO}$.
$\overline{NO}$ *is parallel to* $\overline{ML}$.

In a quadrilateral, sides that do not meet at a vertex are called opposite sides. The opposite sides of a parallelogram are parallel: segments MN and LO are parallel; segments ML and NO are parallel. Opposite sides of a parallelogram also have the same length. $\overline{MN}$ and $\overline{LO}$ are both 5 cm long. $\overline{NO}$ and $\overline{ML}$ are both 3 cm long.

The diagonals of a parallelogram divide each other in half at the point where they intersect. So one way to practice drawing parallelograms is to draw two line segments that divide each other exactly in half where they intersect. Then connect their end points to form a parallelogram.

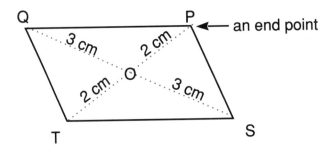

Special Kinds of Parallelograms: Rectangles and Squares

Rectangles and squares are special kinds of parallelograms. Rectangles and squares are parallelograms with four right angles.

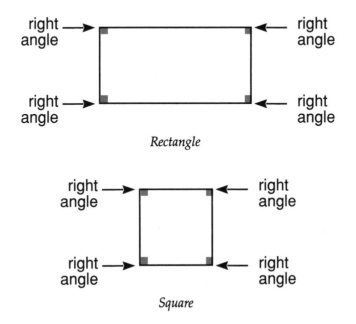

Rectangle

Square

Rectangles can have two sides measuring one length, and two sides measuring a different length. Or, all four sides can be the same length. A rectangle whose four sides are all the same length is called a square.

The diagonals of a rectangle have the same length. That is why one way to form a rectangle is to draw two segments of equal length that divide each other exactly in half, then connect their end points. For example, to draw rectangle ABCD we drew the two red segments of equal length, making sure that they intersected in the middle of each segment. Then we drew segments connecting points A, B, C and D.

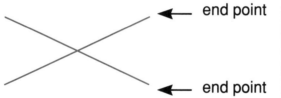
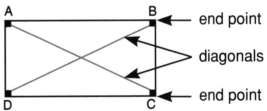

First we drew the two red segments of equal length, making sure they intersect in the middle of each segment.

Then we connected all the endpoints to make rectangle ABCD.

Because a square is a kind of rectangle, the diagonals of a square have the same length. But in a square, the diagonals are also perpendicular to each other. For this reason, to form a square from its diagonals, you must draw line segments that divide each other in half and intersect at right angles. Then you connect their end points.

Square TUSY

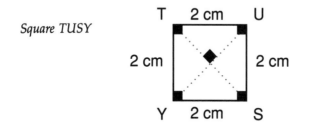

The example below shows you another way to draw a square or rectangle. First we drew segment TU. Then we drew $\overline{UM}$ and $\overline{TO}$ so that they were the same length as $\overline{TU}$ and perpendicular to it. Then we connected points M and O.

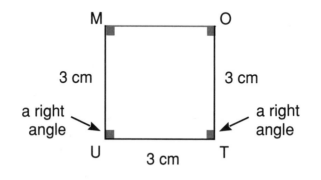

You can also use this method to draw a rectangle.

Circles

A circle is a closed figure, but not a polygon. (Polygons have sides.) All the points on a circle are the same distance from the center of the circle.

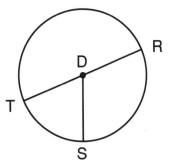

On this circle with center D you can see three segments of equal length: $\overline{DR}$, $\overline{DS}$, and $\overline{DT}$.

A line segment whose end points are the center of a circle and a point on the circle is called a radius of the circle. The plural of radius is radii. Segments DR, DS, and DT are radii of the circle above. Since all the radii of a circle have the same length, we also call the length of any radius of a circle its radius.

A line segment whose end points are both on the circle and which passes through the center of a circle is called a diameter of the circle. Segment RT is a diameter of the circle above. All the diameters of a circle have the same length so we call the length of any diameter of a circle its diameter. The diameter of a circle is always twice as long as its radius.

With a compass, practice drawing circles with a certain radius or a certain diameter. To do this, make a dot for the center of the circle you want to draw, and open the compass to the length of the radius of the circle. Put one point of the compass on a piece of paper. Keeping the point still, swing the arm of the compass around until it draws a circle. Now try opening the compass to a length of 2 centimeters to draw a circle with a radius 2 centimeters.

Since the radius of a circle is always $\frac{1}{2}$ its diameter, open the compass to a length of 3 inches to draw a circle with a diameter of 6 inches.

Division, Part One: One-Digit Divisors

A Way of Writing Division Answers

Let's divide 33 by 5.

$$
\begin{array}{r}
6\ \text{R}3 \\
5\,\overline{)\,3\ 3} \\
-\ \underline{3\ 0} \\
3
\end{array}
$$

33 divided by 5 is 6 with a remainder of 3. 5 is the divisor, and 6 is the quotient. You've already learned that to check a division problem, you multiply the quotient by the divisor and add the remainder.

Now you can begin to use this same form—a multiplication and an addition—as a way of writing division answers.

$$33 = (5 \times 6) + 3 \qquad 3 < 5$$

You write the inequality $3 < 5$ to show that the remainder is less than the divisor. Remember that if the remainder is *not* less than the divisor, the quotient is too small! Here is another example. You can write the answer to 46 divided by 7 like this:

$$46 = (7 \times 6) + 4 \qquad 4 < 7$$

Understanding Remainders

When you do division word problems, you may need to think about your remainders in different ways. Let's look at an example.

Suppose that 31 students are going on a trip in vans, and each van can hold 7 students. How many vans are needed for the trip?

When you divide 31 by 7, you get 4 ($7 \times 4 = 28$) with a remainder of 3. Does the quotient 4 with a remainder of 3 mean you need 4 vans? No. If you only had

4 vans, 3 people would not be able to go on the trip. In this problem the remainder tells us an extra van will be needed. Altogether, 5 vans will be needed for the trip. In this example, having a remainder meant that the quotient had to be increased by one.

Now try the following problem:

> Mrs. Pauli is making surprise baskets for a fund-raising fair. She has 6 baskets and 52 treats to place in them. If she wants all the baskets to have the same number of surprises, how many treats should go in each basket, and how many will be left over for her grandchildren?

Zeros in Quotients

Sometimes when you divide, you need to write a zero as one of the digits of the quotient. As an example we'll look at $922 \div 3$. As you divide, remember to check to make sure that the remainder in each place is less than the divisor.

Divide the hundreds.

$$
\begin{array}{r}
3 \\
3\overline{)9\,2\,2} \\
-\,9 \\
\hline
0
\end{array}
$$

Divide the tens. Since you cannot divide 2 by 3. Write a zero in the tens' place of the quotient.

$$
\begin{array}{r}
3\,0 \\
3\overline{)9\,2\,2} \\
-\,9 \\
\hline
0\,2
\end{array}
$$

Think: $0 < 3$

Bring down the ones.
Divide 22 ones by 3.

Check.

```
    3 0 7 R1
3) 9 2 2
  - 9
    0 2 2
  - 2 1
        1
```

```
      3 0 7
    ×     3
      9 2 1
+         1
      9 2 2  ✔
```

Think: $1 < 3$

Practice writing your answer as a multiplication and an addition, followed by an inequality.

$$922 = (3 \times 307) + 1 \qquad 1 < 3$$

The Number of Digits in a Quotient

Before you begin solving a division problem, figure out first how many digits there will be in the quotient. For example, in the problem $496 \div 3$, you know right away that there will be three digits in the quotient, because you can divide 4 hundreds by 3. Another way to think of this is that $496 > 3 \times 100$. You know the quotient will be at least 100, which is the smallest possible three-digit number.

In the problem $519 \div 6$, you know right away that the quotient will have two digits. You cannot divide the 5 in the hundreds' place by 6 but you can divide 51 tens by 6. Another way to think of this is that $519 < 6 \times 100$. You know the quotient will be less than 100.

Dividing Larger Numbers

You can use the same method to divide larger numbers by one-digit numbers. Here are two examples of dividing a number in the thousands.

```
8) 8 2 5 4
```

```
7) 6 2 3 5
```

You can divide 8 thousands by 8. Begin by dividing the thousands. The quotient will have four digits.

You cannot divide the 6 in the thousands' place by 7. Begin by dividing the 62 hundreds'. The quotient will have 3 digits.

$$\begin{array}{r} 1\ 0\ 3\ 1\ \text{R6} \\ 8\overline{)8\ 2\ 5\ 4} \\ -\ 8 \quad\quad\quad \\ \hline 2\ 5 \quad \\ -\ 2\ 4 \quad \\ \hline 1\ 4 \\ -\ \ 8 \\ \hline 6 \end{array}$$

$$\begin{array}{r} 8\ 9\ 0\ \text{R5} \\ 7\overline{)6\ 2\ 3\ 5} \\ -\ 5\ 6 \quad\quad \\ \hline 6\ 3 \\ -\ 6\ 3 \\ \hline 5 \end{array}$$

In this problem notice that you cannot divide the 2 in the hundreds' place by 8. So you write a zero in the hundreds' place, bring down the 5, and divide 8 into 25 tens.

Remember to check each division problem by multiplication and addition.

Mental Division

Sometimes you can do a division problem in your head, without needing to write out all the steps. Here are two examples.

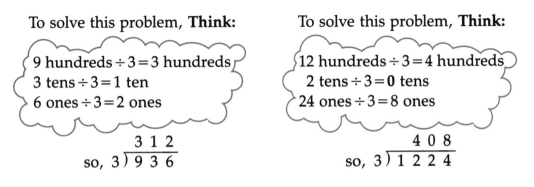

$$3\overline{)9\ 3\ 6} \qquad\qquad 3\overline{)1\ 2\ 2\ 4}$$

To solve this problem, **Think:**

> 9 hundreds ÷ 3 = 3 hundreds
> 3 tens ÷ 3 = 1 ten
> 6 ones ÷ 3 = 2 ones

To solve this problem, **Think:**

> 12 hundreds ÷ 3 = 4 hundreds
> 2 tens ÷ 3 = 0 tens
> 24 ones ÷ 3 = 8 ones

$$\text{so, } 3\overline{)9\ 3\ 6}^{\ 3\ 1\ 2} \qquad\qquad \text{so, } 3\overline{)1\ 2\ 2\ 4}^{\ 4\ 0\ 8}$$

Now you can try solving $6\overline{)1\ 8\ 6\ 6}$ or $7\overline{)7\ 4\ 9}$ in your head.

Factors, Common Factors

A number that divides another number evenly, without a remainder, is called a factor of that number. For example, 4 is a factor of 20, because 4 divides evenly into 20 without leaving a remainder. All the factors of 20 are: 1, 2, 4, 5, 10, 20. All the factors of 24 are: 1, 2, 3, 4, 6, 8, 12, 24.

20 and 24 have three factors in common: 1, 2, and 4. Factors shared by two or more numbers are called common factors.

Notice that 20 has 1 and 20 as factors and that 24 has 1 and 24 as factors. Every number always has at least 1 and itself as factors. Can you explain why this rule is true?

You can divide all even numbers by 2. All even numbers have 2 as a factor.

Practice finding factors and common factors. Find all the factors of 28, 12, 36, 33. Find all the common factors of 28 and 42, of 30 and 45, and of 21 and 63.

Common Multiples

Remember that 18 is a multiple of 6, because $6 \times 3 = 18$. 18 is also a multiple of 9, because $9 \times 2 = 18$. We say that 18 is a common multiple of 6 and 9. Another common multiple of 6 and 9 is 36, because $6 \times 6 = 36$ and $9 \times 4 = 36$. Practice finding common multiples. For example, find three common multiples for 4 and 6.

Division, Part Two: Two-Digit Divisors

Dividing by Tens

When dividing by tens, remember that division is the opposite of multiplication. Here are two examples.

$$30\overline{)90} \qquad\qquad 60\overline{)195}$$

To solve this problem, **Think:** what $\times 30 = 90$? Try different numbers.

$$2 \times 30 = 60$$
$$3 \times 30 = 90$$

$$
\begin{array}{r}
3 \\
3\,0\,\overline{)\,9\,0} \\
-\,9\,0 \\
\hline
0
\end{array}
$$
—Subtract 30×3

Think: $0 < 30$

To solve this problem, **Think:** what $\times 60$ is about 195?

$$60 \times 2 = 120$$
$$\mathbf{60 \times 3 = 180}$$
$$60 \times 4 = 240$$
$$60 \times 4 \text{ is too large}$$

$$
\begin{array}{r}
3 \text{ R15} \\
6\,0\,\overline{)\,1\,9\,5} \\
-\,1\,8\,0 \\
\hline
1\,5
\end{array}
$$
—Subtract 60×3

Think: $15 < 60$

With practice, you will get used to multiplying different possible quotients with the divisor in your head, until you find the quotient that is about right.

Dividing by Two-Digit Numbers

When the divisor is a two-digit number, but not an even ten, round it to the nearest ten to estimate what the quotient will be. Here is an example.

$$2\,8\,\overline{)\,6\,4\,0}$$

To divide the 64 tens by 28, round 28 to 30.
Think: what $\times 30$ is about 64?
$2 \times 30 = 60$.

To divide the 80 ones by 28.
Think: what $\times 30$ is about 80?

$$\mathbf{2 \times 30 = 60}$$
$$3 \times 30 = 90$$
$$3 \times 30 \text{ is too large.}$$

$$
\begin{array}{r}
2 \\
2\,8\,\overline{)\,6\,4\,0} \\
-\,5\,6 \\
\hline
8
\end{array}
$$
—Subtract 28×2

Think: $8 < 28$

$$
\begin{array}{r}
2\ 2 \text{ R24} \\
2\,8\,\overline{)\,6\,4\,0} \\
-\,5\,6 \\
\hline
8\,0 \\
-\,5\,6 \\
\hline
2\,4
\end{array}
$$
—Subtract 28×2

Think: $24 < 28$

Check by multiplying the quotient by the divisor and adding the remainder. Practice writing your answer as a multiplication and an addition, followed by an inequality.

$$
\begin{array}{r}
2\ 2 \\
\times\ 2\ 8 \\
\hline
1\ 7\ 6 \\
4\ 4\ 0 \\
\hline
6\ 1\ 6 \\
+\ \ \ 2\ 4 \\
\hline
6\ 4\ 0
\end{array}
\qquad 640 = (28 \times 22) + 24 \qquad 24 < 28 \quad ✔
$$

Adjusting the Quotient

Sometimes when you round the divisor to the nearest ten, the quotient you try will be too large or too small. Then you need to *adjust* the quotient. Here's an example.

$$36 \overline{)146}$$

You can't divide 14 tens by 36. Divide 146 ones by 36. Round 36 to 40. $40 \times 3 = 120$. Try 3 as a quotient.

$$
\begin{array}{r}
3 \\
36 \overline{)146} \\
-\ 108 \\
\hline
3\ 8
\end{array}
\qquad 38 > 36
$$

The remainder is greater than the divisor. So the quotient you tried was too small. Make the quotient one number larger. Try 4.

$$
\begin{array}{r}
4\ \text{R}2 \\
36 \overline{)146} \\
-\ 144 \\
\hline
2
\end{array}
$$

$$146 = (36 \times 4) + 2 \qquad 2 < 36$$

Here's another example for you to try.

$$13\overline{)851}$$

Divide 85 tens by 13. Round 13 to 10. What $\times 10$ is about 85? $8 \times 10 = 80$. Try 8 tens.

$$
\begin{array}{r}
8 \\
13\overline{)851} \\
-104 \\
\end{array}
$$

104 tens is much larger than 85 tens. You need to try a quotient that is quite a bit smaller. Try 6 tens. 6 works as the quotient for $85 \div 3$.

Now divide the 71 ones. Try using 5.

$$
\begin{array}{r}
65 \text{ R6} \\
13\overline{)851} \\
-78 \\
\hline
71 \\
-65 \\
\hline
6 \\
\end{array}
$$

$$851 = (13 \times 65) + 6 \qquad 6 < 13$$

Always remember whether you have rounded the divisor up or down to find a trial quotient. Once you have found a trial quotient, such as 8 for $13\overline{)85}$ in the problem above, multiply 13×8 in your head to see whether your trial quotient is about right. Being able to multiply combinations like 13×8 in your head makes long division much quicker and easier.

Dividing Thousands

You divide numbers in the thousands by two-digit numbers in the same way.

To solve $32\overline{)6659}$, follow these steps:
1) Divide 66 hundreds by 32.

2) Bring down the 5 tens. You cannot divide 25 tens by 32. Write a zero in the tens' place of the quotient.
3) Bring down the 9 ones. Divide 259 ones by 32. **Think:** what ×30 is about 259?
4) Check your work by multiplying the quotient by the divisor, and adding the remainder to that product.

Check:

```
           2 0 8 R3              2 0 8
  3 2 ) 6 6 5 9               ×  3 2
      − 6 4                     4 1 6
        2 5 9              6 2 4 0
      − 2 5 6              6 6 5 6
            3              +       3
                           6 6 5 9  ✔
```

Practice writing your answer like this:

$$6659 = (32 \times 208) + 3 \qquad 3 < 32$$

Long division is a very good way to practice both multiplication and division, and to learn about the different sizes of numbers. Here are a few long division problems you can use for practice: $39\overline{)\,4132}$, $27\overline{)\,1007}$, $45\overline{)\,2503}$.

Estimating Quotients

When you estimate a quotient, you can round the dividend to a number that makes the division easy, rather than to the greatest place value. Here are two examples that show you how to apply this method.

Estimate $6\overline{)\,3\,8\,3}$
Round the dividend (383) to 360 because you can divide 360 by 6 easily. You cannot divide 400 by 6 easily.

Estimate $2\,8\overline{)\,1\,1\,4\,3}$
Round the divisor to the greatest place value. 28 rounds to 30. 30 does not go into 1000 easily. 30 does go into 1200 easily.

$$\begin{array}{r} 6\,0 \\ 6\,\overline{)\,3\,6\,0} \end{array} \qquad\qquad \begin{array}{r} 4\,0 \\ 3\,0\,\overline{)\,1\,2\,0\,0} \end{array}$$

$383 \div 6$ is about 60. $\qquad\qquad$ $1143 \div 28$ is about 40.

Practice estimating quotients in this way before you divide, to get an idea of about what the answer will be.

Roman Numerals, Time

Roman Numerals

The numerals we use most often—the digits 0, 1, 2, 3, 4, 5, 6, 7, 8, 9—are called Arabic numerals. But you may also come across Roman numerals on clocks and in books.

Here are the Roman numerals from 1 to 10. Look at them carefully, especially the numerals for 4 and 9.

I II III IV V VI VII VIII IX X

Here are the Roman numerals from 10 to 100, counting by tens:

X XX XXX XL L LX LXX LXXX XC C

If you learn the values of the following Roman numerals, you can use these symbols to write numbers into the thousands.

I is 1.	X is 10.	C is 100.	M is 1000.
V is 5.	L is 50.	D is 500.	

Here are two rules:

1) When a Roman numeral that is the same size or smaller comes *after* another Roman numeral, you *add* their values together.

XV is $(10+5)$, or 15 $\qquad$ XXX is $(10+10+10)$, or 30

2) When a Roman numeral that is smaller comes right *before* one that is larger, you *subtract* the smaller one from the larger one.

IV is (5 − 1), or 4   IX is (10 − 1), or 9   XL is (50 − 10), or 40
XC is (100 − 10), or 90

Often you need to use both of these rules to write numbers in Roman numerals. These examples show you how grouping numbers within a long Roman numeral helps you read it:

CDXLVIII is 448

$$
\begin{array}{ccc}
\text{CD} & \text{XL} & \text{VIII} \\
(500-100) + (50-10) & + & 8 \\
400 \quad + \quad 40 & + & 8
\end{array}
$$

MCMLXXXVII is 1987

$$
\begin{array}{cccc}
\text{M} & \text{CM} & \text{LXXX} & \text{VII} \\
1000 + (1000-100) + & 80 & + & 7
\end{array}
$$

We often write a year number like 1987 in Roman numerals. Practice turning numbers that are in Roman numerals, like MCMLXXXVII, into Arabic numerals. Also practice turning numbers that are in Arabic numerals, like 342, 2001, 1215, and 1984, into Roman numerals. What do you notice about writing a number like 2938 in Roman numerals as opposed to Arabic numerals?

Changing Units of Time

There are 24 hours in 1 day.
There are 60 minutes in 1 hour.
There are 60 seconds in 1 minute.

Learn to write amounts of time in different units.

How many minutes are there in 5 hours and 11 minutes?

To find out the answer to this question, multiply 5 by 60 to find how many minutes are in 5 hours. Then add 11 minutes. $(5 \times 60) + 11 = 300 + 11 = 311$. There are 311 minutes in 5 hours and 11 minutes.

How many minutes and seconds are there in 147 seconds?

To find out the answer to this question, divide 147 by 60 to find how many minutes are in 147 seconds. The remainder will be how many seconds are left over that are not part of a whole minute.

$$
\begin{array}{r}
2 \ \text{R27} \\
6\,0\,)\overline{1\,4\,7} \\
-\ 1\,2\,0 \\
\hline
2\,7
\end{array}
$$

There are 2 minutes and 27 seconds in 147 seconds.

Adding and Subtracting Time

When you add and subtract time you may need to regroup, but in a different way. Instead of regrouping so that 10 ones make 1 ten, when you add hours and minutes, regroup 60 minutes as 1 hour whenever there are 60 minutes or more.

Here is an example of adding two times:

A train journey lasts 7 hours and 45 minutes. If the train leaves at 1:43 P.M., when will it arrive at its destination?

You add:

hours minutes

```
      1
   1  :  4 3
 + 7  :  4 5
 ─────────────
         8̶ 8     88 minutes = 1 hour 28 minutes
   9  :   2 8     Add the 1 hour to the other hours.
```

The train will arrive at 9:28 P.M.

You add or subtract minutes and seconds in the same way. When you subtract minutes and seconds, you may need to regroup 1 minute as 60 seconds. Here is an example. Can you find the difference of two times?

Emily ran a race in 37 minutes and 22 seconds. Stella ran it in 28 minutes and 47 seconds. How much faster was Stella's time?

Working with Time Through Noon or Midnight

12 midnight   8:30 A.M.   12 noon   3:00 P.M.   12 midnight

When time switches from A.M. to P.M. at 12 noon, we begin counting hours over again. We do the same thing at 12 midnight, when the time switches from P.M. to A.M. That is why it can take more than one step to figure out the difference between two times when one is A.M. and the other is P.M.

The plane took off at 10:45 A.M. It landed at 1:25 P.M. How long was the flight?

There are different ways you can solve this problem. Here is one. Find out how much time it is from 10:45 A.M. to noon. Then add the time after noon.

Time from 10:45 A.M. to 12:00 noon.

$$
\begin{array}{r}
1\,2 : 0\,0 \\
-\,1\,0 : 4\,5 \\
\end{array}
\quad \text{Regroup} \quad
\begin{array}{r}
5\ 10 \\
1\,1 : \cancel{6}\ \cancel{0} \\
-\,1\,0 : 4\,5 \\
\hline
1 : 1\,5 \\
\end{array}
$$

Add the time from noon to 1:25 P.M., which is 1:25.

$$
\begin{array}{r}
1 : 1\,5 \\
+\,1 : 2\,5 \\
\hline
2 : 4\,0 \\
\end{array}
$$

The flight was 2 hours and 40 minutes long.

Here is another kind of problem to practice. What time is 4 hours before 2:15 P.M.? **Think:** 2 hours before 2:15 P.M. is 12:15 P.M. 2 hours before 12:15 P.M. is 10:15 A.M. So 10:15 A.M. is 4 hours before 2:15 P.M. Counting in this way is another way you can solve problems that go between A.M. and P.M.

Fractions

Equivalent Fractions, Fractions in Lowest Terms

Remember that even if two fractions have different numbers in their numerators and denominators, if they name the same amount they are equivalent.

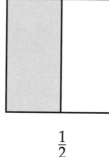

$$\frac{1}{2} \qquad = \qquad \frac{3}{6}$$

You can make an equivalent fraction by dividing or multiplying both the numerator and the denominator by the same number. Here are two examples:

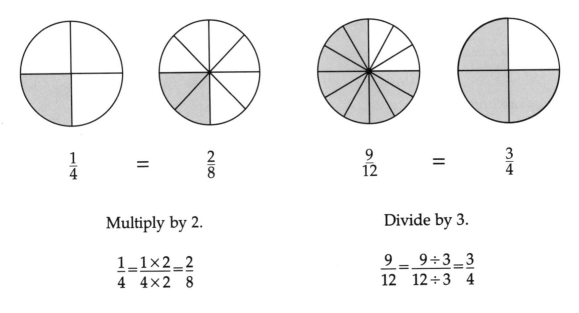

$$\frac{1}{4} \qquad = \qquad \frac{2}{8} \qquad\qquad \frac{9}{12} \qquad = \qquad \frac{3}{4}$$

Multiply by 2.   Divide by 3.

$$\frac{1}{4}=\frac{1\times2}{4\times2}=\frac{2}{8} \qquad\qquad \frac{9}{12}=\frac{9\div3}{12\div3}=\frac{3}{4}$$

A fraction is in lowest terms when its numerator and denominator have no common factor greater than 1. So, to put a fraction in lowest terms, divide its numerator and denominator by common factors, until they have no common factor left greater than 1.

Here are two examples. Put $\frac{3}{9}$ and $\frac{12}{18}$ in lowest terms.

1) $\frac{3}{9}$ You can divide both 3 and 9 by 3. They have 3 as a common factor.

$$\frac{3}{9}=\frac{3\div3}{9\div3}=\frac{1}{3}$$

1 and 3 have no common factor greater than 1. $\frac{1}{3}$ is in lowest terms.

2) $\frac{12}{18}$ You can divide both 12 and 18 by 2.

$$\frac{12}{18}=\frac{12\div2}{18\div2}=\frac{6}{9}$$

You can divide both 6 and 9 by 3.

$$\frac{6 \div 3}{9 \div 3} = \frac{2}{3}$$

There are no more common factors greater than 1. $\frac{12}{18} = \frac{2}{3}$ and $\frac{2}{3}$ is in lowest terms.

You could have done this problem in one step by noticing that 12 and 18 have 6 as a common factor. 6 is the greatest common factor of 12 and 18.

$$\frac{12 \div 6}{18 \div 6} = \frac{2}{3}$$

When you divide the numerator and denominator by their greatest common factor, you put a fraction into lowest terms in one step.

Improper Fractions and Mixed Numbers

When the numerator of a fraction is equal to or greater than the denominator, the fraction is called an improper fraction. Here are some examples of improper fractions: $\frac{5}{5}$, $\frac{7}{4}$, $\frac{12}{3}$, $\frac{18}{5}$. Improper fractions should be written as whole numbers or mixed numbers (remember, mixed numbers have one part that's a whole number and one part that's a fraction, like $2\frac{2}{3}$).

The bar in a fraction means the same thing as the division sign. $\frac{18}{5}$, $18 \div 5$ and $5\overline{)18}$ all name the same number. So to write $\frac{18}{5}$ as a mixed number, do the division problem:

$$\begin{array}{r} 3 \\ 5\overline{)1\ 8} \end{array}$$

$\frac{18}{5}$ is the same as the mixed number $3\frac{3}{5}$. Notice how you write the remainder in this division as a fraction instead of "R3." The remainder (3) becomes the numerator of the fraction. The divisor (5) becomes the denominator of the fraction. A remainder always shows that there is a fractional part left over after a division. You can go back to all the division problems you have done and write the remainders as fractions.

Write the improper fraction $\frac{9}{9}$ as a mixed number or a whole number.

$$9\overline{)9} \quad \frac{1}{} \qquad \text{so, } \tfrac{9}{9}=1.$$

Remember that any number divided by itself is 1. (All division problems can be written as fractions.) So all fractions with numerators equal to their denominators are equal to 1.

$$\tfrac{2}{2},\ \tfrac{3}{3},\ \tfrac{1}{1},\ \tfrac{100}{100},\ \tfrac{197}{197} \text{ all equal 1.}$$

When an improper fraction's denominator divides its numerator without a remainder, the fraction equals a whole number.

$$\tfrac{12}{4} \longrightarrow 4\overline{)12} \qquad \text{so, } \tfrac{12}{4}=3.$$
$$-\underline{12}$$
$$0$$

When you write an improper fraction as a mixed number, make sure to write the fractional part in lowest terms.

Write $\frac{34}{8}$ as a mixed number in lowest terms.

$$8\overline{)34} \quad 4\tfrac{2}{8}$$
$$-\underline{32}$$
$$2$$

Write the $\frac{2}{8}$ part of $4\frac{2}{8}$ in lowest terms.

$$4\tfrac{2}{8}=4\tfrac{2\div2}{8\div2}=4\tfrac{1}{4}$$

Now try your own hand at changing some improper fractions to whole numbers or mixed numbers in lowest terms. You can start with $\frac{25}{3}$, $\frac{14}{4}$, $\frac{25}{5}$, $\frac{56}{10}$.

Writing Remainders as Fractions

Sometimes it makes more sense to write the remainder in a division problem as a fraction. Here is an example. Peter wants to divide a piece of ribbon 15 inches long into 4 equal lengths. How long should he make each length?

He should make each length $3\frac{3}{4}$ inches long. (It would not make much sense to say that he should make each length 3 inches remainder 3 long!) Write the remainder in a division problem as a fraction when it will help the answer make sense.

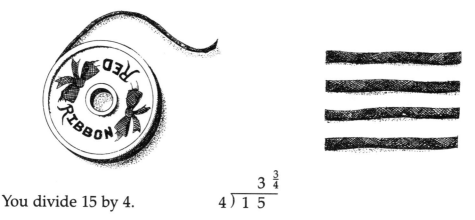

You divide 15 by 4.

$$4\overline{)15} \quad 3\tfrac{3}{4}$$

Adding and Subtracting Fractions

To add fractions that have the same denominator, add the numerators. The denominator stays the same. The picture in the example shows you why you add this way. You are adding the equal parts shown in each numerator. You are not changing the size of the equal parts shown in the denominators.

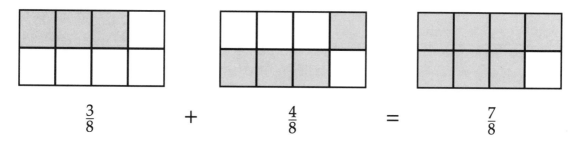

$$\frac{3}{8} \qquad + \qquad \frac{4}{8} \qquad = \qquad \frac{7}{8}$$

Practice adding fractions that have the same denominator. Make sure to write the sum in lowest terms. If the sum is an improper fraction, write it as a whole number or a mixed number in lowest terms. Here are three examples.

$$\frac{5}{9}+\frac{7}{9}=\frac{12}{9}=1\frac{3}{9}=1\frac{1}{3} \qquad \frac{5}{12}+\frac{1}{12}=\frac{6}{12}=\frac{1}{2} \qquad \frac{7}{13}+\frac{6}{13}=\frac{13}{13}=1$$

You subtract two fractions that have the same denominator by subtracting the numerators. The denominators remain the same. Here is an example.

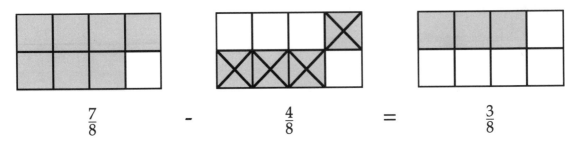

$$\frac{7}{8} \quad - \quad \frac{4}{8} \quad = \quad \frac{3}{8}$$

When you subtract fractions, make sure to write the difference in lowest terms. Here are two examples.

$$\frac{5}{16} - \frac{3}{16} = \frac{2}{16} = \frac{1}{8} \qquad \qquad \frac{5}{12} - \frac{5}{12} = \frac{0}{12} = 0$$

Notice that $\frac{0}{12} = 0$. In $\frac{0}{12}$, you are talking about 0 of 12 equal parts, or 0. Also, $0 \div 12 = 0$. All fractions with a numerator of 0 equal 0.

Decimals

Decimals: Tenths

You can write the fraction $\frac{1}{10}$ as the decimal 0.1. You read both the same way: you say, "one tenth."

The period to the left of the 1 is called a decimal point. The decimal point shows that the value of the digits to its right is anywhere between 0 and 1, like a fraction. A decimal is any number that uses places to the right of the decimal point to show a fraction.

The first place to the right of the decimal point is the tenths' place.

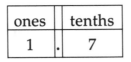

ones		tenths
1	.	7

You can write the mixed number $1\frac{7}{10}$ as the decimal 1.7. You read both the same way: you say, "one and seven tenths."

Decimals: Hundredths

The second place to the right of the decimal point is the hundredths' place. $\frac{1}{100}$ can also be written 0.01.

ones		tenths	hundredths
0	.	0	1

You read both in the same way: "one hundredth."

$2\frac{47}{100}$ =

ones		tenths	hundredths
2	.	4	7

You read both as, "two and forty-seven hundredths."

Notice that when there are both tenths and hundredths in a decimal, you read the tenths and hundredths together in terms of hundredths. Also remember to put an "and" between the whole number part and the fractional part of a decimal, just as in mixed numbers.

Decimals: Thousandths

The third place to the right of the decimal point is the thousandths' place. You can write $\frac{1}{1000}$ as 0.001.

ones		tenths	hundredths	thousandths
0	.	0	0	1

You read both in the same way: "one thousandth."

Notice that as you move from left to right, each place value gets 10 times smaller: first tenths, then hundredths, then thousandths. In the decimal system (the "ten" system), each place has a value ten times smaller than the one to its left.

$$3\frac{857}{1000} = 3.857$$

You read both as "three and eight hundred fifty-seven thousandths." Notice that, because there are thousandths in the decimal, you read the tenths and hundredths in terms of thousandths.

Reading and Writing Decimals, Decimals as Fractions

Practice writing decimals in words. 0.27 is twenty-seven hundredths; 3.8 is three and eight tenths. Notice that you do not reduce eight tenths $\left(\frac{8}{10}\right)$ to four fifths $\left(\frac{4}{5}\right)$. Decimals always have a denominator of 10, 100, 1000, 10,000, etc.

Also practice writing decimals that are in words with digits. Three hundred fifty-four thousandths is 0.354. Five hundred and fourteen hundredths is 500.14.

Practice writing decimals in expanded form. 176.04 is $100 + 70 + 6 + 0.04$. $400 + 5 + 0.2 + 0.007$ is 405.207.

You should also be able to write decimals as fractions and fractions as decimals. $\frac{39}{100}$ can be written 0.39; and 0.02 can be written $\frac{2}{100}$.

Writing Decimals with Zeros

Because the decimal point shows you the value of each digit in a decimal, you can add zeros *after the last digit* of a decimal without changing its value. You can also add zeros *before the decimal point*. All the decimals below are equal.

$$0.5 = 0.50 = 00.50 = 00.500 = .5$$

$0.5 = .5$ You do not have to write a zero before the decimal point. It is a good idea to do so, though, so people notice that there is a decimal point.

In the same way, you can add a decimal point and zeros to whole numbers, without changing them.

$$5 = 5.0 = 5.00 = 5.000$$

No matter how many zeros are added after the decimal point, the decimal point shows that 5 is in the ones' place.

Learn to simplify decimals that have extra zeros.

$$0.120 = 0.12 \text{ but you cannot simplify } 0.102$$
$$37.00 = 37 \text{ but you cannot simplify } 37.004$$

Reading Decimals on a Number Line

We can show decimals on a number line.

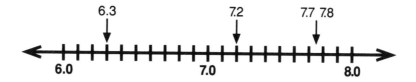

On this number line, each mark shows another tenth. The first arrow is at 6.3. The second arrow is at 7.2. The third arrow is between 7.7 and 7.8. You can see from the number line that $7.2 > 7$. You can also write 7 as 7.0 to make it easier to compare the two numbers: $7.2 > 7.0$. When you compare two decimals, you can add zeros after the last digit of one of them so that they have the same number of places to the right of the decimal point.

On this number line, each mark shows another hundredth. The first arrow is at 7.77. The second arrow is at 7.82.

Comparing Decimals

Remember that when you compare numbers, you start with their greatest place values.

Compare 7.77 and 7.82.

Compare the ones. $7 = 7$
Compare the tenths. $0.7 < 0.8$
So $7.77 < 7.82$

Compare 7.77 and 7.7.
(Remember that you can write
7.7 as 7.70. So compare 7.77
and 7.70.)

Compare the ones. 7=7
Compare the tenths. 0.7=0.7
Compare the hundredths 0.07 > 0.00
So 7.77 > 7.7

Practice comparing decimals in problems like these. Remember the ways in which you can add zeros to decimals without changing their value.
0.04 < 0.27,   0.562 > 0.56 (0.562 > 0.560),   1.02 > 0.102,   and   0.2=0.20
Practice writing numbers that are between two decimals. For example, write four numbers between 6.74 and 7.23.

Rounding Decimals

You round decimals the same way you round whole numbers. To decide whether to round a decimal up or down, look at the digit to the right of the place to which you are rounding.

Round 6.85 to the nearest tenth. Look at the digit to the right of the tenths' place. 6.85 is at least halfway between 6.8 and 6.9. So you round 6.85 up to 6.9.

Round 7.453 to the nearest hundredth. Look at the digit to the right of the hundredths' place. 7.453 is less than halfway between 7.45 and 7.46. So you round 7.453 down to 7.45.

Rounding a decimal to the nearest *whole* number means rounding it to the ones' place, so that there is no fractional part left. Round 76.47 to the nearest whole number. Look at the digit to the right of the ones' place. 76.4 is less than halfway between 76 and 77. So you round 76.47 down to 76.

Practice rounding to the underlined place value in problems like these:

837.5 ⟶ 838   9.258 ⟶ 9.26   2.417 ⟶ 2.4   36.06 ⟶ 36.1

Adding and Subtracting Decimals

You add and subtract decimals the same way you add and subtract whole numbers. You must make sure the decimal points and the place values are lined up correctly. Line up the tenths with the tenths, the hundredths with the hundredths, and the thousandths with the thousandths.

Add 0.167 and 2.346.

$$
\begin{array}{r}
0.1\ 6\ 7 \\
+\ 2.3\ 4\ 6 \\
\hline
2.5\ 1\ 3
\end{array}
$$

Make sure to put the decimal point in your answer.

Subtract 1.846 from 5.072

$$
\begin{array}{r}
4\ \ 10\ 6\ 12 \\
\cancel{5}.\cancel{0}\ \cancel{7}\ \cancel{2} \\
-\ 1.8\ 4\ 6 \\
\hline
3.\ 2\ 2\ 6
\end{array}
$$

Make sure to put the decimal point in your answer.

Sometimes it is helpful to put in zeros when you are adding decimals to help you line up the place values correctly. It is not necessary to add zeros, however, as long as you can keep the place values straight.

Add $9.307 + 8 + 0.53 + 6.2$.

One way is to put in decimal points and zeros.

$$
\begin{array}{r}
9.3\ 0\ 7 \\
8.0\ 0\ 0 \\
0.5\ 3\ 0 \\
+\ 6.2\ 0\ 0 \\
\hline
2\ 4.0\ 3\ 7
\end{array}
$$

Another way is to leave the numbers as they are.

$$
\begin{array}{r}
9.3\ 0\ 7 \\
8 \\
0.5\ 3 \\
+\ 6.2 \\
\hline
2\ 4.0\ 3\ 7
\end{array}
$$

When you subtract decimals, often you *must* put in zeros. Here is an example. When you subtract 2.63 from 5, you must write 5 with a decimal point and two zeros, to match 2.63. Then subtract.

$$
\begin{array}{r}
4\ 9\ 10 \\
\cancel{5}.\cancel{0}\ \cancel{0} \\
-\ 2.6\ 3 \\
\hline
2.3\ 7
\end{array}
$$

Money and Decimals

The cents' point in money is the same as the decimal point. You read $0.35 as "35 cents," but it also means "35 hundredths of a dollar." A cent is a hundredth of a dollar.

Practice writing amounts of money either with cent signs or as decimals with dollar signs. For example, 7¢ can be written as the decimal $0.07. To find the total of $13.00, $6.75, 8¢, and 78¢, first write all the amounts as decimals with dollar signs. Then add.

$$\begin{array}{r} \$ \ 1 \ 3.0 \ 0 \\ 6.7 \ 5 \\ 0.0 \ 8 \\ + \quad 0.7 \ 8 \\ \hline \$ \ 2 \ 0.6 \ 1 \end{array}$$

When you are subtracting money, you may need to put in zeros, just as when you are subtracting with other decimal numbers.

Probability, Changing Units of Measurement, Word Problems

Probability

The probability of an event is the chance that it will happen. Suppose there are four balls of the same size in a container you can't see inside. Two are red, one is green, and one is blue. Larry reaches in and draws out one ball. What is the probability that it is green?

The four balls are the same size. There are four equally likely outcomes, or things that can happen, when Larry reaches in and draws out a ball. One ball is green. So Larry's chance of getting a green ball is 1 out of 4, or $\frac{1}{4}$. We say, "The probability of Larry getting a green ball is $\frac{1}{4}$." Because there are 2 red balls, the probability of Larry getting a red ball is $\frac{2}{4}$ or $\frac{1}{2}$. The probability of Larry getting a blue ball is $\frac{1}{4}$.

Learn to figure out the probabilities of events like these. For example, on this spinner what is the chance that Melissa will spin a 3 or a 5?

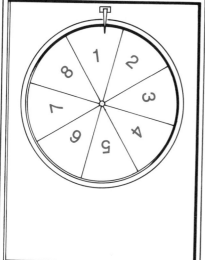

There are 8 sections of equal size. So there are 8 equally likely outcomes. The probability of Melissa getting a 3 or a 5 is 2 out of 8 or $\frac{2}{8}$. Now put this probability in lowest terms.

When you flip a coin, there are two equally likely outcomes, heads or tails. The probability of getting heads is $\frac{1}{2}$, and the probability of getting tails is $\frac{1}{2}$.

Working with U.S. Customary Units of Measurement

Here are some equivalences among the units in the U.S. Customary system of measurement. An equivalence shows that two things that appear different are really equal values.

Length	Weight	Capacity
1 ft = 12 in	1 lb = 16 oz	1 c = 8 fl oz (fluid ounces)
1 yd = 3 ft	2000 lb = 1 t (ton)	1 pt = 2 c
1 mi = 5280 ft		1 qt = 2 pt
1 mi = 1760 yd		1 gal = 4 qt

Learning to change from one unit of measurement to another takes practice. Here are some examples.

1) 1 gal = _____ pt

From the table of equivalences you know that 1 gal = 4 qt. Since there are 2 pints in 1 quart, you multiply the 4 quarts in a gallon by the 2 pints in a quart to find how many pints there are in a gallon. There are 2 × 4 pints in a gallon.

$$1 \text{ gal} = 4 \text{ qt} = (2 \times 4) \text{ pt} = 8 \text{ pt}$$

2) 8 lb 3 oz = _____ oz

To solve this problem, you need to find out how many ounces are in 8 pounds, and then add 3 ounces. From the table of equivalences you know that 1 pound = 16 ounces. Since there are 16 ounces in 1 pound, there are 16 × 8 ounces in 8 pounds. To finish the problem, add the 3 remaining ounces to the product of 16 × 8 ounces.

$$
\begin{aligned}
8 \text{ lb } 3 \text{ oz} &= (16 \times 8) \text{ oz} + 3 \text{ oz} \\
&= \quad 128 \text{ oz} \ + 3 \text{ oz} \\
&= \qquad 131 \text{ oz}
\end{aligned}
$$

3) $\frac{1}{2}$ mi = _____ ft

You know from the table of equivalences that 1 mile has 5280 feet. Remember that to find $\frac{1}{2}$ of any number, you divide it by 2.

$$1 \text{ mi} = 5280 \text{ ft}$$
$$\frac{1}{2} \text{ mi} = 5280 \div 2 = 2640 \text{ ft}$$

$$\begin{array}{r} 2\,6\,4\,0 \\ 2\overline{)5\,2\,8\,0} \end{array}$$

As you keep practicing changing units of measurement in problems like these, you'll want to memorize the equivalences in the table above. That way you can switch from one unit of measurement to another without having to look at a table.

Working with Metric Units of Measurement

In many other countries, from France to Taiwan, a different system of measurements, called the metric system, is far more commonly used than U.S. Customary units. More and more metric units are being used for measurement in our own country, too.

Here is a table of metric equivalances.

Length	Mass	Capacity
1 cm = 10 mm (millimeters)	1 cg = 10 mg	1 cl = 10 ml
1 m = 1000 mm	1 g = 1000 mg	1 l = 1000 ml
1 m = 100 cm	1 g = 100 cg	1 l = 100 cl
1 km = 1000 m	1 kg = 1000 g	1 l = 1000 ml

Because the metric system is based on the decimal system, it is easy to change from one metric unit to another. It's like working with place value. 3 km = _____ m? Since 1 km = 1000 m, you multiply by 1000 to change kilometers to meters. 3 km = 3000 m. 400 cm = _____ m? Since 100 cm = 1 m, you divide by 100 to change centimeters to meters. 400 cm = 4 m. Practice changing units of measurement in the metric system.

Metric measurements can be written as decimals. For example, a centimeter ruler is often divided in tenths, just as an inch ruler is divided in sixteenths. Each tenth is a millimeter.

This paper clip is 2.7 centimeters long. Since each tenth of a centimeter is equal to 1 millimeter, you could also say that the paper clip is 27 millimeters long. In the same way 6.8 cm = 68 mm. Learn to measure lengths to the nearest tenth of a centimeter, or to the nearest millimeter.

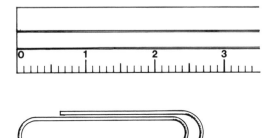

Word Problems

Practicing word problems that involve more than one step can be fun because in each step you have to stop and think about what kind of operation is best to use. Here are two examples.

1) A bottle of Brand X olive oil with 32 fluid ounces costs $4.80. A bottle of Brand Y olive oil with 1 cup 4 fluid ounces costs $1.92. Which brand costs more per fluid ounce? ("Per" means "for each.") How much more?

First you must see how many ounces total are in Brand Y, so that you know the number of ounces in each bottle. 1 cup equals 8 fluid ounces. 1 cup 4 fluid ounces equals 8 fluid ounces plus 4 fluid ounces, which equals 12 fluid ounces. Then you must divide the price of each bottle by the total number of ounces it contains to find out how much 1 ounce of olive oil costs for each brand.

You divide an amount of money the same way you divide other numbers. Place the decimal point in the quotient above the decimal point in the dividend.

Brand X   Brand Y

$$\begin{array}{r} \$\,0.1\;5 \\ 3\;2\,\overline{)\;\$\;4.8\;0} \\ -\;3\;2 \\ \hline 1\;6\;0 \\ -\;1\;6\;0 \\ \hline 0 \end{array}$$

$$\begin{array}{r} \$\,0.1\;6 \\ 1\;2\,\overline{)\;\$\;1.9\;2} \\ -\;1\;2 \\ \hline 7\;2 \\ -\;7\;2 \\ \hline 0 \end{array}$$

Then compare the price per ounce of each brand. Brand X costs 15¢ an ounce. Brand Y costs 16¢ an ounce. Brand Y costs 1¢ more per ounce than Brand X.

2) 21 yards of fence at A-OK Hardware cost $232.89. How much will 58 yards of the same fence cost?

First you must divide $232.89 by 21, to find the cost per yard.

$$\begin{array}{r} \$\;\;\;1\;1.0\;9 \\ 2\;1\,\overline{)\;\$\;2\;3\;2.8\;9} \\ -\;2\;1 \\ \hline 2\;2 \\ -\;2\;1 \\ \hline 1\;8\;9 \\ -\;1\;8\;9 \\ \hline 0 \end{array}$$

Then you multiply the cost per yard ($11.09) by 58 to find the cost of 58 yards.

$$\begin{array}{r} \$\;1\;1.0\;9 \\ \times\;5\;8 \\ \hline 8\;8\;7\;2 \\ 5\;5\;4\;5\;0 \\ \hline \$\;6\;4\;3.2\;2 \end{array}$$

58 yards of fence will cost $643.22.

Geometry, Part Three—Similar Figures, Area, Volume, and Points on a Grid

Similar Figures

Remember that congruent figures have both the same *shape* and the same *size*.

We say two figures are similar when they have the same shape, but not necessarily the same size. When two figures have the same shape *and* the same size, they are both similar and congruent. All congruent figures are similar, but not all similar figures are congruent.

For example, rectangles ABCD and HIJK are similar. Though they have different sizes, they have the same shape.

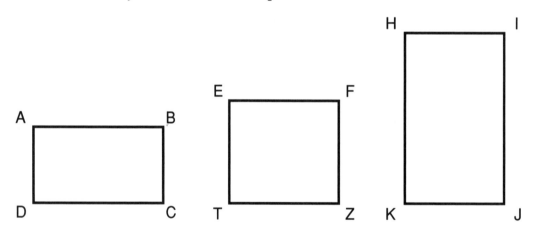

Rectangles ABCD and EFZT are not similar. They do not have the same shape.

All squares are similar, and all circles are similar.

Formula for the Area of a Rectangle

The length and width of a rectangle are called its dimensions. A rectangle has two dimensions. All plane figures have two dimensions. For example, triangles and circles also have two dimensions. (Line segments and lines only have one dimension: their length.)

The length of a rectangle is the length of either of its two longer sides. The width of a rectangle is the length of either of its two shorter sides.

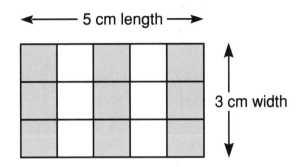

There are 5×3 square centimeters in this rectangle. Its area is 15 cm². You can find the area of a rectangle by multiplying its length by its width.

Here is the formula for the area of a rectangle. A formula is an equation written with letters that tells you a relationship that is always true. In this formula, A stands for the area of a rectangle, l for its length, and w for its width.

$$A = l \times w \text{ or } Area = length \times width$$

You can always find the area of a rectangle by multiplying its length by its width. Later on, you will learn many other formulas in mathematics.

Problems Using the Formula for the Area of a Rectangle

You always measure area in square units.

Some U.S. Customary units of area:	Some metric units of area:
mi² (square mile)	km² (square kilometer)
yd² (square yard)	m² (square meter)
ft² (square foot)	cm² (square centimeter)
in² (square inch)	mm² (square millimeter)

From this table you can see how to read each of the square units. For example, 12 m² is read, "twelve square meters." You should be able to find the areas of rectangles using any of these square units.

Here are some examples of the kinds of problems you can solve using the formula for the area of a rectangle.

1) What is the area of this rectangle? To find the area of a rectangle, you multiply its length by its width. $27 \times 24 = 648$. The area of this rectangle is 648 square feet.

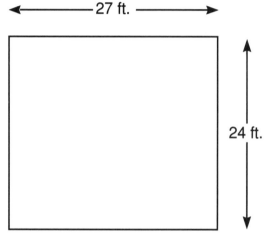

2) Because the length of a square is the same as its width, you can multiply the length of any side by itself to find the area of a square. To find the area of a square with sides of 4 yd, multiply 4×4. $4 \times 4 = 16$. The area of a square with sides of 4 yd is 16 yd².

3) How many square inches are there in a square foot? There are 12 inches in 1 foot.

$12 \times 12 = 144$

A square foot.

There are 144 in² (square inches) in 1 ft² (square foot). Notice that there are *not* 12 square inches in a square foot, even though there are 12 inches in a foot! Changing units of area is different from changing units of length. Work out how many mm² there are in a cm², how many ft² there are in a yd², and how many cm² there are in a m².

4) You know the length of this rectangle (12 cm) and its total area (84 cm²). Find its width.

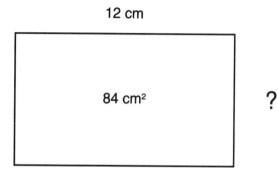

12 cm

84 cm²

?

You know that 12 cm × _____ cm = 84 cm². So you must divide the area by the length to find the width:

$$\begin{array}{r} 7 \\ 1\,2\,\overline{)\,8\,4} \\ -\,8\,4 \\ \hline 0 \end{array}$$

The width is 7 cm.

When you know the measurement of one dimension of a rectangle and its total area, you can divide to find the measurement of the other dimension.

Perimeter and Area

In Book Three of this series, we learned that perimeter is the distance around a figure. Figures can have the same perimeter, but different areas.

Remember that opposite sides of a rectangle have the same length. When you add the length and width of a rectangle, you get half of its perimeter. To find the whole perimeter, multiply the sum of the length and the width by 2.

The formula for the perimeter (P) of a rectangle is:

$$P = 2 \times (l + w)$$

This is the same as $P = l + l + w + w$.

You can use the formula above to find the perimeter of each of the rectangles below.

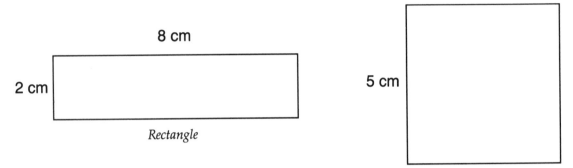

Rectangle

Square

The perimeter of the first rectangle is:

$$2 \times (8 \text{ cm} + 2 \text{ cm}) = 2 \times 10 \text{ cm} = 20 \text{ cm}$$

The perimeter of the second rectangle is:

$$2 \times (5 \text{ cm} + 5 \text{ cm}) = 2 \times 10 \text{ cm} = 20 \text{ cm}$$

The rectangles have the same perimeters. But their areas are different. The area of the first rectangle is 16 cm². The area of the second rectangle is 25 cm². Notice that the second rectangle is a square. (Even if they have the same perimeters, rectangles that are closer to being squares will have the largest areas.)

Solids

Here is a new kind of solid: a pyramid.

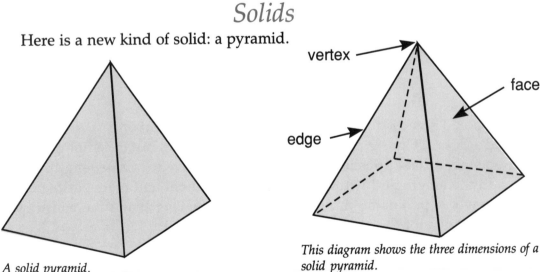

A solid pyramid.

This diagram shows the three dimensions of a solid pyramid.

Remember that a flat surface of a solid is called a face. Learn to identify what kinds of plane figures are formed by the faces of certain solids.

The top and bottom of a cylinder are circles. All the faces of a rectangular prism are rectangles. A sphere has no faces at all.

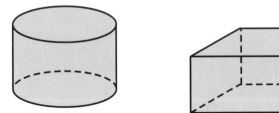
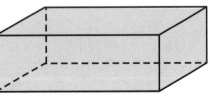

Cylinder	*Rectangular Prism*	*Sphere*
two flat circular faces		*no flat faces*
no vertices		*no vertices*

Volume

The volume of a figure is how much space it occupies. You measure space in cubic units. One example of a cubic unit is a cubic centimeter. The abbreviation for cubic centimeter is cm^3.

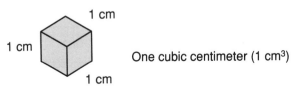

One cubic centimeter (1 cm^3)

Notice that a cubic centimeter is a cube. All cubic units are cubes.

By counting cubic units, you can find the volume of a figure—how much space it occupies. Sometimes you have to count cubic units that you know are there but that you cannot see.

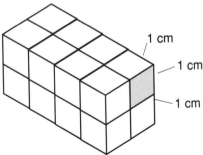

1 cm
1 cm
1 cm

You can count cubic units that are hidden by thinking about the pattern of those that you can see. On one layer of this rectangular prism, there are 8 cubes. There are two layers. $8 \times 2 = 16$. There are 16 cubic centimeters in the rectangular prism.

The volume of the next figure is 40 cm³. Practice finding the volume of solids by counting cubic units.

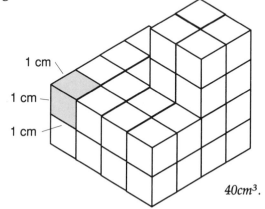

40cm³.

Points on a Grid

The location of a point on a grid is named by an ordered pair. For example, the location of point A is named by the ordered pair (2,1). The first number of an ordered pair tells you how many units to the right a point is from zero. The second number tells you how many units up a point is from zero. Point A is at (2,1): you get to point A from zero by going 2 units to the right, then 1 unit up. Point B is at (5,3), 5 units to the right of zero and 3 units up.

Learn to name the location of points on grids with ordered pairs. For example, point C is at (1,3). Also learn to find the points located by ordered pairs. For example (4,5), locates point G. See if you can find it on the grid.

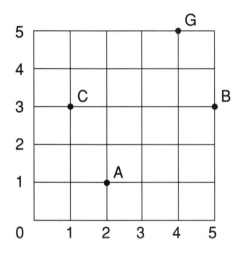

V.

NATURAL SCIENCES

Introduction to Life Sciences

FOR PARENTS AND TEACHERS

Here children are introduced to ancient forms of life through the study of fossils and fossil formation. They also learn about the human body's circulatory system.

A child's early knowledge of the natural world must be gained chiefly through hands-on experience, not merely from books. Direct experience of fossils and the fossil record is, of course, more difficult for a child to acquire than with the life science topics we have presented so far, and we have therefore suggested activities that would give children direct analogies for fossil development in their own experience. In addition, we also suggest the following activities for adults and children:

• Study shells and ferns and compare them to pictures of fossils to draw comparisons between the two.

• If possible, obtain some turf and observe it minutely on a firsthand basis.

• Visit a fossil collecting site. The *Centennial Field Guide* of the Geological Society of America (Boulder, Colorado) lists many fossil collecting sites.

• Visit a museum that has fossils on display.

So important is direct experience in early science teaching that some experts have rejected the very idea of scientific book-learning for young children. But book-learning should not be neglected altogether. It helps bring system and coherence to a young child's developing knowledge of nature, which is often a very disorderly and complex process, and different for each child. A systematic approach to the life sciences provides essential building blocks for deeper understanding at a later time. And we shouldn't forget that some children like book-learning even more than they like experiments and field trips. Both kinds of experience are needed to ensure that huge gaps in knowledge will not hinder later understanding.

Life Sciences

THE HISTORY OF THE EARTH
AND ITS LIFE FORMS

The Fossil Record

If you wanted to learn what happened during the Middle Ages, what would you do? You would probably go to the library and find a book about the Middle Ages (or you could turn to the World Civilization section of this book). The history of humankind has been recorded for thousands of years, and if you want to know what happened at a certain time, all you have to do is

Three paleontologists carefully digging up the 250,000-year-old fossil remains of a woolly mammoth. Later in this section you can see a picture of a mammoth as we think it looked.

find a book and read about it. Even before history was written in words, it was drawn in pictures by people who lived in caves.

But how do we know what the earth was like before people were around to write or draw about it? This is a question studied by geologists, scientists who study the earth. *Geo* means earth in Greek, and is the basis for other earth-related words like geography, geometry (which started out as a way to measure land), and geology, which is the study of the earth. A special type of geologist, known as a paleontologist, studies the earth's past. *Paleo* means ancient in Greek. Paleontologists can figure out some of the things that happened on earth millions and millions of years ago by "reading" layers of rock from ancient times.

One way they do this is by studying fossils. Fossils help tell the story of life on earth because they are the traces or outlines of plants and animals that lived millions of years ago, when ancient rock formed. (Most fossils are found in rock, though some traces of plant and animal life are also found in hardened tree sap, ice tundra or glaciers, and in tar or peat beds.) The fossils are at least as old as the rock around them. If we figure out how old the rocks are, we will then know what kinds of creatures lived during certain time periods and what the climate was like. And we can tell how these creatures and the earth's surface changed over time. Before we read about how fossils tell the story of life on earth, let's read about how they are formed.

Fossil Formation

Fossils are found most often in sedimentary rock. You probably know what sediment is. It's made up of the mud, sand, and decayed bits of plants and animals that settle down to the bottom of a lake or ocean. To see this happen, put some dirt in a glass of water and stir it up. Leave it alone for a few hours. You will then see sediment in the bottom of the glass. As the sediment in ancient lakes, rivers, and seas built up, bones, teeth, shells, bodies of animals, and parts of plants were covered over by more layers of sediment. These layers then hardened, and great pressure caused them to form into rock. When the rock hardened around a dead animal, or its tracks, or a plant, these things became fossils preserved in the rock.

Types of Fossils

Fossils form within rock in one of several ways. Sometimes, dead animals or plants rot away and leave a hollow space in the rock that is the same shape as the once-living animal or plant. This is called a mold fossil. If the mold fills with water, minerals from the water build up and form the shape of the plant

This is a mold fossil of a kind of bony fish. These fish, ancestors of modern-day trout and goldfish, first developed in the Mesozoic era.

Cast fossils such as these were so common along beach areas in England during the 1800's, that many hunted for fossils as a hobby.

or animal. This is called a cast fossil. If, instead of filling a mold, minerals gradually replace the cells of a dead plant or animal, they can form a rocklike fossil that looks much like the live plant or animal. This is called a petrified fossil. Petrified wood is one example of this kind of fossil.

Have you ever seen traces

These petrified tree trunks in Yellowstone National Park are also examples of cast fossils. Even the roots, which you cannot see in this picture, were petrified long ago.

This is a true-form fossil of a grasshopper in the hardened sap called amber.

of a bird or human's footprints in mud? Footprints or trails of animals that are preserved in rock are called trace fossils. In dry regions, animal footprints can be covered with slowly falling dust that many years later turns into rock under pressure.

Sometimes, hard remains of animals, like teeth, bones, and shells, are preserved. They are called true-form fossils. Even soft-bodied insects have been preserved as true-form fossils. This happened when the insect was covered with sticky tree sap, which became rock-hard. After millions of years, one can still see the whole insect inside its amber (hardened sap) case.

Reading the Rocks

Since sedimentary rock forms in layers, paleontologists believe that fossils found in the same layer of rock probably lived during the same time period. Look at the picture of sedimentary rock layers. Which layer of sedimentary rock do you think is the oldest? Which would be the youngest? Why?

Layers of sedimentary rock.

The Dating Game: How Old Is the Earth?

All living things contain a substance called carbon 14. Carbon 14 slowly changes into nitrogen gas after living things die. By measuring the amount of carbon 14 that is left in a fossil, scientists can determine its age. They can therefore tell the age of the rock in which the fossil was found. The carbon 14 dating method is used to determine the age of rocks up to 50,000 years old.

To find the age of rocks up to 4.5 billion years old, scientists use the uranium-lead method. Uranium is a radioactive substance that turns into lead over a long period of time. (You can read more about radioactivity later in this book in the biography of Marie Curie.) It takes 4.5 billion years for half of the uranium found in a rock to turn to lead. If a rock had equal amounts of uranium and lead, it would therefore be 4.5 billion years old. The oldest rock ever found is 4 billion years old. Scientists believe that the age of the earth is about 4.6 billion years.

Making Fossils

Materials:
   Soft, dry clay
   scissors
   plaster of Paris
   water
   milk cartons
   petroleum jelly
   large rubber bands
   toothpicks
   shells of various shapes and sizes

1. Cut the top off a milk carton with scissors, so you have a square box.

2. Following the instructions that come with the plaster of Paris, mix a batch of plaster of Paris with water and let it harden slightly.

3. Cover a shell with a thin layer of petroleum jelly.

4. Pour plaster of Paris into the milk carton, filling it about halfway.

5. Gently press the shell into the plaster of Paris, then leave your project overnight so the plaster will harden.

6. The next day, rub some petroleum jelly on the top of the plaster, and pour some new plaster on top. Let it harden overnight.

7. The following day, use scissors to cut open one side of the milk carton, and remove the plaster block. Gently separate the two halves of plaster, and remove the shell. What kind of fossil have you made?

8. Now lightly rub some petroleum jelly into the depression made by the shell.

9. Press some clay into the depression. Fill the depression until the clay is slightly rounded on top, and cover it with the other half of the plaster block, pressing down hard. Wrap a couple of rubber bands around the block, and let it sit overnight.

10. The following day, remove the rubber bands, and separate the blocks. You may have to pry the clay gently from the block with toothpicks. What kind of fossil is this?

Telling the Earth's Story

Once they have matched rock layers and fossils that are the same age, paleontologists can figure out what life was like on earth during that time period. They look at what is called the "fossil record" to tell what kinds of animals and plants were living at the time. From the kinds of fossil plants found, they can tell what the climate was like, because they know what kind of climate certain plants must live in. For instance, in Antarctica people have found fossils of plants that need warm temperatures and lots of moisture. This means that Antarctica had a warm, wet climate at one time.

Scientists can trace the history of how different animals developed by comparing fossil bones of the same kind of animal found in different layers of rock that were laid down thousands of years apart. For example, fossil bones of horses found in different rock layers show that horses have changed in size over thousands of years. The older bones are much smaller than the bones of horses today.

Next to this fossil of a mesohippus—an ancient ancestor of our horse—you can see a model showing how scientists think the living mesohippus might have looked. The mesohippus lived during the Cenozoic era and was about the size of our modern-day sheep.

Scientists can also tell how the surface of the earth has changed by studying the location of fossils. They know, for example, that certain mountains must have been under the ocean at some point, because fossils of sea creatures have been found on top of these mountains. Also, fossils of the very same plant have been found in similar rock in India, South America, Africa, and Antarctica. How could the same plant and rocks be found in four separate places? Scientists have a theory that it is because these continents were at one time connected, but slowly drifted apart. You can read more about the theory of continental drift in the Physical Sciences section of this book.

Dividing the Earth's Story into Chapters

Paleontologists have used the information from studying rocks and the fossil record to divide prehistoric time into four large periods, called eras. Prehistoric means "before history," or before history was written down.

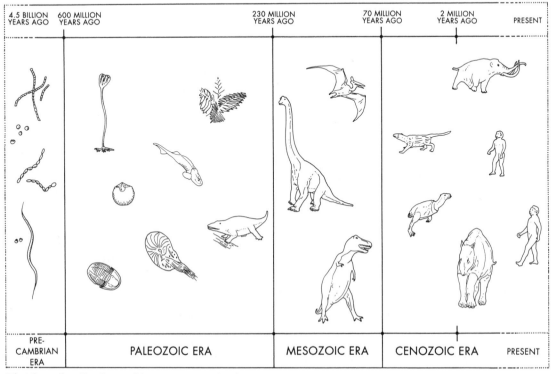

Thanks to fossils, the earth's eras can now be characterized by the different life forms that lived during each.

The oldest and longest era is called the Precambrian (pree KAM bree en) era. It began when the earth was first formed, about 4.6 billion years ago. During this era, the earth's crust formed, and simple creatures such as single-celled bacteria and animals without backbones appeared.

Next came the Paleozoic (pay lee eh ZOH ik) era, which began 600 million years ago. This is known as the "age of ancient life." Simple plants and animals with backbones lived and developed during this period.

The Mesozoic (mez eh ZOH ik) era began about 230 million years ago. It is known as the "age of middle life." Flowering plants appeared during this time, and the dinosaurs roamed the earth.

Then came the Cenozoic (sen eh ZOH ik) era, the one in which we live today. This era began about 70 million years ago, and is known as the "age of recent life" or the "age of mammals." This is the age in which many kinds of animals disappeared, or became extinct, and the age in which man first appeared. Let's read about these eras in greater detail to see what life was like then.

The Precambrian Era

Very little is known about life in the Precambrian era, because few rocks or fossils have been found from this period. Scientists believe that the early part of the era was marked by violent earthquakes that occured as the earth's crust was forming. Volcanoes spewed gases into the air, helping to form the atmosphere—an envelope of gases surrounding the earth. Oxygen was later released into the atmosphere by early forms of plant life.

The earliest forms of life were probably single-celled bacteria and blue-green algae. Later in the era, multicelled jellyfish, sponges, worms, and other animals without backbones evolved. Animals with no backbones are called invertebrates. Why do you think very few fossils have been found of these animals?

The Paleozoic Era

It is believed that in the beginning of the Paleozoic era, there was only one large continent on earth, called Pangaea. It was covered with ice because it was located near the South Pole. (You can read more about Pangaea in the Physical Sciences section of this book.) Invertebrates lived in the seas then, and fish evolved. Fish were the first vertebrates—animals that had backbones to protect their spinal cords. Crablike animals called trilobites (TRY luh bytes) also evolved at the beginning of this era. Like crabs, trilobites had hard shells on the outside to protect them.

Scientists think that about 400 million years ago, Pangaea drifted north toward the equator, causing the ice sheet to melt. The melting ice formed shallow lakes and swamps on the land, and the climate became moist and humid. Mountains began to form, and sedimentary layers sank into the ground. Scientists think that some creatures that were capable of changing adapted to these new conditions and survived. Seaweeds and land plants arose that were similar to modern-day ferns and evergreens. And fish developed fins and lungs. Some of these fish were able to leave the water and spend time on land. These animals may have become amphibians (am FIB ee ans), animals that live both in the water and on land. Can you name some present-day amphibians?

Scorpions and millipedes, air-breathing creatures, developed too. Insects also evolved, and late in the era, reptiles followed. Can you name some present-day reptiles?

When the era ended, trilobites had become extinct. How might the presence of trilobites in a rock layer help paleontologists?

The evolution of fish during this era was a milestone in the history of the earth. Some scientists now believe that fish are the ancestors of all vertebrates, including reptiles, amphibians, birds, and mammals.

A trilobite is an ancient shellfish that can be recognized by the three lengthwise sections on its body. It became extinct millions of years ago, but we still find many trilobite fossils today.

The Mesozoic Era

The huge continent Pangaea slowly separated into the seven present-day continents during the Mesozoic era. The earth's climate varied from moist to very dry, but cooled off at the end of the era.

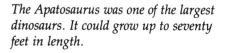

The Pteranodon lived during the Mesozoic era.

Dinosaurs were the dominant animal during this period. The word dinosaur means "terrible lizard." Among these animals were the largest land animals in the history of the earth. But not all dinosaurs were big. Some were as small as dogs.

The Apatosaurus was one of the largest dinosaurs. It could grow up to seventy feet in length.

The dinosaurs ruled the earth for more than 100 million years, but by the end of the Mesozoic era, they had become extinct. No one really knows why, although there are several different theories.

Very small mammals and the first birds also arose during this era. Common plants included cone-bearing and palmlike trees. Flowering plants developed near the end of the Mesozoic era.

N*national Geographic's periodical for children,* World History, *has an article on fossils on pages 26–29 of the July 1985 issue. The issue costs $1.60. Call (800) 638-4077 to order it.*

An amusing, engaging paperback with many terrific activities and fossil "fun-facts" is The Fossil Factory: A Kid's Guide to Digging Up Dinosaurs, Exploring Evolution, and Finding Fossils *by Niles Eldredge, Gregory Eldredge, and Douglas Eldredge (Addison-Wesley). This book also contains an appendix of locations in twenty-eight states and Canada where fossils can be seen and studied in nature.*

The Cenozoic Era

The early climate of the Cenozoic era was hot and moist, and swamps covered large areas of land. Flowering plants and forests became numerous, and grasslands developed. By the middle of the era, more mountain ranges began to form.

Mammals were common during this period. The mammals of the early Cenozoic era were very different from the mammals of today. But by the middle of the era, those primitive mammals had disappeared and were replaced by modern ones such as horses and whales. Humans also appeared in the fossil record at this time.

Late in the Cenozoic era, temperatures began to cool and huge areas of land were covered with sheets of ice called glaciers. During this cold period, known as the first ice age, large mammals called mammoths arose. Mammoths had very heavy, woolly coats. The earth eventually warmed up and then cooled again in another ice age. When the glaciers finally melted again, temperatures became mild. Like the dinosaurs, mammoths eventually became extinct. Why do you think that happened?

We are still living in the Cenozoic era. Animals and plants continue to develop, but they do it so slowly that we do not notice it.

Woolly mammoths like this one became extinct about twelve thousand to fifteen thousand years ago.

How the Earth's Story Unfolded

As far back as 550 B.C., a Greek named Anaximander proposed an explanation for the variety and similarities of living creatures. He believed that all life began in water. Over time, he said, water creatures developed legs, crept onto land, grew fur, and finally took human form. Anaximander did not have evidence to support his theory, but as we've just read, he was not far off from the theory of evolution that is widely accepted today.

Before the story of life on earth was pieced together from the fossil record, scientists argued for many years about whether plants and animals developed slowly over time, or whether the different kinds came suddenly. The idea that animals and plants developed slowly over time is called evolution. It was not until the 1850's that people observed physical evidence leading to a theory about evolution. The thinker who made the most important contribution on this subject was an Englishman named Charles Darwin.

Darwin was interested in how different kinds of species of animals started. He observed that similar plants and animals that were separated by *distance* usually had different traits or characteristics. He also observed that the same thing happened when similar plants and animals were separated by *time* in the fossil record. He asked himself, "Why do creatures separated in time or place

Charles Darwin.

become different from one another after a long time has passed—so different that they become a new species?"

Darwin made some observations that helped answer his question: (1) Living creatures have more offspring than can survive; (2) There is variation in these offspring; (3) Some variations help the offspring survive the many challenges of life, increasing the probability of survival; (4) Those that survive pass on their survival traits to *their* offspring. These survival traits change as conditions change. For instance, if a new ice age comes and the weather gets cold, offspring that can stand the cold better will live, and the others will die. Darwin said that this process of adaptation gradually causes species to change over time.

Later evidence found by paleontologists studying fossils in the twentieth century continues to support Darwin's ideas. But people still debate whether evolution explains the origins of plant, animal, and human life. Different scientists today have slightly different theories of evolution. Some very religious people do not accept the theory of evolution at all because it seems to conflict with their accounts of creation. Other religious people say that the theory of evolution does not conflict with the Bible, because the biblical account of creation was meant to be a kind of simile, or poetic figure of speech, about what really happened. People get very angry over these disagreements, but no matter what belief one holds, everybody should know about both the theory of evolution that scientists have made as a result of studying the earth's fossil record and other accounts of creation.

The Human Body and Health

The Circulatory System

The circulatory system pumps and carries blood throughout the body. It is made up of the blood, the blood vessels, and the heart. From the lungs, the blood picks up oxygen and carries it to the cells. From the digestive system, the blood picks up nutrients and carries them to the cells. From the cells, the blood carries away waste products.

The Blood

How does the blood do its work? It is made up of liquid and solid parts, and each has a job to do. The solid part of the blood is made up of red blood cells, white blood cells, and platelets. Red blood cells carry the oxygen. They turn bright red when they leave the lungs, carrying oxygen. White blood cells are larger than red blood cells, but there are fewer of them in the blood. They help the body fight infection and disease. Some white blood cells surround and "eat" invaders, like viruses or bacteria, when they discover them in the blood or in cells. Platelets, tiny bits of cells carried around in the blood, help stop bleeding. They clog the openings in blood vessels caused by cuts and help start the process of forming a blood clot, which will eventually become a scab as the body begins to heal.

The liquid part of the blood is called plasma. Oxygen and nutrients from the digestive system dissolve in the thin, clear plasma, and are carried where they are needed. The plasma also dissolves wastes from the cells. These wastes are then excreted, or sent out of, the body.

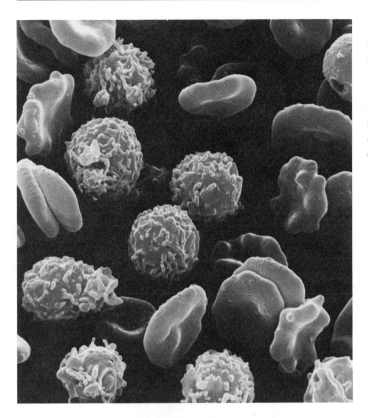

This photo of red and white blood cells shows them as they would be seen under a microscope—magnified to many times their real size. The red blood cells look like doughnuts with the center not quite punched out. The round cells with the bumpy surfaces (lymphocytes) are one kind of white blood cell.

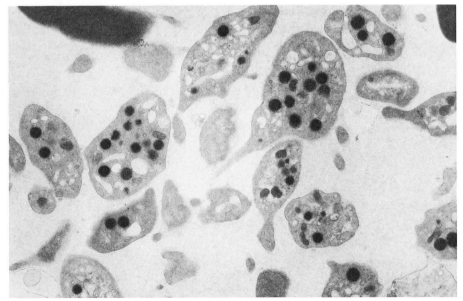

Platelets, shown as you would see them under a microscope and magnified to many times their real size.

The Blood Vessels

The blood vessels—arteries, veins, and capillaries—serve as indoor plumbing for the body's blood. These hollow, stretchy tubes carry the blood along in one direction. Arteries carry blood away from the heart. You can remember this easily if you remember that the words "arteries" and "away" both begin with *a*. Veins take the blood back to the heart. You can remember that because *v* comes after *a*.

Capillaries are tiny blood vessels that connect arteries and veins. You can look at your arm and see some of your veins, and you can feel your artery pulse in the inside of your wrist. But capillaries are so small that you cannot see them. There are billions of them—more than three billion—in your body!

Capillaries do an important job in the circulatory system because they distribute the blood to the cells. Arteries and veins are the pipelines, but the tiny capillaries are the places where the blood actually does its work of feeding the cells and taking away their "trash." Through the thin capillary walls, nutrients and waste materials are exchanged back and forth with the cells.

The Heart

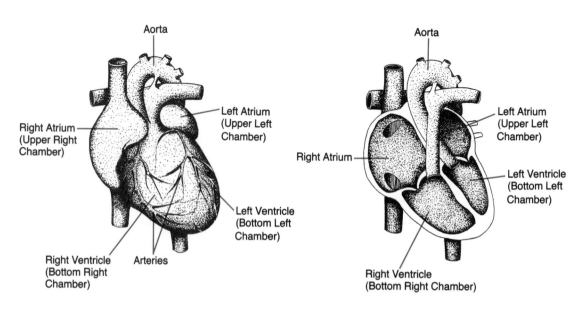

A diagram of the human heart.

This drawing shows the heart cut in half so that you can see inside the four chambers.

If your heart stopped beating, you would soon die. Why? The heart is responsible for keeping blood pumping throughout the body. Without the oxygen and nutrients carried by the blood, the cells of the body can't live.

The heart is a hollow muscle about as big as your fist. It has four chambers, two on the left, and two on the right side. The upper right chamber receives blood from the veins. This blood doesn't contain any oxygen. The bottom right chamber pumps this blood to the lungs, where it picks up oxygen. The upper left chamber then receives the oxygen-rich blood from the lungs. The bottom left chamber pumps the blood to the cells in the rest of the body through the aorta, a large artery, which comes out of the top of your heart.

Following the Circuit

Now that you've read about the parts of the circulatory system and what they do, let's trace the circuit the blood makes. We'll begin with the clean blood in your heart. The heart pumps the clean, oxygen-carrying blood through arteries that carry it out to capillaries in your fingers, toes, or scalp. When blood passes through the capillaries, it gives up oxygen and nutrients to body cells. It also picks up water and waste products including carbon dioxide, or CO_2, from body cells. The blood then passes from the capillaries to the veins. The veins carry blood to the kidneys and skin, where water and certain waste products are sent out of your body through urine and sweat. Then the veins take the blood to your heart. Your heart pumps this blood, which still contains carbon dioxide gas, to the lungs. In the lungs,

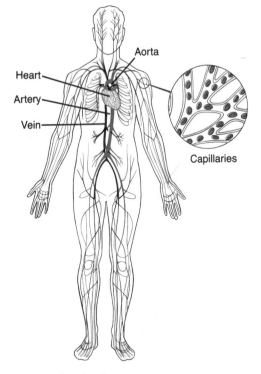

The circulatory system.

the carbon dioxide is exchanged for oxygen. When you breathe out, this carbon dioxide leaves the body. Finally, veins carry the clean, oxygen-carrying blood to the heart again, where it begins the whole journey once more.

Stopping Up the System

Just as plumbing can become clogged, so can our blood vessels. One of the major reasons for this clogging is fat cells that are carried in the blood. Fat sticks to the sides of arteries, and builds up. Sometimes in older people it has built up so much in the arteries that supply the heart muscle that very little blood can pass through to reach the heart. Just like all body cells, heart cells die if they don't receive oxygen and nutrients from the blood. So when blood vessels become clogged, preventing blood from passing freely to the heart muscle, heart cells die. This is one cause of a heart attack. During a heart attack, the heart beats irregularly and eventually stops. Eating foods that have little fat and getting regular exercise, starting from the time you are young, are ways of preventing heart attacks when you are older.

The Respiratory System

Most of the time, you probably don't think much about breathing, unless, of course, you get a head or chest cold. Breathing is an involuntary action, meaning our brain takes care of it without conscious effort on our part. But it is a very complicated process, involving many more body parts than just the brain and lungs. Let's try a simple exercise to see how many body parts are involved.

Take a deep breath of air. What do you feel? Try to follow the air as it passes through your mouth and nose, down your windpipe, and into your lungs. Do you feel your lungs filling with air as your chest expands? What about when you breathe out? Do you feel your chest wall and lungs pushing the air out? Do you feel your lungs lose air like an untied balloon? How does the air feel as it passes out of your nose and mouth? Is it warm or cool? Dry or moist? How many parts of your body are involved in breathing? These body parts make up your respiratory system, which is the system that brings oxygen to your blood and picks up carbon dioxide from your blood so that your body can get rid of it.

Let's look at a detailed drawing of the respiratory system to see how it brings air into and out of the body, and oxygen to the blood.

Trace the movement of air into and out of the body on the diagram as you read how respiration takes place. When you breathe in, your diaphragm (DIE uh fram), a thin sheet of muscle just below your lungs, moves down. This

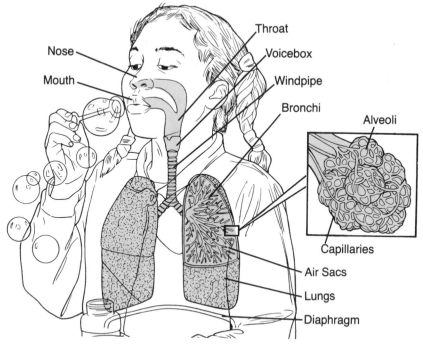

The respiratory system.

helps cause air to enter your mouth or nose, where it is warmed, moistened, and filtered. Air passes down your throat and moves past your voice box. Next, it travels down your windpipe, and into tubes in your lungs called bronchi. These bronchi branch into smaller tubes and finally into millions of tiny air sacs called alveoli, which are only one cell thick. Oxygen passes from the air in the alveoli into the capillaries and is carried away by the blood. At the same time, carbon dioxide carried by blood in the capillaries passes into the air sacs and is passed out of the body when you exhale.

A Health Tip

Healthy habits can also help keep the respiratory system running smoothly. Not smoking is one way to keep your lungs healthy. If you ever see a pack of cigarettes or a cigarette ad in a magazine, you will notice a warning from the U.S. government's health spokesperson, the surgeon general, that cigarette smoking is a serious health hazard. Cigarette smoke causes the alveoli in the lungs to enlarge by merging into one another. As a consequence, there are

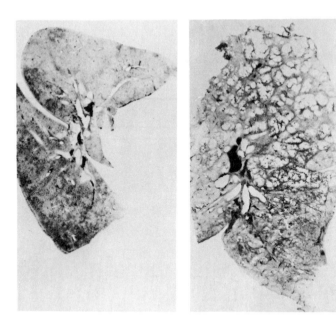

The healthy lung on the left has alveoli (air sacs) that are too small to be seen in this picture. On the right, the lung tissue of a heavy smoker shows the enlarged alveoli that can make it hard to breathe.

fewer places for oxygen to be passed to the blood, and the cells in the body of a smoker sometimes don't get enough oxygen. In addition, smoking increases the number of infections, such as pneumonia, that occur in the lungs. Smoking also greatly increases the risk of developing lung cancer, which kills thousands of people every year. Smoking can even harm people who do not smoke: the number of these infections and diseases is higher for nonsmokers who live and work with smokers than it is for nonsmokers who don't.

Exercise can make the respiratory system stronger, just as it makes the heart muscle stronger. Did you know that when you play games like kickball or jump rope, you make your heart pump faster, and your lungs work harder? Physical fitness can be fun, and sometimes you don't even notice you are doing it!

Introduction to Physical Sciences

FOR PARENTS AND TEACHERS

The topics in this section concern the physical characteristics of our planet, including such dramatic geological events as earthquakes and volcanoes, the effects of weather, and the sources of energy and the effects of its use.

While not all children come to school with equal amounts of experience and knowledge of the physical world, all children have some firsthand experience of the earth and the weather. An important task for science teaching in the early grades is to build upon the knowledge children already have, fill important gaps, and promote activities that enliven the learning of this expanded knowledge.

To encourage activities that help focus a child's interest on the ways of the physical world, adults may want to:

• Encourage rock collections to help children learn more about the earth's surface. Books such as *Rocks & Minerals* (a book in the Eyewitness Series published by Alfred A. Knopf) will help children identify the rocks in their collections and learn more about the geological forces that produced those rocks.

• Compare the composition and formation of man-made "rocks" (e.g., cement rubble) with naturally occurring rocks.

• Keep a daily log of hours of daylight, wind direction and inches of rainfall in your area for a month.

• Observe wind movements while flying a kite.

• Place a block of salt someplace where it can be "weathered" by wind and rain. Observe and measure the effects of weather on the block regularly.

• Have children list all the things at home that would be affected by a power outage.

Physical Sciences

The Whole Earth and the Inside Story

When you imagine what the planet earth is like, what do you see? A big blue and brown ball? What do you think the inside of that ball looks like? Some balls, such as beach balls, are hollow on the inside. Others, like softballs or baseballs, are solid all the way through.

The earth is neither hollow on the inside nor solid all the way through. It's made of different layers, some solid, some liquid, or both. These layers are called the crust, the mantle, and the core. They vary not only in the type of material found within them, but in their temperature and their width. If we could cut the earth in half we could look at each of these layers and see how they differ in thickness. Let's study a picture of how that would look.

The earth's thin crust, or outer layer, is mostly rock and varies in thickness from 3 to 34 miles. Below the crust is the mantle, a layer of mostly solid rock about 1,800 miles thick. The mantle is very, very hot—about 5,400° F in some

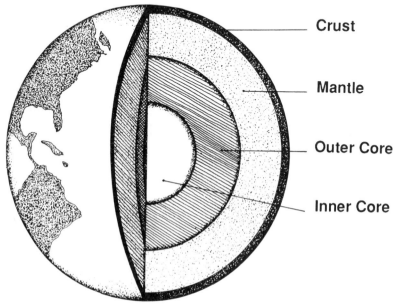

Layers of the earth.

spots. Farther into the center of the earth is the core. It is about 2,200 miles thick, and extremely hot—about 7,200° F. Scientists believe the core has two parts, an outer core and an inner core. The outer core is a liquid layer made up of melted iron and nickel. The inner core is made up of solid iron and nickel.

Since geologists, the scientists who study the earth, can't cut our earth in half, how do they figure out what's inside it? They use the clues from geological activities such as earthquakes and volcanoes to come up with theories, or educated guesses.

Earthquakes and the Earth's Plates

What would happen if you rubbed your thumb very hard against a ripe peach? Its skin would wrinkle, and it might split open. This is what happens to the earth's crust during an earthquake. When an earthquake occurs, the earth's crust shakes, buckles, cracks, or bends. But what force causes this movement, the way your thumb causes the peach skin to move? To answer this question, we must first read more about the earth's mantle and crust.

After measuring the temperature of gases released during earthquakes and volcanoes, geologists have decided that the mantle is hot enough in some places to melt solid rock. Geologists believe this melted rock, called magma, rises toward the crust because it is lighter

As a result of an earthquake, the land in this photograph has shifted so that the bridge no longer spans the stream. What other effects of the earthquake do you see?

than the solid rock around it. In the crust, it forms pools in open areas between rocks. Pressure from the heat of the magma forces it into cracks that have formed in the earth's crust.

Think about the crust of a loaf of bread. What happens as the bread bakes, and the heat and gases cause the loaf to expand? The crust has to expand also, and as it becomes more solid, it cracks in places to allow the gases to escape.

Geologists believe the earth's crust is under the same kind of pressure and has been for millions of years. Therefore, they have decided that it must not be smooth and connected all over, but rather must be made up of pieces or plates that fit together and cover the mantle.

According to geologists, there are about ten plates that make up the crust of the earth. The plates lie very close together, but they can and do move in response to the pressure from built-up heat and gases. The crust's plates sometimes push against each other, move apart, or slide past each other, making the earth shake during what we call an earthquake. This pressure can also cause volcanoes to erupt, which we will read about a little later.

Faults

Between the plates are great cracks in the earth's crust called faults. Serious earthquakes occur most often in areas adjacent to these faults. The San An-dreas Fault in the state of California is very famous because earthquakes are common there. The city of San Francisco is located near the San Andreas Fault. Do you remember hearing about the earth-quake that occurred there

Part of the San Andreas Fault in California. The fault makes a slight dip in the land that looks like a vertical line in the middle of the photograph.

in October 1989? Bridges and buildings collapsed, and many people were killed and injured.

There is also a fault that runs along the bottom of the Pacific Ocean near Japan. Many earthquakes occur along this fault, too. When an earthquake occurs out at sea, it sometimes causes a huge wave to form. These huge waves are known as tsunamis (soo NAH mees) from the Japanese for "harbor wave." (You may also hear them called tidal waves, though they have nothing to do with tides.) Tsunamis can be as high as two hundred feet when they reach land. That's as tall as a full-grown redwood tree! As you can imagine, a wave that size can be very destructive.

Look at the map below. This map shows the areas where earthquakes and volcanoes most commonly occur. Can you see how this information helped geologists figure out how many plates make up the earth's crust? Can you also see how geologists have determined the location of the major faults?

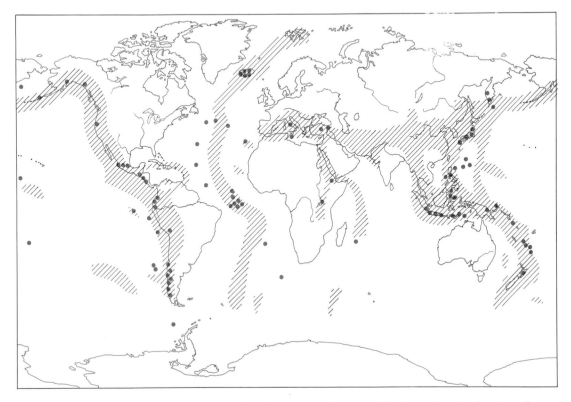

The lines on this map mark areas where earthquakes commonly occur. The dots show the location of volcanoes.

Volcanoes

In May 1980, a mountain in Washington state called Mount St. Helens erupted and became an active volcano. Before it erupted, this mountain looked much like the others around it, but geologists could tell something was going to happen. More and more small earthquakes were occurring in the area, and the ground around Mount St. Helens had begun to swell. Finally, the mountain's top blew off, spewing hot gases, ash, and melted rock all over its sides. Let's find out what caused this mountain to become an active volcano.

Like all volcanoes, Mount St. Helens is located above a pool of magma, melted rock that came from the earth's mantle. As we read in the earthquake section, sometimes the pressure under the earth's crust builds due to the heat and gases generated by magma pools. This pressure can cause earthquakes, or it can force the land on the earth's surface to swell the way the land around Mount St. Helens did. When the pressure is great enough, a thin spot in the crust, such as the top of Mount St. Helens, pops off, just like a bottle cap. The magma shoots to the surface through this opening.

Geologists call the magma that reaches the earth's surface lava. Steam and other gases and ash shoot into the air and lava flows down the sides of the mountain. These materials are all very hot, and they burn up everything they touch. Once the lava hits the air, though, it begins to cool. As it cools, it becomes solid and stops flowing.

Here is a picture of Mount St. Helens during the 1980 eruption. You can see the huge cloud of volcanic ash, the lava flow on the mountainside, and the layer of sooty air hanging over the landscape.

Not all magma reaches the surface of the earth in such a dramatic way. Sometimes it finds its way to a crack in the crust and oozes slowly out to the earth's surface. Geologists call this a lava flow. They measure the temperature of the gases that escape with the lava flow in order to estimate temperatures inside the earth. Once the lava cools and hardens, geologists can find out what it is made of by breaking off pieces and analyzing them.

Take another look at the map showing where earthquakes and volcanoes occur. As you can see, earthquakes and volcanoes both occur in the same areas of the earth's crust. Can you understand why geologists believe that volcanoes and earthquakes are caused by the same thing?

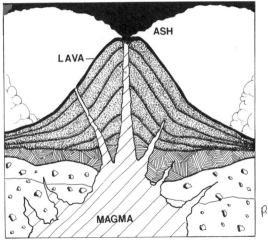

A volcano erupts: hot magma forces its way through cracks in the earth's crust and erupts on the surface as lava.

The lava flow from a Hawaiian volcano called Kilauea hardened into a formation that looks almost like the folds of drapery.

Predicting and Measuring Earthquakes and Volcanoes

Scientists have been studying earthquakes and volcanoes for many years in order to predict when they might occur and warn people ahead of time.

Geologists use an instrument called a seismograph to record earthquake and volcano activity. If you have read Book Two of this series, you may have learned about Chang Heng's seismograph. This seismograph, made during the Han dynasty, looked like a statue decorated with dragons and frogs. The seismograph used today has an ink pen on it that is attached to a long arm.

Seismograph.

The arm is weighted down, and attached to a spring, which causes the arm to bounce when the instrument is disturbed. When an earthquake occurs or a volcano rumbles, the arm bounces, and the pen moves up and down, leaving marks on a piece of paper. The stronger the movement of the earth, the more the pen moves.

Before a large earthquake or a volcanic eruption, there is usually a lot of small earthquake activity. Geologists try to predict when a large earthquake is coming or a volcano is about to erupt by using a seismograph to record how often these small earthquakes happen.

When an earthquake does occur, geologists measure the height of the pen marks to figure out how strong it was. A number from one to nine is assigned to each quake, depending on its strength; nine indicates the strongest quake, one is the weakest. The scale is designed so that each number indicates a quake ten times more powerful than the previous number. An earthquake of strength seven is ten times more powerful than a quake of strength six. An earthquake that measures seven or above is considered a major earthquake. This scale of numbers is called the Richter scale after Charles Richter, the scientist who invented this method of measuring earthquakes.

A free teacher's packet on volcanoes is available from the U.S. Geological Survey, Eastern Distribution Branch, 604 South Pickett Street, Alexandria, VA 22304; or the Western Distribution Center, Box 25286, Federal Center, Denver, CO 80225.

Continental Drift

It is thought that the earth's seven continents were once attached to one another, forming one large continent (you may have already read a little bit about this in the Life Sciences section of this book). Scientists call this super-continent Pangaea (pan GUY ah). Over a very long period of time, the pressures inside the earth that caused earthquakes and volcanoes cracked the crust of Pangaea, dividing it into several plates. Continued pressure forced the plates to move apart, and Pangaea broke into smaller pieces. These smaller pieces became the continents we know today. We call this the theory of continental drift, because the continents drifted apart. Scientists believe the plates on which the continents float are still moving, but very, very slowly.

There are several clues that have led scientists to the theory of continental drift. One is the fossils that are found in the rocks of different continents. The fossils of certain prehistoric animals that could not swim far are found both in South America and in Africa. Geologists think that, since these animals couldn't cross the Atlantic Ocean, the two continents were joined at one time.

Another clue is the shape of the continents. Let's look back at the map of the world to see why this is so. Can you see how South America fits next to Africa like a puzzle piece?

When they separated, the continents divided the large body of water that covered three quarters of the earth's surface into sections. We call these sections oceans. The four major oceans of the world are the Atlantic, the Pacific, the Indian, and the Arctic. Can you find them on a map?

PANGAEA

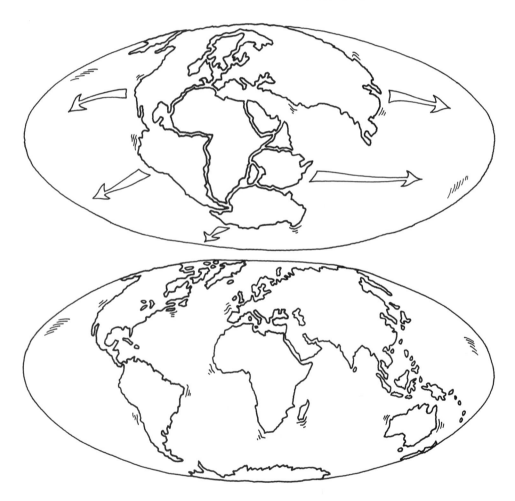

PRESENT

You can see how the plates of Pangaea drifted to the location of our present-day continents.

On the Surface: Making Mountains

Movement of the plates making up the earth's crust also causes mountains to form. This usually takes a very long time, except in the case of volcanic mountains, which can form more quickly. The Hawaiian Islands are actually the top part of volcanic mountains that stick up out of the Pacific Ocean. From what you've already learned about volcanoes, can you explain how these islands were made?

Another group of mountains are called folded mountains. These are formed when two plates collide, and the crust where they meet is bent and buckled into folds. Imagine two small rugs being pushed together end to end. The rugs fold more and more as you continue to push them toward one another. The Appalachian Mountains in the Eastern United States are folded mountains.

Sometimes the rocks that make up the two colliding plates are so hard that they simply won't fold. Imagine two blocks being pushed together end to end. You could push and push, but those blocks wouldn't fold. If you could push hard enough, eventually one or both blocks would crack and tilt. Or one block would slip above the other. Mountains formed in this way are called fault-block mountains, because they consist of blocks of rocks separated by faults. The Tetons in northwest Wyoming are fault-block mountains.

Mountains can also form when magma forms a pool between layers of rock, and has no outlet. The magma builds up, and begins to push against the layers of rock above it. These layers bend upward and form a dome-shaped mountain on the surface. The Black Hills in South Dakota are an example of dome mountains.

Part of the Teton mountain range.

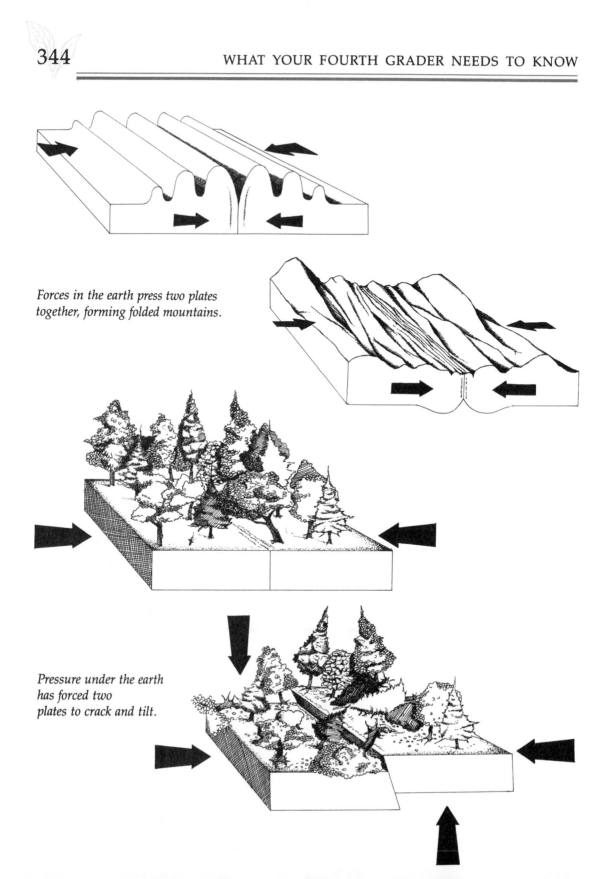

Forces in the earth press two plates together, forming folded mountains.

Pressure under the earth has forced two plates to crack and tilt.

Under the Ocean

The same forces that make mountains on the continents also make mountains on the part of the earth's crust that is under the sea. Sometimes these mountains stick out above the water, like the Hawaiian Islands do. But the tops of many mountains are covered by water, so we never see them. These mountains make the floor of the ocean uneven instead of flat. There are peaks and valleys on the ocean floor just as there are on land. One very deep valley in the Pacific Ocean is called the Mariana Trench. This huge trench, as deep as 36,000 feet in some places, could easily contain a mountain higher than Mount Everest!

It is very cold and dark in the Mariana Trench. This is the deepest place in all the oceans on earth, and the sun can't even come close to reaching the bottom. Colder ocean currents sink right into the trench, and keep warmer currents out. The plants and animals that live deep in the trench have adapted to the cold, dark conditions in fascinating ways. Next time you go to the library, you might want to look for a book about fish that live in the deepest parts of the sea.

Rocks and Minerals

As we've already read, much of the inside of the earth is made of solid rock. The crust is mostly rock, and so is the mantle. Rocks are found everywhere on the surface of the earth—on mountains and in the desert, on the floor of the ocean, and on the plains. Rocks are actually broken-off pieces of the earth's crust.

There are many different kinds of rocks, and they have different properties that allow us to tell them apart. Some rocks are smooth, others are rough; some are hard, others are soft; some are shiny and others are dull. Rocks have different properties because they are formed differently and made of different types of minerals. (Minerals are solid chemical substances.) Just as a cake made of chocolate is different from a cake made of bananas, rocks differ depending on what is in them.

One very common mineral found in rocks is quartz. Quartz comes in a variety of colors. Sand is made mostly of quartz. Diamond is another mineral you might know since it is used in jewelry. Diamond is one of the hardest minerals and is therefore used to cut rocks and other hard things like glass.

Quartz is the most common mineral in the earth's crust. It can be found in a pure form or mixed with other minerals. This photograph shows quartz mixed with mica, a shiny, flaky mineral. The quartz is the lighter-looking material.

Properties of Rocks and Minerals

Materials:

A few rocks collected from a playground or around your home (try to pick out rocks that look different from one another)

a steel mallet strong enough to split open rocks

hard surface for splitting the rocks

a mineral chart if possible

1. Examine the rocks to determine how they look and feel, and record your findings, keeping track of which rock is which (you may want to label them with numbers).

2. Split the rocks with a steel mallet (a teacher or parent may want to do this), and examine their mineral content, comparing it with a mineral chart.

3. Group rocks with similar attributes, and develop a way to classify your rocks.

If you want to read more about rocks, **Rocks and Minerals** *by The Natural History Museum (Eyewitness Books Series) (Knopf) is a good place to start.*

Rock Formations

There are three rock formations, or classes, in which rocks are placed according to the way they were formed: igneous, sedimentary, and metamorphic. Igneous rock forms from cooled and hardened magma. The word igneous comes from a Latin word meaning fire. Granite and obsidian are igneous rocks.

Sedimentary rock forms when layers of minerals or decayed plants and animals are squeezed together under pressure. (In the Life Sciences section of this book you learned that sediment is soil, rocks, bones, leaves, teeth, and other kinds of materials that drop to the bottom of a lake or an ocean.)

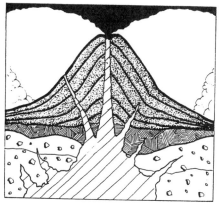

When the magma from this volcano cools, it will form igneous rock.

Sedimentary rock is usually found near rivers. Can you think why? Sandstone is a sedimentary rock.

Metamorphic is a word that means changed in form (you may remember reading about the metamorphosis of the butterfly in Book Two of this series). Metamorphic rock is made of either igneous or sedimentary rock that has been changed in form by forces within the earth, such as pressure or temperature. Quartz is the main ingredient of quartzite, a metamorphic rock.

Pressure can turn the layers of sediment on the bottom of this river into sedimentary rock.

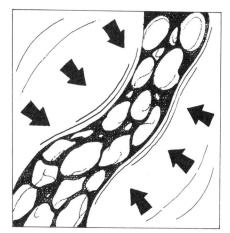

Pressures inside the earth cause the formation of metamorphic rock.

Chips Off the Old Block

Large pieces of rock found in the earth's crust and formed in one of the three ways mentioned above are known as parent rocks. Have you heard the expression "she's a chip off the old block"? It is sometimes used to describe how children look and act just like their parents. Boulders and smaller rocks are chips off the old block, too. They have the same or similar properties as their parent rock. For example, pebbles found along the shoreline of a lake are usually similar in color to the cliffs above them.

Weathering and Erosion

How do boulders and smaller rocks get separated from their parent rock? There are many ways. Human activity and the forces of nature—such as rain, wind, ice, and temperature—can cause rocks to be separated from the parent rock. To understand more about the whole process, let's divide it, as geologists do, into two parts. We'll use the term "weathering" when we refer to rocks being broken down into smaller pieces. And we'll use the term "erosion" when we refer to rocks being moved away from the location of the parent rock. First let's see how weathering can happen.

Types of Weathering

One kind of weathering is called physical weathering, because only the physical properties of the rock, such as its size and shape, are changed. For example, physical weathering happens when water drips into cracks in a mountainside and freezes if the temperature becomes cold enough. When the water in the crack forms into ice, it expands, forcing the crack to widen. If the crack is widened enough, pieces of rock will break away from the parent rock.

Physical weathering can also happen when a plant seed falls into a crack in a rock that is filled with enough soil for the plant to sprout. If a plant grows, its roots can get big enough to put pressure on the sides of the crack. This pressure can force the crack farther apart, and the rock may even split completely as a result.

In a different kind of weathering, the actual minerals of the rock are affected by a chemical change. We call this process chemical weathering. For example, rainwater can mix with carbon dioxide in the air to form a weak acid. This acid rain changes the minerals in rocks, weakening them so that the rocks either wear slowly away or break off easily. (You can read more about acid rain later in this book.)

See how acid rain has eroded this statue's nose, head, and side?

Types of Erosion

Once the rock is broken into smaller pieces by the forces of weathering, it may be eroded (moved away from the parent rock) by water, glaciers, and wind.

The action of water on rocks can have a powerful eroding effect. The constant waves of big lakes and oceans can not only weather the rocky shore by breaking or rubbing away at rocks, but also move rocks and sand away from the waterside. The action of water on sand can lead to beaches being washed away and re-formed someplace else. And the running water of a stream or river can form a deep canyon.

The Grand Canyon was created by the weathering and eroding action of a river. Over millions of years, the water of the Colorado River picked up tiny pieces of rock and carried them along. Just as sandpaper wears wood smooth, those tiny rocks scoured out the walls of the Grand Canyon, breaking down the mighty rock into tiny pieces, which the river swept away. These pieces were then deposited further downstream, in places where the river slows down. The process is still going on today.

Erosion can change the land in other ways, too. For example, the Mississippi River, like the Colorado, carries large amounts of tiny rocks and soil in its waters and deposits them downstream as sediment. The Mississippi deposits its sediment where it empties into the Gulf of Mexico. The sediment built up this way at the mouth of a river is called a delta. Deposited sediment forms soil rich in nutrients, so deltas are often fertile farming areas.

In the case of the Mississippi River, sedimentation is usually a good thing. But sedimentation can also choke a river. Sometimes so much dirt builds up that the river can no longer flow. When this happens occasionally at the mouth of the Mississippi, the sediment must be dug out, or dredged.

The Grand Canyon is about 280 miles long and has an average depth of 1 mile. Its sides show colorful strata of sandstone, limestone, and shale. Some of the rocks formed a billion years ago and are among the oldest rocks in the world!

Large sheets of moving ice and snow, called glaciers, can also erode the land by moving tremendous amounts of rocks and soil. Glaciers are like huge rivers of ice, and as they flow slowly downhill, they scrape up the earth beneath them and push it along. Glaciers are often big enough to cover mountains, and they can level whole hills and carve out valleys as they move along. Many of the features of our country were formed by the eroding action of glaciers. Let's read about one of these features, the Great Lakes.

The Saskatchewan Glacier in Canada is part of a series of connected glaciers called the Columbia Icefield, which formed during the ice ages. Do you remember from the Life Sciences section what the ice ages were and when they happened?

How the Great Lakes Were Formed

About twelve thousand years ago, North America experienced an ice age. Temperatures were much colder than they are today, and the ice and snow that fell did not melt. It packed together to form glaciers that moved down from Canada and covered land as far south as southern Illinois and central Long Island. These glaciers created long, low hills with the rocks and soil they pushed in front of them. When temperatures warmed up again, the glaciers melted, and left enormous holes behind in the places where they scraped away rock and soil. These holes filled with meltwater and rainwater and became lakes. That is how the Great Lakes were formed.

How Rock Becomes Soil

Have you ever seen the side of a building that has been sandblasted? Sandblasting wears away the outer layer of paint or grime on buildings. The wind can act on rock faces in much the same way that a sandblaster wears away paint and grime on a building: it picks up tiny particles of sand, dirt, or rock and whips them against hard surfaces like rock, wearing away the rock's face. On softer rock, the wind sometimes acts like a sculptor and creates incredible statues.

This is a view of Monument Valley, a sandy plain that extends into Arizona and Utah. Over time wind eroded the valley and left the large towerlike formations, called buttes, you see here. They are made of red sandstone.

What becomes of the bits of rock produced by weathering, carried by water, ice, and wind, and deposited far from their source? Mostly these bits mix with rotted plants and animals and form soil. There are two main layers in soil, which you can see if you dig a deep hole.

The top layer, which is darker, is called topsoil. It contains the greatest amount of dead plant and animal material, also called humus. It is where most of the nutrients for plant growth are contained. Topsoil is very important to all living things. Given what you've already learned about plants and the food chain, can you explain why?

Subsoil is the name of the layer below the topsoil. Subsoil is mostly bits of rock with some nutrients. Most plant roots do not reach this layer. Subsoil rests on a layer of solid unweathered rock called bedrock.

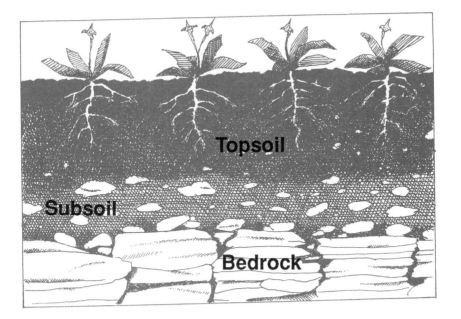

The Dust Bowl Era

People can contribute to erosion, too. Sometimes their activities cause severe erosion, as they did in the 1930s in the region of the Great Plains known as the Dust Bowl. (The Dust Bowl got its name because periods of drought or near-

It's hard to imagine being caught in a duststorm. But this picture from the time of the Dust Bowl can help you see what it was like.

drought occur regularly in the region.) From about 1900 through the 1930s, farmers in the south-central United States plowed the soil over and over again, year after year. They left few areas unplowed where prairie grass once grew and held the topsoil in place. They did not grow anything to cover the land when their main crops weren't growing. They also left the soil uncovered once the crops were harvested. These practices led to a disastrous period of drought in which the thousands of acres of uncovered topsoil dried to dust. Strong winds then swept over the plains, picked up the dust and carried it hundreds of miles away. What was once rich farmland became exposed subsoil—cracked, dry, and useless to farmers.

Weather

Have you ever planned an outdoor party, and had to cancel it because of rain? Or have you heard about or experienced the damaging effects of a tornado, flood, or hurricane? If you have experienced or heard about these weather effects, you probably already understand why people are so concerned with the weather.

Weather is the condition of the atmosphere in a certain place. It can be sunny and warm or cold, rainy, and windy. The study of weather is called meteorology. Meteorologists are people who try to predict what the weather will be like. Since there are many different factors that affect weather, this can be a difficult job.

Our Atmosphere

To understand what makes different types of weather, we must first read about our atmosphere and how the sun and the earth affect its temperature.

The atmosphere is an envelope of gases around our earth. We think of it as being made up of different layers. Moving out from the earth, the first four are sometimes called the troposphere (TROHP uh sfear), the stratosphere (STRAT uh sfear), the mesosphere (MEZ uh sfear), and the ionosphere (eye ON uh sfear). The layer closest to the earth, the troposphere, contains the air we breathe. This is also the layer where most clouds are formed.

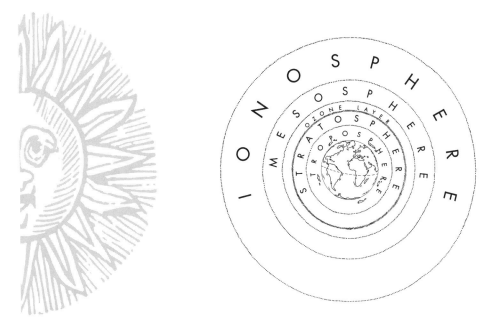

The earth's atmospheric layers. Part of the stratosphere is the ozone layer, which filters out dangerous radiation before it enters our atmosphere.

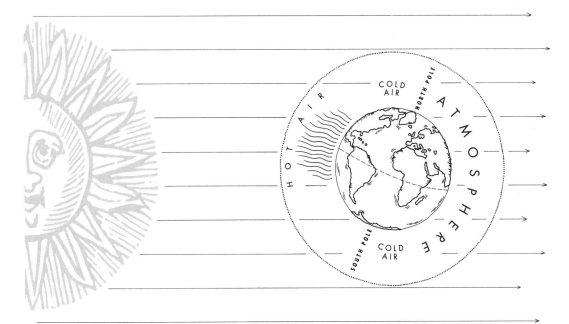

The air over the equator and over the continents is warmer than the air above the North and South Poles.

Hot and Cold Air

The sun's rays warm the atmosphere, but only a little, when they pass through it. It is the heat that is reflected from the earth that really warms the atmosphere. The atmosphere is not heated evenly, however, for two reasons. One, land reflects more heat than water. So the air over land is warmer than that over water. Two, the sun's rays strike certain areas more directly because of the way the earth is tilted. For this reason, the air above the equator, the imaginary line that circles the earth horizontally, is much warmer than the air above the North and South Poles. The North and South Poles are the northern and southern ends of the earth's axis, the imaginary line around which the earth rotates. The cool air above the poles keeps large blocks of floating ice, called icebergs, from melting. They, in turn, keep the air above the poles cool.

Air Movement

Air is made up of gases. As air is heated or cooled at the earth's surface, it begins to move. Heated air rises, because its molecules are further apart than those of cool air. This makes heated air less dense, so it floats up above cooler air. The denser, cooler air moves down to replace the heated air and becomes heated itself, starting the process over again. This movement of air is what we call wind.

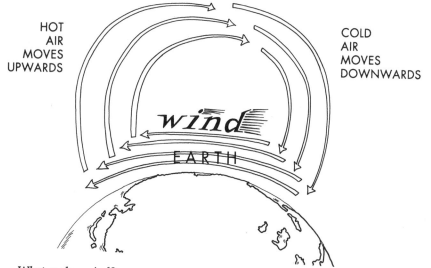

HOT
AIR
MOVES
UPWARDS

COLD
AIR
MOVES
DOWNWARDS

wind

EARTH

What makes wind?

The wind created by moving air masses is responsible for moving clouds across the earth's surface. In the United States, our air masses move in a general pattern from west to east. This is due in part to the jet stream, a band of wind in the upper troposphere that blows from west to east. Because these winds blow most commonly in one direction and are responsible for our weather patterns, we call them prevailing winds. The word prevailing means the most common, or the greatest.

You can read more about wind and weather in Feel the Wind *by Arthur Dorros (A Let's-Read-&-Find-Out Science Book, published by Crowell Junior Books).*

How Air Masses Affect Weather and Climate

Large, slow-moving bodies of heated or cooled air are called air masses. Air masses form over North America and affect our weather. There are seven major air masses in North America: three in the north, and four in the south. Northern air masses are usually cooler *high pressure* systems, while southern air masses are warm, *low pressure* systems. Air pressure is the weight of the air pressing down on the earth, and air pressure systems are the ways different parts of the air press down on the earth.

Air masses can also be wet or dry, depending on whether they form over very dry land, such as the desert, or wet areas, such as the oceans. The wet Tropical Atlantic air mass forms over the warm currents of the Gulf Stream, and travels up the eastern coast of the United States.

The three northern and four southern air masses tend to meet over an area covering the parts of North America that the most number of people live in. This is known as the zone of mixing or the temperate zone. Most of the United States is in the temperate zone. Because the number of hot and cold air masses is almost the same, they tend to balance each other out, and the temperate zone has warm summers, cold winters, and moderate spring and fall temperatures.

The general pattern of weather found in any region is known as climate. So, we say that the United States in general has a temperate climate. What's the climate like where you live?

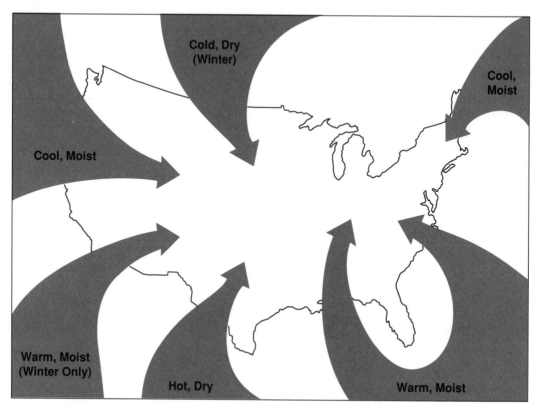

The major air masses over North America.

Clouds and Water Vapor

Clouds are actually collections of water droplets that have attached themselves to bits of dust or smoke in the air. There are several different kinds of clouds, which vary in shape and height above the earth: cirrus, stratus, and cumulus. Cirrus clouds form high in the sky, and are feathery or curly. They are sometimes called "mare's tails." The appearance of cirrus clouds generally means that the weather will change soon. Stratus clouds form in flat sheets that usually cover the sky. They are usually a sign of stormy weather. Cumulus clouds look like big piles of cotton balls and are usually seen during fair weather. They can become storm clouds if they pile up and get thicker.

Not all water in the air is in the form of drops. Some of it is in the form of a gas called water vapor. You are probably familiar with one kind of water vapor, steam. Another term for water vapor in our atmosphere is humidity. Warm air can hold more water vapor than cold air can. That's why, in the summer, drops

Cirrus clouds—feathery and curly, high in the sky.

Stratus clouds can be found high in the sky or touching the ground (as the ones in this photograph do). Stratus clouds that touch the ground are called fog.

Cumulus clouds— puffy piles of clouds.

appear on a glass filled with a cold drink. When the air around the drink is cooled slightly by the coldness of the drink inside, water vapor in the air becomes liquid again and condenses on the glass. Because high amounts of humidity often make people feel uncomfortable, meteorologists try to report the expected humidity on hot summer days. That way people can choose clothing and plan their activities to help them feel less uncomfortable.

A Cloud Record

For a week, check the sky at least twice a day, in the morning and in the afternoon. Write down what type of clouds you see and what sort of weather you are having. At the end of the week, try to figure out if there is a pattern between the clouds you've seen and the weather you've had.

For a second week, follow the steps you did above and cut out the weather forecast from the paper (check with a parent first) to put in your daily record. At the end of the second week, see if you can figure out the relationship between cloud changes and weather.

Precipitation

Clouds lose their water droplets when they can't hold any more moisture. Then the water falls to the earth as precipitation. Rain is one form of precipitation. Sleet, snow, and hail are also forms of precipitation. Water in these various forms falls to the earth and collects in rivers, lakes, and oceans. It eventually evaporates, or turns from a liquid into water vapor. The vapor condenses on dust particles and forms water droplets. Clouds are formed again when many of these water droplets come together. As the clouds become full, they drop their water as precipitation, and the water cycle continues. (Did you make the model ecosystem suggested in Book Three of this series? If you did, you may have noticed it had its own water cycle.)

The red arrows show the water cycle: (1) Clouds lose their water droplets in the form of precipitation. (2) Precipitation collects in rivers, lakes, and oceans. (3) Water evaporates. (4) The water vapor collects on dust particles in the form of clouds, and the cycle begins over again. The role plants play in the water cycle is shown here with the gray arrows, and you will learn about this in Book Five of this series.

Fronts

When warm and cold air masses first meet, they do not immediately mix. The edge along which they meet is called a front.

If the cold air mass pushes under the warm air mass, the place where they meet is known as a cold front. Cold fronts often bring storms, becuse they force warm air to rise swiftly. When this happens, the warm air cools rapidly, forming heavy clouds that quickly drop precipitation.

Thunderheads, a special type of cumulus cloud, form this way. Thunderheads lead to violent thunderstorms with lightning and thunder. You may think of lightning as a dangerous, electrical charge that jumps from clouds to

The characteristic funnel shape of a tornado.

strike the earth. But lightning also jumps from cloud to cloud or moves within a single thunderhead. As the lightning moves through a cloud, it causes air to expand. This expanding air makes a loud noise we call thunder. Although both lightning and thunder occur at the same time, we see lightning before we hear thunder because light travels faster than sound.

If a warm air mass moves over a cold one, the boundary formed by the warm air is known as a warm front. Warm fronts do not cause dramatic changes in weather, but they can bring on storms. Because the warm air slowly moves over the cold, it cools slowly. This causes many different types of clouds to form. As the clouds thicken, they begin to drop their precipitation.

Storms called tornadoes form when cold fronts move in above warm fronts, and the hot air begins to spin as it rises. This forms a huge funnel-shaped cloud. The winds inside tornadoes sometimes reach five hundred miles per hour. Tornadoes travel over land, and when they touch down, they are very destructive. Meteorologists figure out when the weather conditions might lead to a tornado, and they issue a "tornado watch."

Hurricanes are another type of violent storm. Hurricanes form over warm oceans near the equator, usually between the months of June and November when the air is warmest. Large amounts of water evaporate from the ocean because the temperature is so warm, and this warm, moist air rises quickly. It cools quickly, too, causing a strong, whirling storm of high winds and heavy rains to form.

Rainbows

Have you ever seen a rainbow before, during, or after a storm? Rainbows form when the sun reflects off particles of dust and water droplets in the air. Each droplet bends and reflects light the way a prism would. Regular white light is made of different colors, and prisms split white light into these different colors. All the colors show up in a rainbow because millions of drops of water in the air act like tiny prisms.

Measuring the Weather

Meteorologists are very concerned with accurately predicting what the weather will be like. When you consider all the people who are affected by weather—farmers, airplane and boat pilots, and people who might plan outdoor parties—you can see how valuable an accurate forecast is. The United States Weather Service in Asheville, North Carolina, gathers weather information for the entire country, and sends it to forecasters and reporters across

There are several kinds of barometers. The arrow on this one moves clockwise with rising barometric pressure.

the nation. This information comes from six hundred different weather service stations, four times a day.

Meteorologists at weather service stations use many different tools to help them predict the weather. They use barometers to measure air pressure over

Here is a computerized weather map. You may see maps like these on TV, during the weather report on the news. This one shows a hurricane on the Gulf of Mexico. Where is the hurricane?

periods of time. Rising air pressure usually means the weather will be fair. Falling air pressure may mean a storm is approaching.

Information from barometers can be compared with satellite photographs to predict weather. Weather satellites are machines that are launched into space and set to orbit the earth in a special pattern. They have TV cameras on board, which send signals to receivers on earth. The signals are made into pictures that are used for computerized weather maps. These weather maps show swirls of clouds in different places, and can be used to track storms.

Energy Sources

Human beings use energy to warm themselves and to make things move. The first people who walked the earth, before the discovery of fire, could not use some of the sources of energy that we use today. They had the sun's heat to provide warmth, but when they wanted to make things move, they had only their own bodies to help them. (Our bodies, as you've read, get energy from the food we eat.) Later, humans learned to use the energy stored in wood to make fires for heat and light. They used the energy of horses, donkeys, and camels for transporting themselves and for hauling loads. The Egyptians harnessed the energy of the wind by making sails for their boats. And ancient people learned to use the energy of falling water to turn wheels that could grind grain. Thus, fire, animals, wind, and water were sources of energy that made people's lives easier in earlier times.

Today, we use energy from electric power plants, fuels like oil and gasoline, and other sources. We can fly from Washington, D.C., to London, England, in half a day—using energy from fuel in a jet engine. We can wash and dry clothes using energy from electricity to operate washing machines and dryers. A New Yorker can eat a peach picked in Georgia, because the energy in gasoline and other fuels runs the trucks and trains that carry the peaches to the grocery store. We can read a book or play a tennis match long after the sun has gone down by using electric lights. All these things are possible because of energy. But, as we learned in Book Three, we pay a price for using all this energy. We use up the coal and oil stored beneath the earth, and when we burn them we put harmful materials into our air and water.

Electricity

You already know that a lot of the energy we use comes from electricity brought to our houses through wires. When you turn on a light bulb, electricity flows through a wire and heats a filament in the bulb to make light. When electricity flows through a heater, a wire inside gets hot and warms us.

Most of the electricity that we use comes from our ability to make electrons move through a wire. (You can read about electrons and simple electric circuits in Book Three of this series.) We are able to move electrons through wire because scientists discovered a remarkable thing—that there is a connection between electricity and magnets. If you move electrons through a wire, a magnetic field forms around the wire, consisting of magnetic lines of force. More important, if you move a coil of wire across a magnetic field, the opposite thing happens—electrons flow through the wire. All our power plants that make electricity rely on this connection between electricity and magnetism, using heat or other energy to move wires and magnets near each other in order to make electricity flow through wires.

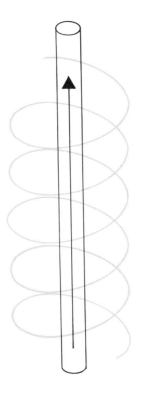

Magnetic lines of force form around a wire that conducts an electric current.

When electric power plants use heat to move wires near magnets, they usually do that by turning water into hot steam. Have you ever seen steam lifting up the lid of a pot on the stove or blowing out of a kettle? In a power plant, the hot steam is sent through nozzles pointed at blades attached to a round pole or shaft that turns when the blades are hit by the steam. When the shaft turns, we have succeeded in changing heat into a turning motion. Now we must convert the turning motion into electricity by using a machine called a generator.

A modern generator is a very complicated machine, but you can see how it works by looking at a simple one driven by water. This single generator is

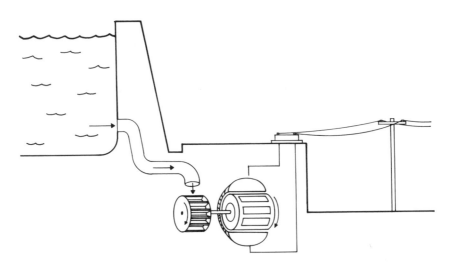

Water from a dam is channeled to flow over the blades of a shaft, causing the shaft to turn. The turning motion of the shaft is then converted into electricity by the generator.

much like the very first generator, made in 1831 by a physicist named Michael Faraday. Faraday knew that if you moved copper near a magnet, you would get electricity. He decided to spin a copper disk between the poles of a horseshoe magnet. As the disk spun, he let one end of a wire rub against the center and the other against the edge of the disk. The spinning of the disk near the magnet made electricity flow continuously through the wire. The circular movement of the copper plate near a magnet made the first electric generator! Modern generators are huge machines with complicated coils of wire and pieces of iron, but they are all based on the principles behind Faraday's simple invention.

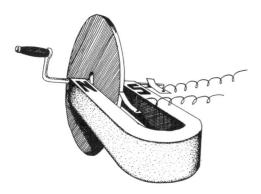

Michael Faraday's first generator.

The Fossil Fuels—Coal, Oil, and Natural Gas

The energy for many of our electric power plants, cars, trains and airplanes comes from burning natural gas, coal, oil, and petroleum products manufactured from oil, such as gasoline and kerosene. The gas, oil, and coal that we find underground are made from carbon, which is an element contained in all living things. Scientists think that the carbon in coal, oil, and natural gas comes from the remains of plants and animals that lived and died millions of years ago. As the bodies of these ancient creatures decayed, coal, oil, and natural gas were formed. Because the remains of ancient creatures are called fossils, we call these carbon fuels fossil fuels.

Coal is a black rocklike material found underground. Though much coal is mined in the United States, most of the world's supply is found in the Commonwealth of Independent States (formerly the Soviet Union). Coal can be burned to produce heat and, more frequently, electricity.

Fossil remains also formed oil, a liquid fuel found beneath the ground and under the oceans. The gasoline, diesel fuel, and jet fuel that power our cars, ships, and planes are made from oil.

The third fossil fuel, natural gas, is often found along with oil deposits. It is used for cooking and heating. Check the kitchen stove, furnace, hot water heater, or clothes dryer in your home to see if one or more of those appliances runs on natural gas.

Fossil Fuels and the Environment

The smoky exhaust from cars and factories that burn fossil fuels can damage the environment. This is a serious problem, because the three fossil fuels provide most of the world's energy.

Remember that coal, oil, and natural gas are the remains of ancient creatures, and that all living things contain the element carbon. When fossil fuels are burned, the carbon reacts with oxygen in the air. That chemical reaction produces the heat we gain by burning these fuels. But when carbon combines with oxygen, a gas called carbon dioxide is also produced, and it builds up in the air. Many scientists think that this build-up of carbon dioxide contributes to an environmental problem known as global warming. The earth warms up because the carbon dioxide keeps heat from escaping back into space. If there is too much carbon dioxide in our atmosphere, too much heat is trapped and the earth may grow too warm. Polar ice caps could melt, making the oceans rise. Coastal cities could be flooded. The climatic patterns of the earth could change in harmful ways.

Using a toothbrush and soapy water, Dr. Jessica Porter cleans the oil from a seabird at the animal rescue center in Valdez, Alaska.

Using and transporting oil can injure lakes and oceans. For example, in March 1989 the tanker *Exxon Valdez* was carrying oil from Alaska to a refinery in California. The *Exxon Valdez* ran aground, and millions of gallons of oil were spilled into Prince William Sound, one of North America's richest marine habitats. Many fish, mammals, and birds were killed.

When oil and coal are burned, gases are produced that rise into the air and combine with moisture in the clouds. Some scientists believe that the product formed, called acid rain, is a serious environmental threat. Experiments show that acid rain removes important minerals from the soil, minerals that plants need to grow. Lakes can fill up with acid rainwater until fish and algae cannot live in them anymore. But one report, commissioned by the United States Congress, claims that acid rain does less damage than originally thought to lakes, rivers, and forests. Scientists are still debating this issue.

Although scientists argue about the dangers of acid rain and global warming, they agree on one thing: fossil fuels won't last forever. Because the world's supply of coal, oil, and natural gas is dwindling, we need to work harder to develop new energy sources.

Hydroelectricity

The prefixes "hydra" and "hydro" mean "water." A fire hydrant is a water outlet. If you are dehydrated, your body needs water.

Hoover Dam was built across the Colorado River between Nevada and Arizona in 1931–36. One of the largest hydroelectric power plants in the United States is located on this dam.

Hydroelectricity is electrical current produced from the energy of falling water. Hydroelectric power plants are constructed near rivers flowing down steep grades. A dam is built across the river so that the water flow can be regulated. On the upstream side of the dam, a huge volume of water is stored in a reservoir. As water spills over the dam, it drops through pipes to a powerhouse. Here the energy of the falling water pushes the blades on a turning shaft and is changed to electrical energy.

Nuclear Energy from Fission

Energy is produced when carbon and oxygen come together to make carbon dioxide. But a lot more energy is produced when certain elements come apart. For instance, when an atom of the heavy element uranium is broken into two lighter atoms, energy is released. This process of breaking apart the atom is called fission, from the Latin word that means "to split." When people speak of "splitting the atom," they are talking about fission. The energy of fission can be very destructive if it is in the form of an atomic bomb. But scientists have learned how to slow down the fission of uranium so they can control the energy and use it for productive purposes.

The controlled release of energy from atomic fission is what makes heat in a nuclear power plant. The heat is used to make steam. After that, the steam is

This photograph shows some of the effects of an exploding fission bomb, especially the characteristic "mushroom" cloud. This cloud is made of bomb particles, small bits of radioactive materials, water droplets, and particles of dirt carried up by the wind.

sent to turn a generator, just as in a power plant where the heat is produced by the burning of fossil fuels.

But there is a great controversy over nuclear power. Unless fission is carefully controlled, too much energy may be released too quickly, and the power plant and surrounding areas might be damaged or destroyed. The fission process makes radioactive elements (called radioactive wastes), some of which can hurt us if they contaminate the air we breathe and the water we drink. In 1986, a disaster occurred in the Commonwealth of Independent States at the nuclear power plant in Chernobyl. A foolish experiment, one for which the plant was not designed, caused a terrible accident. Dozens of workers were killed and poisoned. Radioactive material entered the soil, air, and water around Chernobyl. Many thousands of people had to flee their homes. Today, and for years to come, no one can live or grow things around Chernobyl.

Nuclear power plants are carefully designed so they can never explode like an atom bomb, but it is important that a cooling system be used to remove the heat produced by fission in order to avoid damage. The most serious nuclear accident in the United States occurred in 1979 at the Three Mile Island plant in Pennsylvania. There were no deaths, and no one ever got sick as a result of the accident because the amount of radioactivity released was extremely small. But the accident at Three Mile Island was serious because a lot of equipment and property was destroyed.

The towers of the Three Mile Island nuclear power plant are used for cooling the reactors. After the accident, one of its two reactors was closed.

Unlike the burning of fossil fuels, fission does not produce acid rain, and does not cause global warming. Engineers are designing a new generation of nuclear reactors that are safer than the old ones. They are exploring new methods of disposal of radioactive wastes. And scientists are learning how radioactive elements can sometimes be used to heal people. For example, cobalt-60, which can be made in a nuclear reactor, is used to treat cancer.

Is nuclear power safe, or are the risks greater than the benefits? If we reject nuclear power, what energy source will provide the power that it now furnishes? These are questions to think about the next time you turn on a light.

Wind and Solar Energy

Problems with fossil fuels and nuclear fission have motivated people to search for new energy sources. For example, thousands of windmills provide the city of San Francisco with some of its electrical power.

The world's largest solar energy plant, located in California's Mojave Desert, furnishes some electricity for the city of Los Angeles. Mirrors are used to focus sunlight on tubes of mineral oil. The oil gets so hot that it can be used to boil water. The steam produced drives generators.

Of course these "new" sources of energy really aren't new at all. The sun and wind have provided clean energy for thousands of years. But solar and

Some of the windmills that provide San Francisco with electrical power.

A solar energy plant in the Mojave Desert.

wind power have limitations. Windmills take up a lot of land in proportion to the amount of energy they produce. What happens if the wind stops blowing? And what happens to the people who rely on solar power if the clouds come out for too long?

Geothermal Energy

Do you recall that the inside of the earth is very hot? Geo means earth and thermal refers to heat. Geothermal energy, then, describes electricity produced from the heat deep inside the earth.

Rain seeps into the earth through deep cracks in the surface called fissures. The earth's heat turns this water to steam, which rises through the fissures to the surface. There it can be trapped and used to spin turbines and run generators.

Geothermal energy is almost as clean as energy provided by the wind and sun. But it's not produced everywhere. And even where it is available, its use can cause problems. Recently in the state of Hawaii, people got angry because tropical rain forests were being bulldozed to make way for geothermal drilling.

Nuclear Fusion

Why does the sun shine? In the center of the sun, two hydrogen atoms can fuse together, making helium. This process, called thermonuclear fusion, has been repeated many times every instant since the sun's birth. It creates the energy we see as light and feel as heat.

On the earth, we can split atoms for energy. But can we fuse them? Until recently it was thought that to fuse atoms it would be necessary to heat them to millions of degrees Fahrenheit. This is not easy to do on the earth. But scientists all over the world are working to create nuclear fusion. If they someday succeed in fusing the ordinary hydrogen found in water, we will have cleaner energy than is today produced by fission or fossil fuels. It would be very hard to run out of fusion energy—one cup of water contains enough hydrogen atoms to supply electricity for an entire day and night to all the factories and homes of a small city.

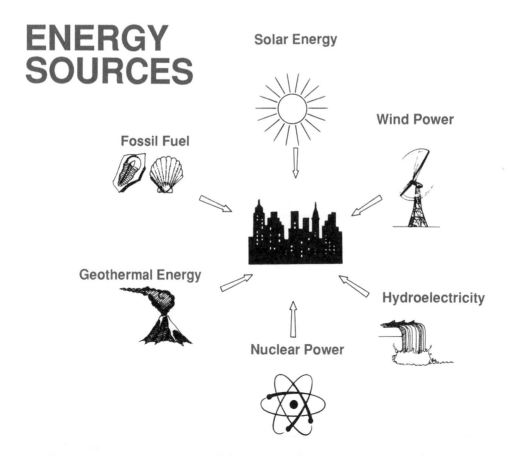

ENERGY SOURCES

Solar Energy

Wind Power

Fossil Fuel

Geothermal Energy

Hydroelectricity

Nuclear Power

Stories of Scientists

Marie Curie

Do you know the saying "a double-edged sword"? It's used to describe something that has two results, one good and one bad. Major scientific advances are often like that, offering humans wonderful benefits along with heavy responsibilities.

Take, for instance, the element radium (an element is a substance that cannot be broken down into other substances). Radium is radioactive, meaning it actively radiates, or gives off, particles smaller than atoms. These sub-atomic particles can be directed at unhealthy cells and used to cure cancer and tumors. But exposure to radioactivity can also harm healthy cells and make you very sick. It can even kill you.

Marie Curie was the scientist who discovered radium. She was born in Warsaw, Poland, in 1867. At age twenty-four, she left Poland to pursue her studies elsewhere because there were no Polish colleges for women. She received two degrees—one in physics and another in mathematics—from the University of Paris, also known as the Sorbonne. While in Paris, she met and married Pierre Curie, a well-known physicist and professor.

Reading that the element uranium gives off emissions very much like X-rays, Marie Curie got an idea. She began to test every known element for radioactivity. She soon discovered that a mineral called pitchblende was even more radioactive than pure uranium. That meant it had to *contain* an un-discovered element that was much more radioactive than uranium! In order to prove her theory, Marie Curie had to have a pure sample of the new element. Because his wife's investigations were potentially so important, Pierre abandoned his own research and joined her search for the mystery element.

Working together in a cold, drafty shed, the Curies began to separate radium from tons of pitchblende. Marie dissolved the powdered mineral and boiled it in huge metal pots for hours at a time. Pierre used chemicals to separate the resulting compounds, throwing away whatever was not radioactive. It took four years to extract a pure sample of radium, which only makes up a one-millionth part of pitchblende.

During these years, the Curies breathed radioactive gas, ate radium in their food, and handled it with their bare hands. Scientists estimate that the radiation in their laboratory was one hundred times the amount considered safe today. Marie Curie's linen-covered notebooks are *still* too radioactive to handle. The Curies observed in themselves the physical effects of radiation poisoning: extreme fatigue, burns that wouldn't heal, pains in the limbs, nagging colds and coughs. But they also noticed that radiation harmed tumors (unusual and sometimes dangerous growths of cells) more quickly than it harmed healthy cells. Radiation really was a double-edged sword. Too much was harmful, but careful

Marie Curie at work in her Paris laboratory.

use of radiation might actually cure some diseases. The world rejoiced at news of an innovative tool for treating tumors. In 1903 Pierre and Marie Curie received a joint Nobel Prize for their work.

After her husband's death in a carriage accident, Marie Curie continued their work alone. She even took over Pierre's teaching duties, becoming France's first female professor. She later received a second Nobel Prize. During World War I, she equipped a fleet of cars and vans with X-ray equipment that could be transported to the edge of a battlefield. Thanks to her, some 1,100,000 wounded men received X-rays and were treated more effectively.

Driven by unquenchable curiosity, Marie Curie not only found a new element, she blazed new paths of thinking along the way. "I am among those who think that science has great beauty," she said. "A scientist in his laboratory is not only a technician; he is also a child placed before natural phenomena which impress him like a fairy tale."

Alexander Fleming

Alexander Fleming was born on August 6, 1881. He was one of eight children of a Scottish farmer. When he was thirteen he left Scotland and moved to London, where he worked in a shipping office until an uncle died and left him a small inheritance. Fleming used this money to study at the St. Mary's Hospital Medical School.

Young Dr. Fleming served in the Royal Army Medical Corps in France during World War I. Like other physicians, he struggled to treat terribly infected wounds with antiseptics—medicines that stop infection. But Fleming noticed that while antiseptics killed bacteria, they caused other serious problems by destroying the white blood cells that make up a body's natural defense against disease. This discovery fueled Fleming's lifelong search for a substance that would destroy

Alexander Fleming.

bacteria without harming tissue or weakening the body's defenses.

After the war, he worked in a cluttered laboratory growing deadly bacteria and their possible enemies in shallow dishes. For years he tested the effectiveness of many attackers of bacteria. But the bacteria always won. Then, on a hot September afternoon in 1928, Fleming picked up a specimen from a stack of unwashed experiments left under an open window. He noticed that the bacteria culture had been invaded by a mold. Ordinarily, Fleming's next step would have been to "chuck the contaminated dish into the sink," but there was something different about this one. There was an empty margin around the mold, and nearby bacteria colonies were transparent or ringed with clear drops of moisture. It appeared that the mold was stopping the growth of the lethal bacteria or even destroying it!

The mold turned out to be an antibiotic, or bacteria killer. Fleming named the mold "penicillin." Further tests revealed that penicillin destroyed bacteria that caused illnesses like pneumonia, without interfering with the body's own disease-battling leukocyte (white blood cells). Despite Fleming's amazing results, the world remained relatively uninterested in penicillin for many years because no one was able to isolate and test a pure sample. Fleming patiently nursed his mold cultures, and other scientists began to study penicillin in their research labs. Without Fleming's persistence, a ground-breaking opportunity would have been missed.

In 1939, two British doctors finally isolated and extracted pure penicillin and used it successfully to treat laboratory mice. By 1943 English and American factories were mass-producing penicillin. Now diseases like rheumatic fever, scarlet fever, and pneumonia that once usually killed people could be prevented or cured. A new era of medicine had dawned.

The world showered Alexander Fleming with honors as supplies of penicillin were shipped around the globe and reports of its amazing results circulated widely. Alexander Fleming won a Nobel Prize for medicine in 1945. Since that time, penicillin has saved millions of lives—all because an accident was observed by a scientist who was prepared to investigate what it meant. Scientists have a saying that Fleming's great discovery illustrates: "Fortune favors the prepared mind."

Elizabeth Blackwell

Sometimes a person's whole life can be changed in an instant. Elizabeth Blackwell's life changed one afternoon in 1844 when she went to visit a friend who was dying. As Blackwell later described the scene, the dying woman asked her why she did not think of studying medicine, since she was smart and healthy. When Elizabeth reminded her friend that there were no women doctors, the woman sighed and said that if she had been treated by a "lady doctor," she might not be dying.

At that time, it was not considered proper for women to talk about or know anything about the human body. Elizabeth's sick friend had been so ashamed to mention her internal problems to a man that she hid her pain for too long. When she finally sought treatment, it came too late to save her life.

Elizabeth couldn't get the dying woman's suggestion out of her mind. She decided to devote her life to medicine. She was prepared for this radical step because her parents had taught all their sons and daughters to help other people. The Blackwells knew what it was like to be needy. They had once been rich in their homeland of England, but they ran into hard times and immigrated to the United States when Elizabeth was eleven years old. Elizabeth's father died soon after the move, and the family opened a small school to pay their bills.

To earn money for her medical training, Elizabeth took a teaching job in North Carolina. It happened that the principal of the school where she worked was a medical doctor. He had lots of medical books, and Elizabeth was free to read them when her teaching work was done.

She wrote to twenty-nine medical schools asking for admission. Most didn't even reply, and the ones that did were very rude. Friends suggested that she dress up as a man to attend medical school, but Elizabeth wanted to be accepted for what she was. A small medical college in New York finally said "yes." Elizabeth graduated in 1849 at the head of her class, the first woman in the United States to receive a medical degree.

Elizabeth Blackwell.

No American hospital would hire Dr. Blackwell, so she went to Europe seeking experience. She was able to get work in a French hospital for women. Then she worked in a famous British hospital. When she returned to the United States she opened her own clinic, the New York Infirmary for Indigent Women and Children. The clinic's patients were very poor; few had ever seen a doctor before.

Elizabeth Blackwell worked at her clinic, wrote articles, and made speeches teaching women about nutrition for babies, the need for exercise and clean air, and the importance of keeping your house and body clean. Her clinic grew into an institution that included a medical college for women. Over the next ninety years, more than a million patients were treated at the clinic she helped start.

Elizabeth Blackwell made many sacrifices. She even lost an eye to infection after caring for a sick baby. Nevertheless, she remained determined to teach women to care for their own bodies and those of their children. She was also determined to open new career opportunities for other women. Today, almost 100,000 American women doctors follow in her footsteps.

Daniel Hale Williams

Have you ever been in a hospital? If so, you probably saw doctors and nurses moving through the brightly lit corridors dressed in spotless white uniforms. Most modern hospitals have shiny instruments and beds with clean sheets. But they were not always such nice places. In fact, in the 1800's hospitals were pretty frightening. Many hospitals, especially those that admitted African-Americans, were filthy, full of germs, and overcrowded. At that time, doctors washed their hands *after* an operation, instead of before!

But not Daniel Hale Williams (1856–1931). He was one of the first medical students to learn new methods of preventing infection. Williams entered medical school in 1880, graduated three years later, and set up an office in downtown Chicago. "Doctor Dan" worked hard and became a popular member of the community. He served as the doctor at a home for orphans, as teacher at Chicago Medical College, and as the surgeon who treated injured employees of the city railroad company.

Some people grumbled that his light-colored skin lessened his experience of racial discrimination, but Dr. Williams knew what it meant to be denied his rights because he was black. Like other black doctors, Williams was not allowed to work in a hospital. He watched, helpless, as black patients received inferior care and as talented young black women were turned away from nursing schools. His anger grew into a fierce determination to build a medical center that would care for all patients, regardless of their race. With the support of his many friends, Daniel Hale Williams opened the doors of America's first interracial hospital on May 4, 1891.

Although "Doctor Dan" saved

Daniel Hale Williams.

many lives at Provident Hospital, he became famous as a result of one operation. On July 9, 1893, Provident's horse-drawn ambulance brought in a young man who had been stabbed in the chest during a knife fight. When examinations showed that James Cornish's heart had been punctured, Dr. Williams decided to operate. (When you remember that there were no X-rays, antibiotics, or blood transfusions, you'll understand what a courageous decision this was!) Six doctors watched as Williams cut open the patient's chest, repaired a torn artery, and stitched the membrane around the still-beating heart. Fifty-one days later, James Cornish left the hospital a well man.

SEWED UP HIS HEART read one of the headlines that appeared around the world. When news of the first ever heart surgery reached our nation's capital, President Grover Cleveland invited Daniel Hale Williams to become head doctor of the badly run-down Freedman's Hospital, in Washington, D.C., which served mostly black patients. When Williams first took over Freedman's Hospital, 10 percent of all surgical patients died. After his improvements, that figure dropped to 3 percent. Williams's excellent work earned him a position at Chicago's largest hospital. He also became the only black member of the American College of Surgeons.

Daniel Hale Williams helped establish at least forty nursing schools and high-quality hospitals to care for black patients. Throughout his life, he refused to compromise a person's right to health care because of race or poverty.

Illustration and Photo Credits

The Metropolitan Museum of Art, The Cloisters Collection, Gift of John D. Rockefeller, Jr., 1937. (37.80.6): 131

The Metropolitan Museum of Art, Gift of John S. Kennedy, 1897 (97.34): 169

Monticello /© 1992 Robert C. Lautman: 194

Courtesy of Museum of Fine Arts, Chinese and Japanese Special Fund, Boston: 155

Alexander Hamilton; John Trumbull; National Gallery of Art, Washington; Andrew W. Mellon Collection: 192(a)

Susan Nees: 46(b)

Courtesy of The New-York Historical Society, New York City: 193

Philbrook Museum: 199

Photo Researchers, Inc.
  © J. Allan Cash: 107
  © Stephanie Dinkins: 109
  © Carl Frank: 103, 104
  © Lowell Georgia: 372
  © Adam Hart-Davis: 349
  © 1976 Tom McHugh: 319
  © Hank Morgan: 373
  © David M. Phillips, The Population Council: 327(a,b)
  © Laurence Pringle: 106

© Bucky Reeves, National Audubon Society: 315(a)
© Art Rothstein: 353(b)
© Robin Scagell: 89
© Jerome Wexler: 346
© Dr. Paul A. Zahl: 316(b)

Rheinisches Landesmuseum, Bonn: 116

Joel Smith: 180, 358

Sophia Smith Collection, Smith College, Northampton, Massachusetts: 40

Photographs by Marvin Trachtenberg: 226, 233, 235

Guiseppe Trogu: 66, 91, 320, 342, 354, 355, 356

United States Geological Survey
  N.W. Carkhuff, B: 350
  Earthquake Info. Bull., 181: 340
  E. B. Hardin, 1572: 315(b)
  C. B. Hunt, 911: 322
  J. P. Iddings, 325: 316(a)
  H. E. Malde, 62: 351
  Mt. St. Helens, 2: 338
  D. A. Swanson, 3: 339
  R. E. Wallace, 241: 336
  I. J. Witkind, 4: 335
  I. J. Witkind, 1262: 343
  I. J. Witkind, 178: 352

Text Credits

Poetry

"Afternoon on a Hill" by Edna St. Vincent Millay from *Collected Poems* by Edna St. Vincent Millay. Copyright © 1917, 1945 by Edna St. Vincent Millay. Harper & Row Publishers.

"Clarence" by Shel Silverstein from *A Light in the Attic* by Shel Silverstein. Copyright © 1981 by Evil Eye Music, Inc. Reprinted by permission of HarperCollins Publishers.

"Dreams" by Langston Hughes from *The Dream Keeper and Other Poems* by Langston Hughes. Copyright © 1932 by Alfred A. Knopf, Inc. and renewed 1960 by Langston Hughes. Reprinted by permission of the publisher.

"The Frog" by Hilaire Belloc from *The Complete Verse of Hilaire Belloc* by Hilaire Belloc. Published by Pimlico, a division of Random Century. Reprinted with permission of the Peters Fraser & Dunlop Group Ltd.

"Humanity" by Elma Stuckey from *The Collected Poems of Elma Stuckey* by Elma Stuckey. Copyright © 1975 by Precedent Publishing. Copyright © 1987 by Elma Stuckey. Reprinted by permission of Transaction Publishers.

"Life Doesn't Frighten Me" by Maya Angelou from *And Still I Rise* by Maya Angelou. Copyright © 1978 by Maya Angelou. Reprinted by permission of Random House, Inc.

"The Rhinoceros" by Ogden Nash from *Verses From 1929 On* by Ogden Nash. Copyright © 1933 by Ogden Nash. First appeared in *The New Yorker*. Reprinted by permission of Little, Brown and Company.

"Things" by Eloise Greenfield from *Honey, I Love* by Eloise Greenfield. Text copyright © 1978 by Eloise Greenfield. Reprinted by permission of HarperCollins Publishers.

Songs

"Do Re Mi" (from *The Sound of Music*). Lyrics by Oscar Hammerstein II. Music by Richard Rodgers. Copyright © 1959 by Richard Rodgers and Oscar Hammerstein II. Copyright renewed. Williamson Music owner of publication and allied rights throughout the world. International copyright secured. All rights reserved.

Stories

"The Glittering Cloud," retold from the original story from *On the Banks of Plum Creek* by Laura Ingalls Wilder. Copyright © 1937 by Laura Ingalls Wilder, renewed © 1963 by Roger L. MacBride. Reprinted by permission of HarperCollins Publishers.

Index

About the Author

E. D. Hirsch, Jr., a professor at the University of Virginia, is the author or editor of ten books, including *Cultural Literacy*, *The Dictionary of Cultural Literacy*, and *A First Dictionary of Cultural Literacy*. He and his wife Polly live in Charlottesville, where they raised their three children.

*"The best year of teaching I ever had. This year has
been so much fun: fun to learn, fun to teach."*

Joanne Anderson, Teacher,
Three Oaks Elementary School
Fort Myers, Florida

COLLECT THE ENTIRE CORE KNOWLEDGE SERIES

ISBN	TITLE	PRICE
41115-4	What Your 1st Grader Needs To Know	$22.50/$28.00Can
41116-2	What Your 2nd Grader Needs To Know	$22.50/$28.00Can
41117-0	What Your 3rd Grader Needs To Know	$22.50/$28.50Can
41118-9	What Your 4th Grader Needs To Know	$22.50/$28.00Can
41119-7	What Your 5th Grader Needs To Know	$22.50/$28.00Can
41120-0	What Your 6th Grader Needs To Know	$22.50/$28.00Can

READERS:

The titles listed above are available in your local bookstore. If you are interested in mail ordering any of the
Core Knowledge books listed above, please send a check or money order only to the address below (no C.O.D.s
or cash) and indicate the title and ISBN book number with your order. Make check payable to Doubleday
Consumer Services (include $2.50 for postage and handling). Allow 4–6 weeks for delivery. Prices and
availability subject to change without notice.

Please mail your order and check to:
Doubleday Consumer Services, Dept. CK
2451 South Wolf Road
Des Plaines, IL 60018

EDUCATORS AND LIBRARIANS:

For bulk sales or course adoptions, contact the Bantam Doubleday Dell Education and Library Department. Outside New York
State call toll-free 1-800-223-6834 ext. 9238. In New York State call 212-492-9238.

FOR MORE INFORMATION ABOUT CORE KNOWLEDGE:

Call the Core Knowledge Foundation at 1-800-238-3233.

CK-9/93